THE SQUIDDER

IDW™

IDW · 78SQUID · 44 FLOOD

THE SQUIDDER

FOR 44FLOOD

BEN TEMPLESMITH

CREATOR, EXECUTIVE PRODUCER,
WRITER, ARTIST & LETTERS
(& WHATEVER ELSE HE CAN THINK OF)

KASRA GHANBARI

EXECUTIVE PRODUCER, ART WHISPERER

TYLER CRANE

PRODUCER, LOGISTICS, REDBULL ENTHUSIAST

MENTON 3

SPIRIT GUIDE

CHRIS RYALL

SENSEI

Collection Edits by Justin Eisinger and Alonzo Simon.

ISBN: 978-1-63140-205-0

18 17 16 15   1 2 3 4

www.IDWPUBLISHING.com
IDW founded by Ted Adams, Alex Garner, Kris Oprisko, and Robbie Robbins

Ted Adams, CEO & Publisher
Greg Goldstein, President & COO
Robbie Robbins, EVP/Sr. Graphic Artist
Chris Ryall, Chief Creative Officer/Editor-in-Chief
Matthew Ruzicka, CPA, Chief Financial Officer
Alan Payne, VP of Sales
Dirk Wood, VP of Marketing
Lorelei Bunjes, VP of Digital Services
Jeff Webber, VP of Digital Publishing & Business Development

Facebook: facebook.com/idwpublishing
Twitter: @idwpublishing
YouTube: youtube.com/idwpublishing
Instagram: instagram.com/idwpublishing
deviantART: idwpublishing.deviantart.com
Pinterest: pinterest.com/idwpublishing/idw-staff-faves

So, here we are then.

I'm knackered. A bit warm, as my studio has no windows and Spring is well and truly heating up. The fan drones on as I contemplate how I got to this point.

I've just formatted the last story page of the last chapter of this book. This sucker is finally done.

THE SQUIDDER started as a bunch of rambling ideas I'd write down in my iPhone notes as I'd ride the New York City subway back and forth. Where I lived, the line had no phone coverage. My subway trips couldn't be polluted with Facebook, Twitter, or any of the thousand other things most people occupy their time with if they can, when stuck in a moving metal box for more than two minutes. So I sat there, over the months, typing out notes as my thoughts would wander, forced to be alone with my own imagination… and this… thing… was born. Born of my love for Dolph Lundgren films and the Road Warrior, and for my unnatural love of tentacles and squidly things.

For some people, creating comes naturally. Others have to work hard to come up with things. And then of course, there's those that've never had an original idea in their lives. These strange creatures can often be found in middle management, corporate positions and political offices. For most of my life, things just came to me. Brain fruit, naturally growing in my head, ready to be plucked and with luck, cooked up into something edible for anyone who'd stupidly give me the time of day. I've been lucky, always have, and I know it. But then for a few years, I decided to make life hard for myself, with various personal events, both good and bad. For a few years there, I fell into a rut and surrounded myself with people who literally sucked the creativity out of me. All was not good. Not good at all. It's been a long, slow process of ditching the bad influences and people, regaining motivation and finding that spark again. Of figuring out where I came from and where I should be going. I've had the great fortune to meet some amazingly creative people who brought me back to who think I once was. In large part, that's why 44FLOOD exists for all of us here, and why this book has wound up in your hands. Because we all found our passions and those of you who kickstarted us were willing to let us indulge them. You pay our rent, allow us to eat and still do the things that come from within us creatively. There's a debt there I don't think can ever be repaid.

Anyway, this book, I hope, brings me full circle. As a creator and someone who cares about creator rights. This is the first project I own 100%. My sense of investment in it isn't like anything I've experienced before, and I have you Kickstarter folks to thank. So thank you, from the bottom of my heart. I hope you like it.

Since this journey started as some loose notes, progressed to a project that secured funding to actually happen, to now, finally being a finished book, it seems like a lifetime has passed. I've moved cities, met the love of my life, lived through some horrible heartbreaking situations, met so many who I now consider family and figured out what direction my path should truly take. With a little luck, I hope you enjoy this book as much as I did creating it. It's helped me rediscover my love for the medium, for art, writing and above all, finishing things.

HAIL SQUID.

-Ben Templesmith
Chicago 2014

FOR ASH, MY LOVE, WHO REMINDED ME OF THE IMPORTANT THINGS
IN LIFE. FOR IO AND RINGO, FOR THE CAT HAIR IN EVERYTHING. AND
FOR THOSE WHO EMPOWER CREATIVES EVERYWHERE, TO SIMPLY
CREATE.

HAIL SQUID.

CHAPTER ONE

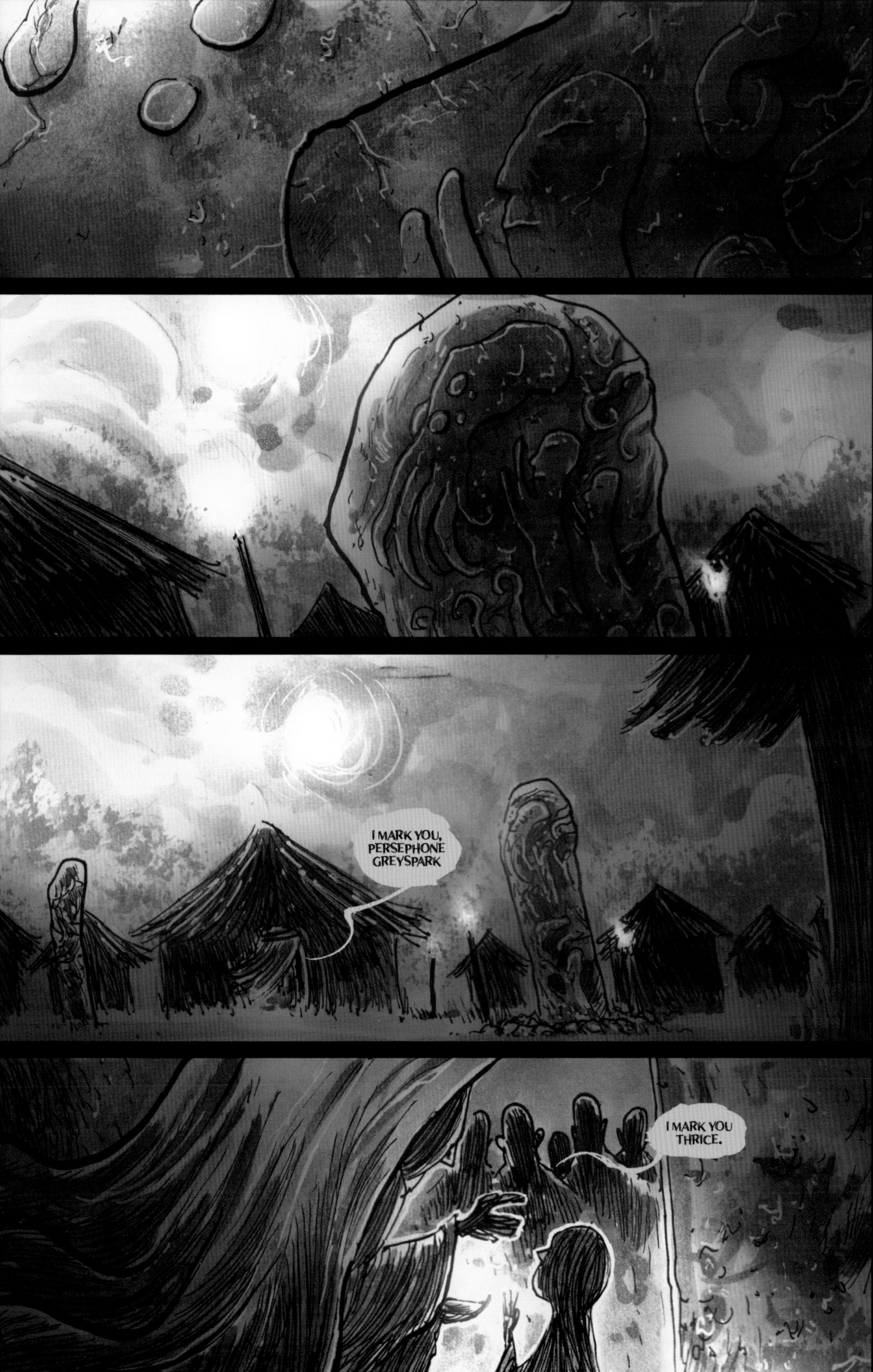
I MARK YOU, PERSEPHONE GREYSPARK
I MARK YOU THRICE.

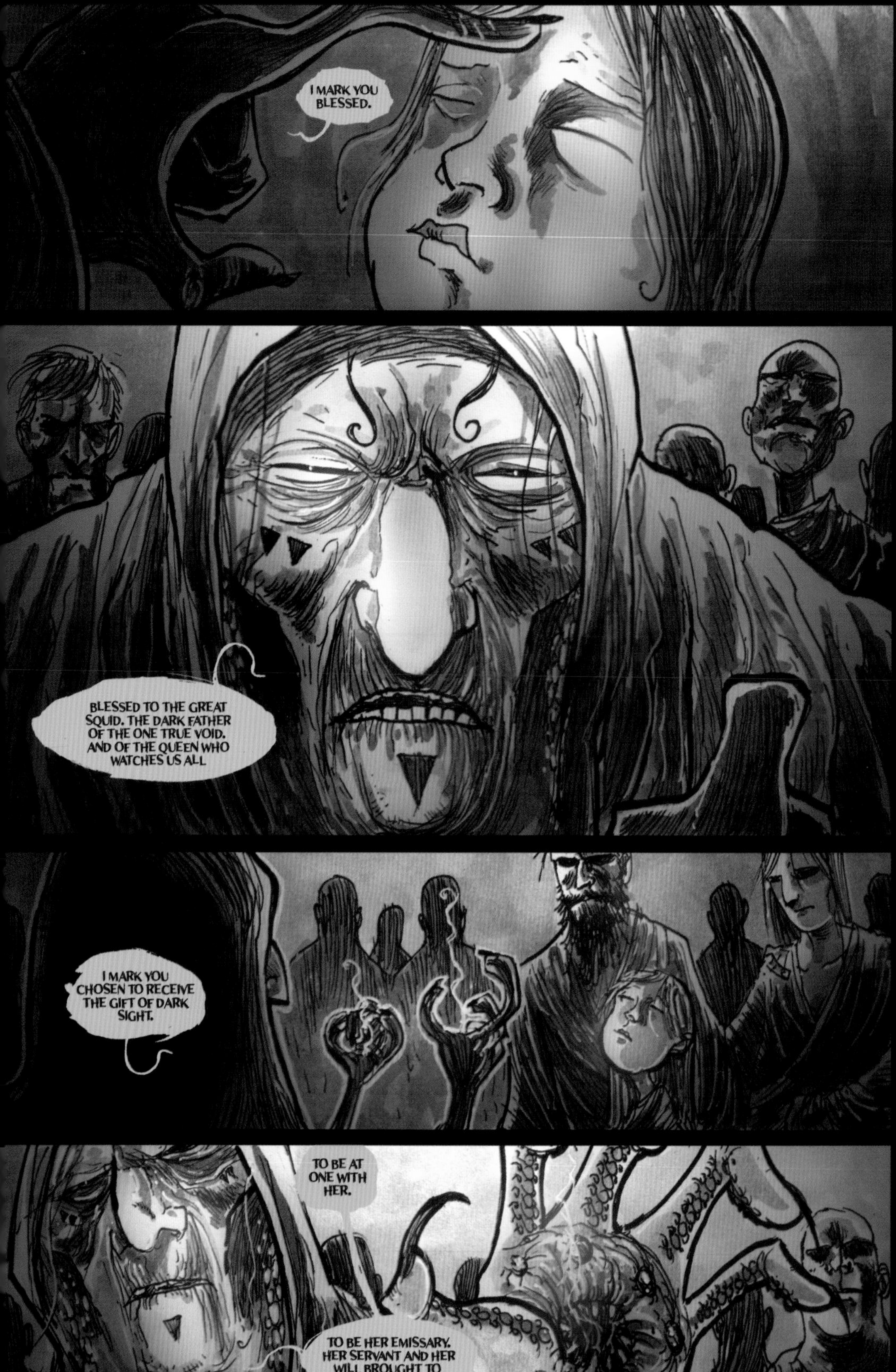
I MARK YOU BLESSED.
BLESSED TO THE GREAT SQUID. THE DARK FATHER OF THE ONE TRUE VOID. AND OF THE QUEEN WHO WATCHES US ALL
I MARK YOU CHOSEN TO RECEIVE THE GIFT OF DARK SIGHT.
TO BE AT ONE WITH HER.
TO BE HER EMISSARY. HER SERVANT AND HER WILL BROUGHT TO ACTION.

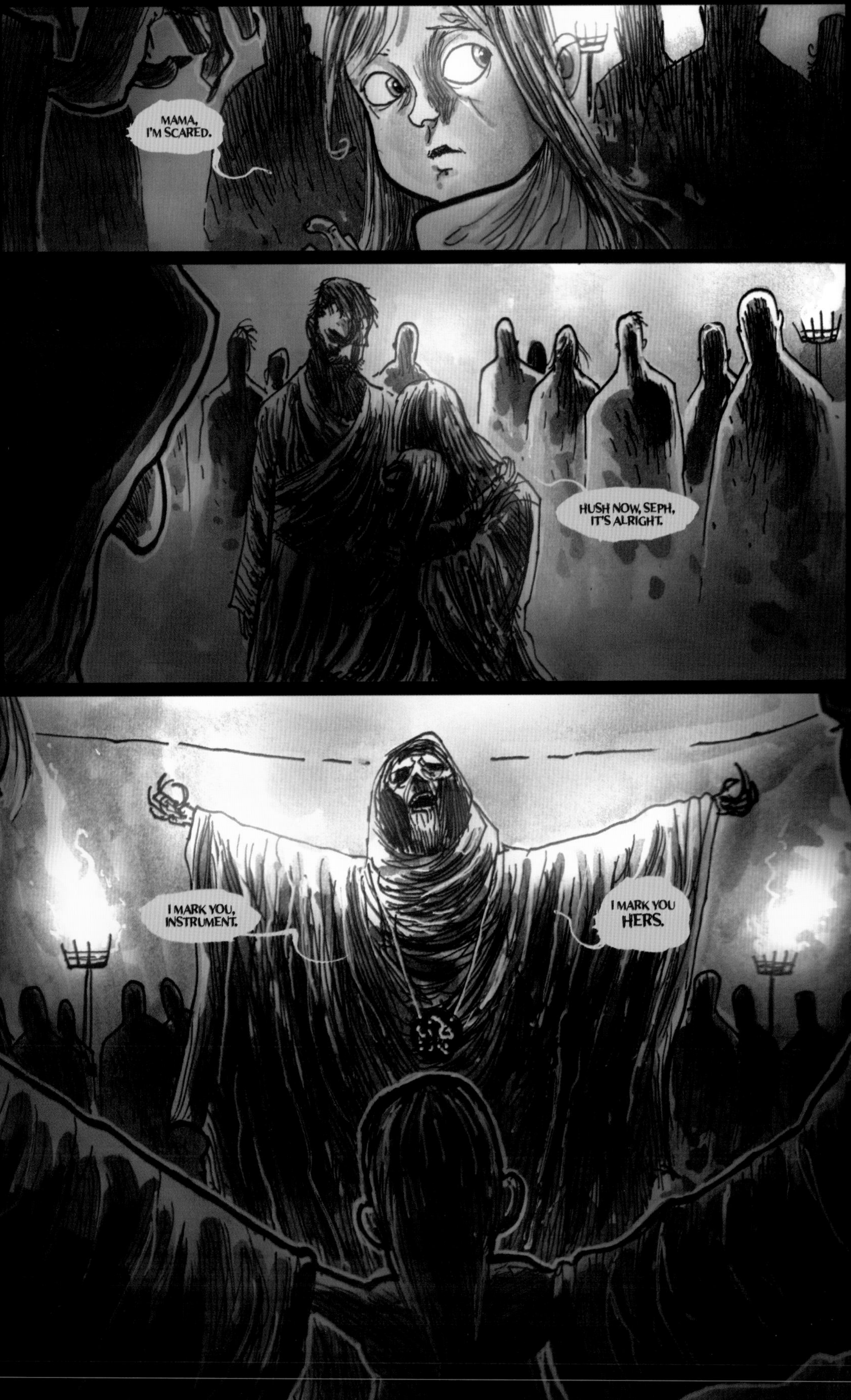
MAMA, I'M SCARED.
HUSH NOW, SEPH, IT'S ALRIGHT.
I MARK YOU, INSTRUMENT.
I MARK YOU HERS.

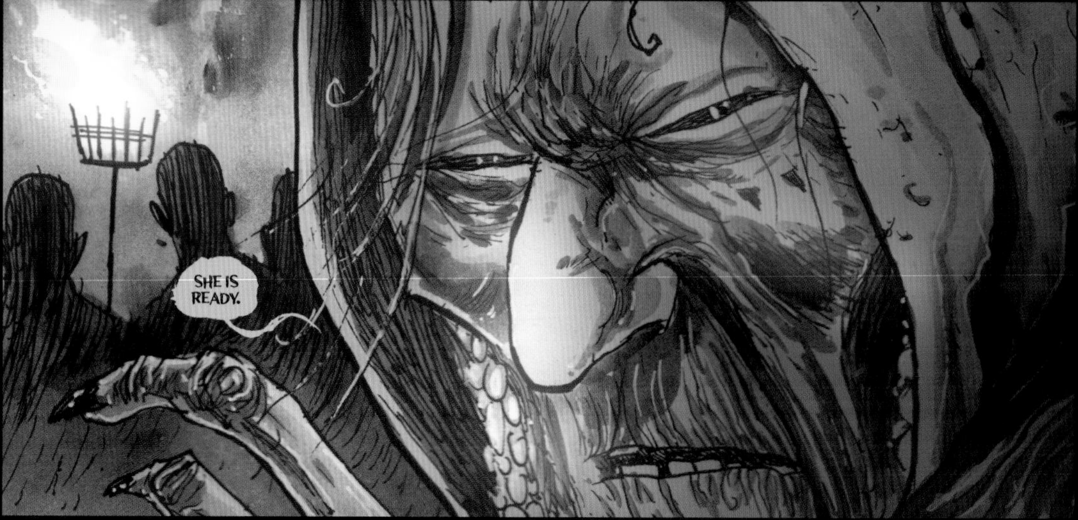
SHE IS READY.

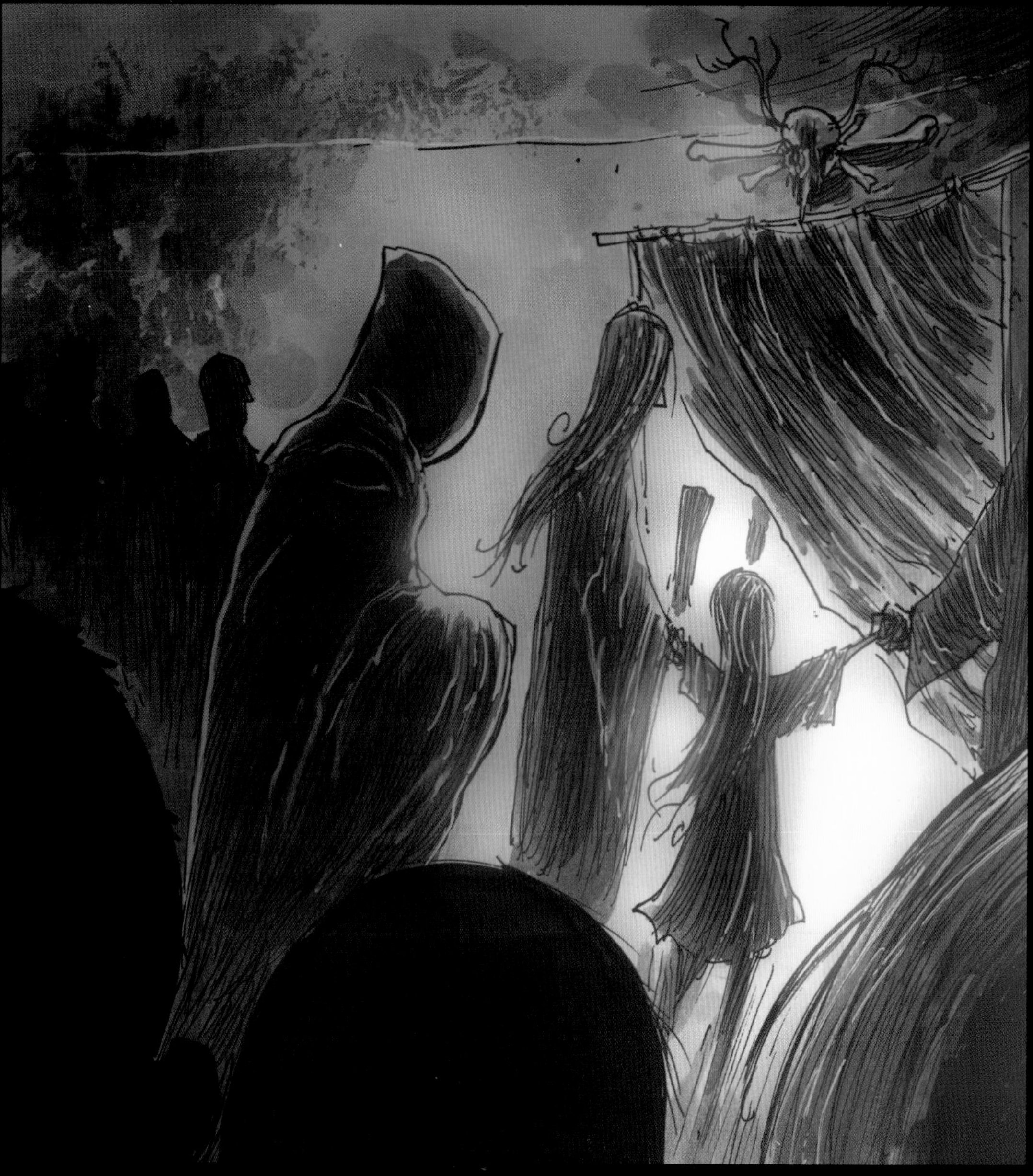

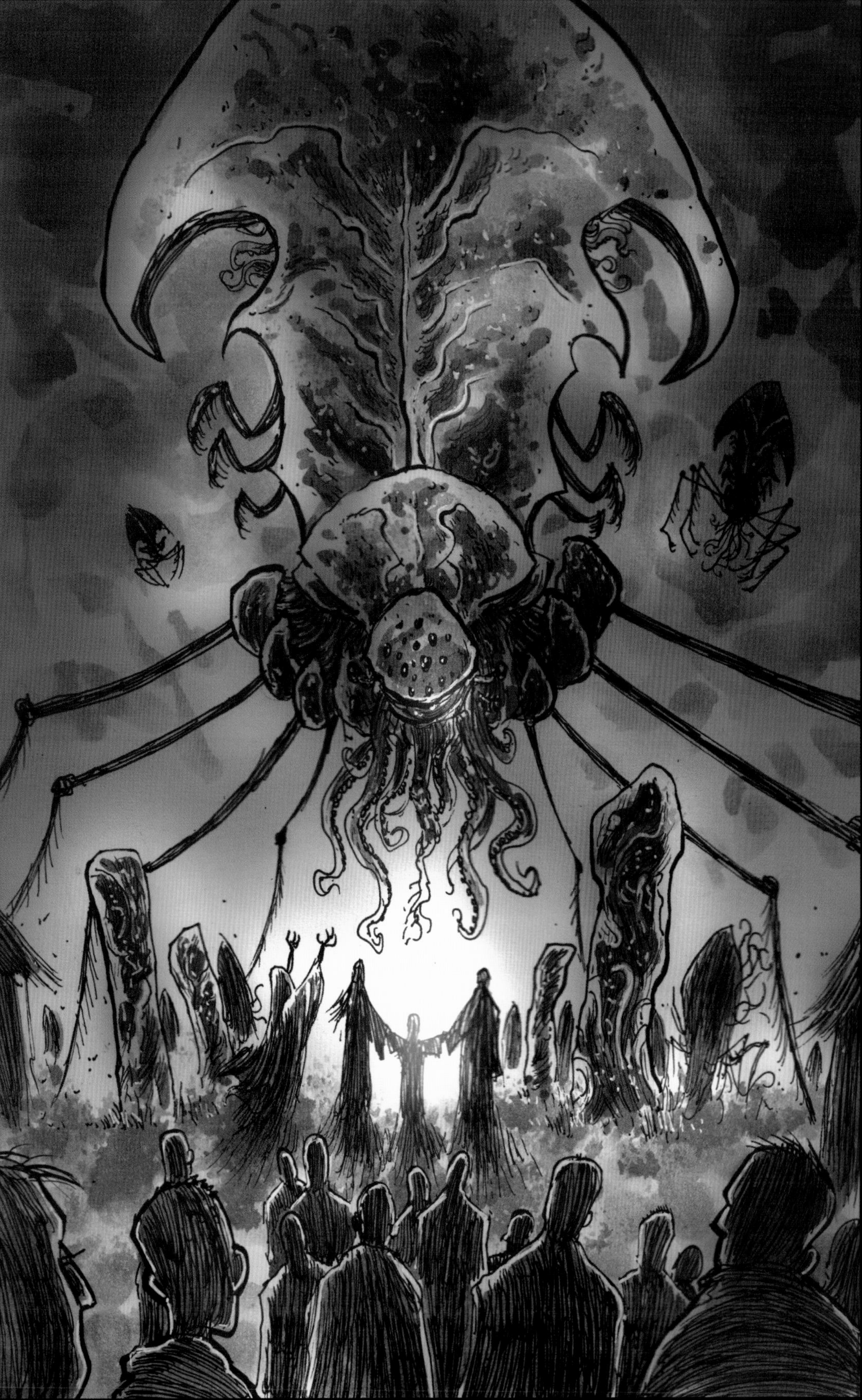

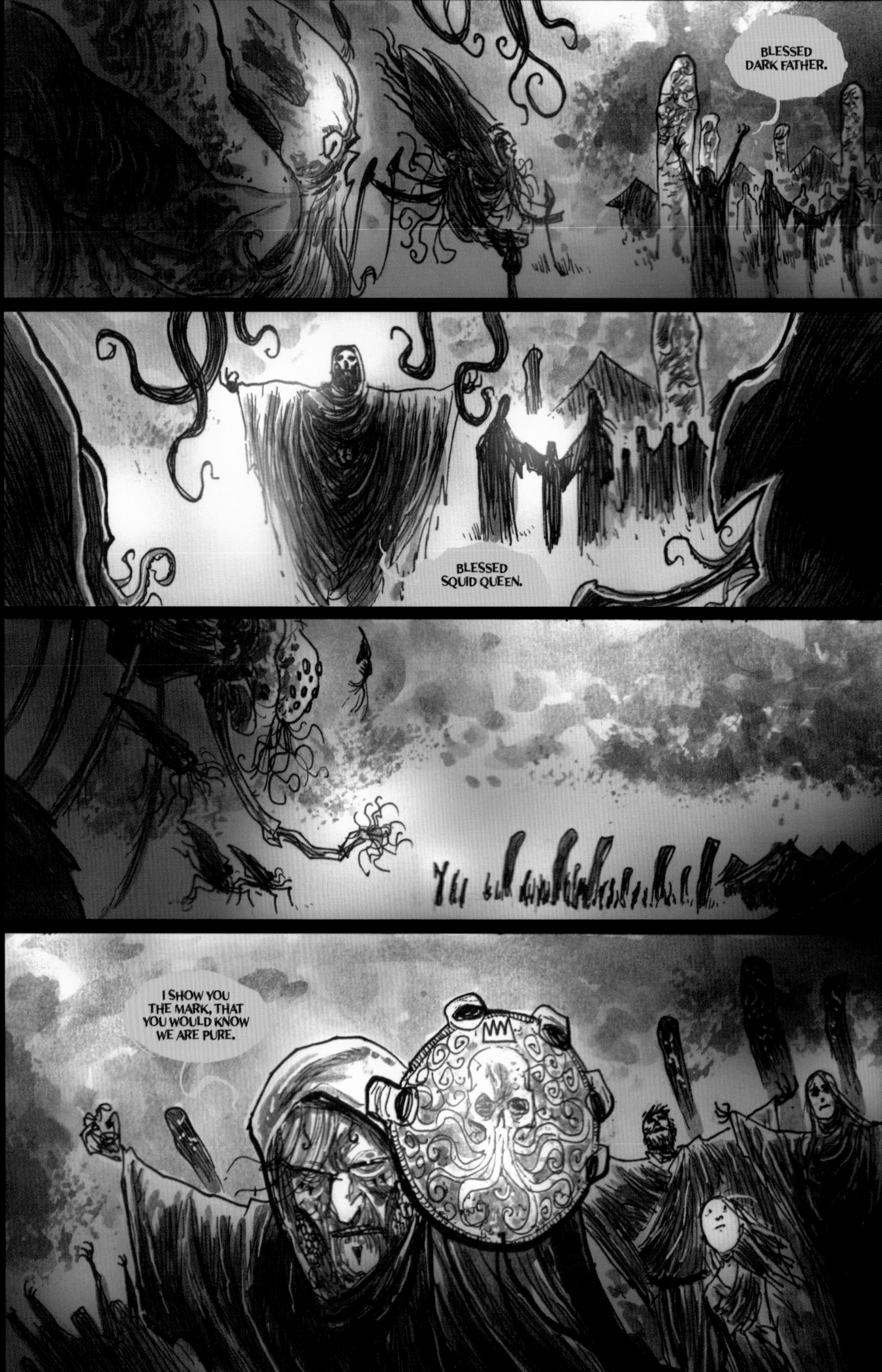
BLESSED DARK FATHER.
BLESSED SQUID QUEEN.
I SHOW YOU THE MARK, THAT YOU WOULD KNOW WE ARE PURE.

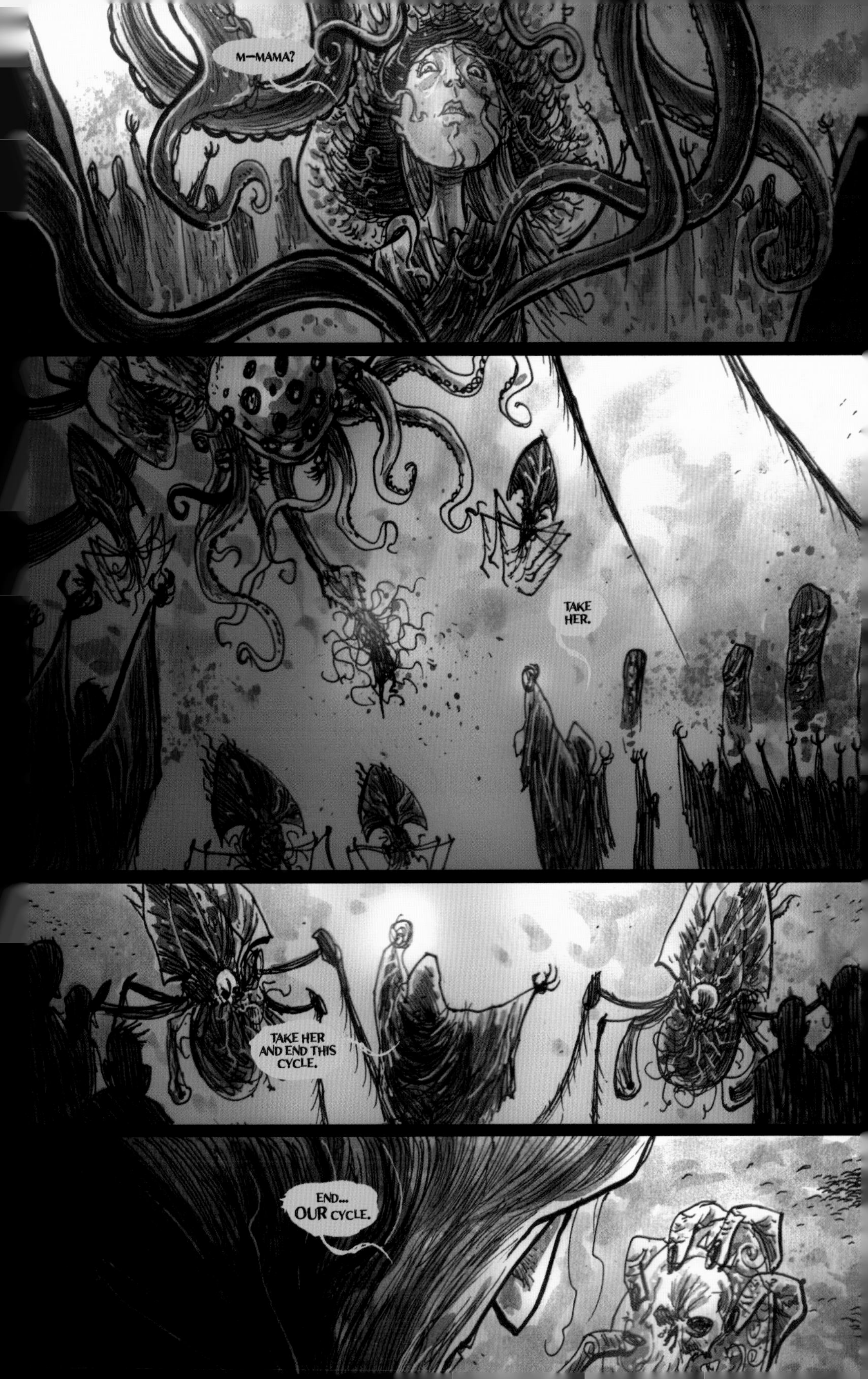
M—MAMA?
TAKE HER.
TAKE HER AND END THIS CYCLE.
END... OUR CYCLE.

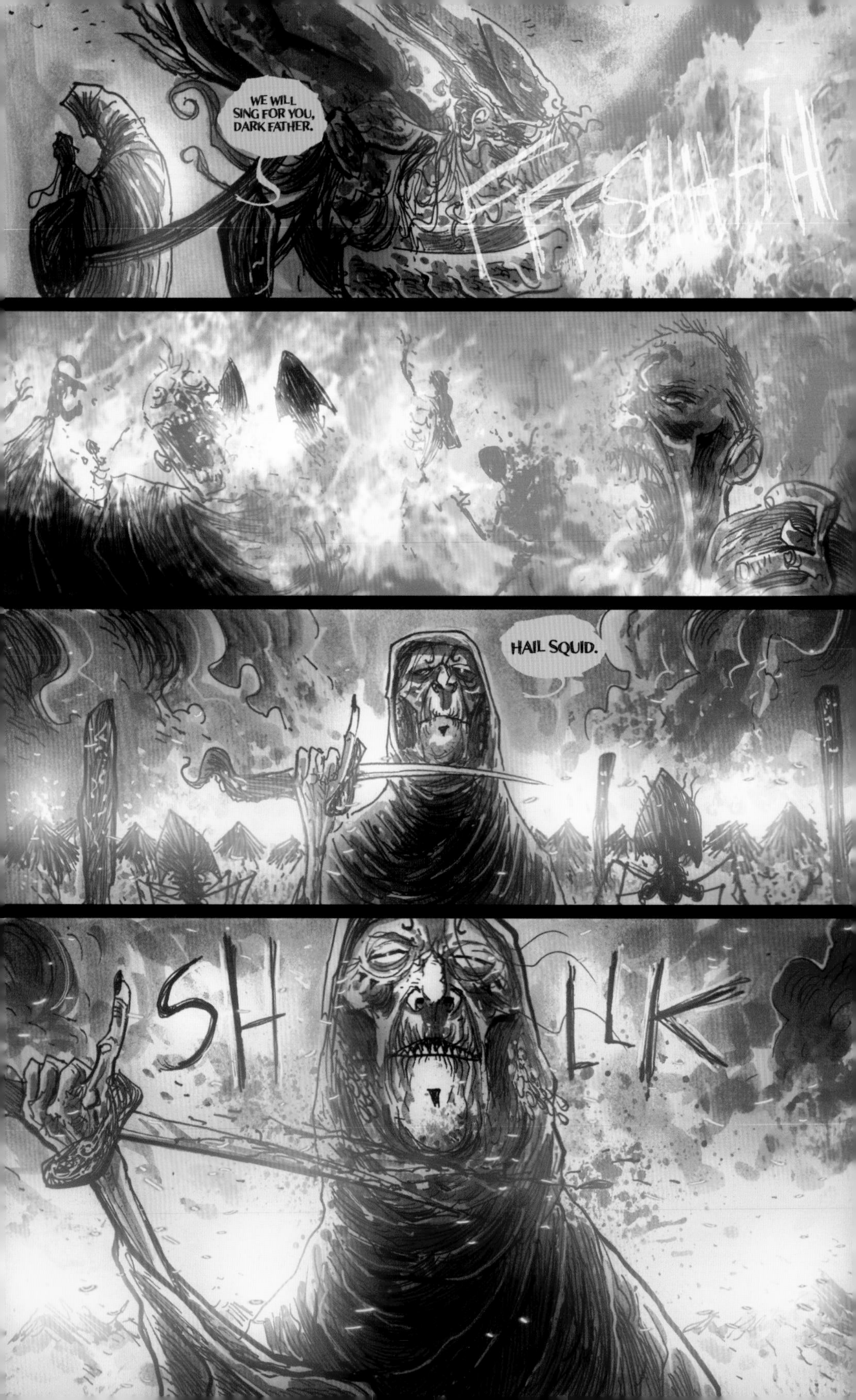
WE WILL SING FOR YOU, DARK FATHER.
FFSHHHH
HAIL SQUID.
SH LLK

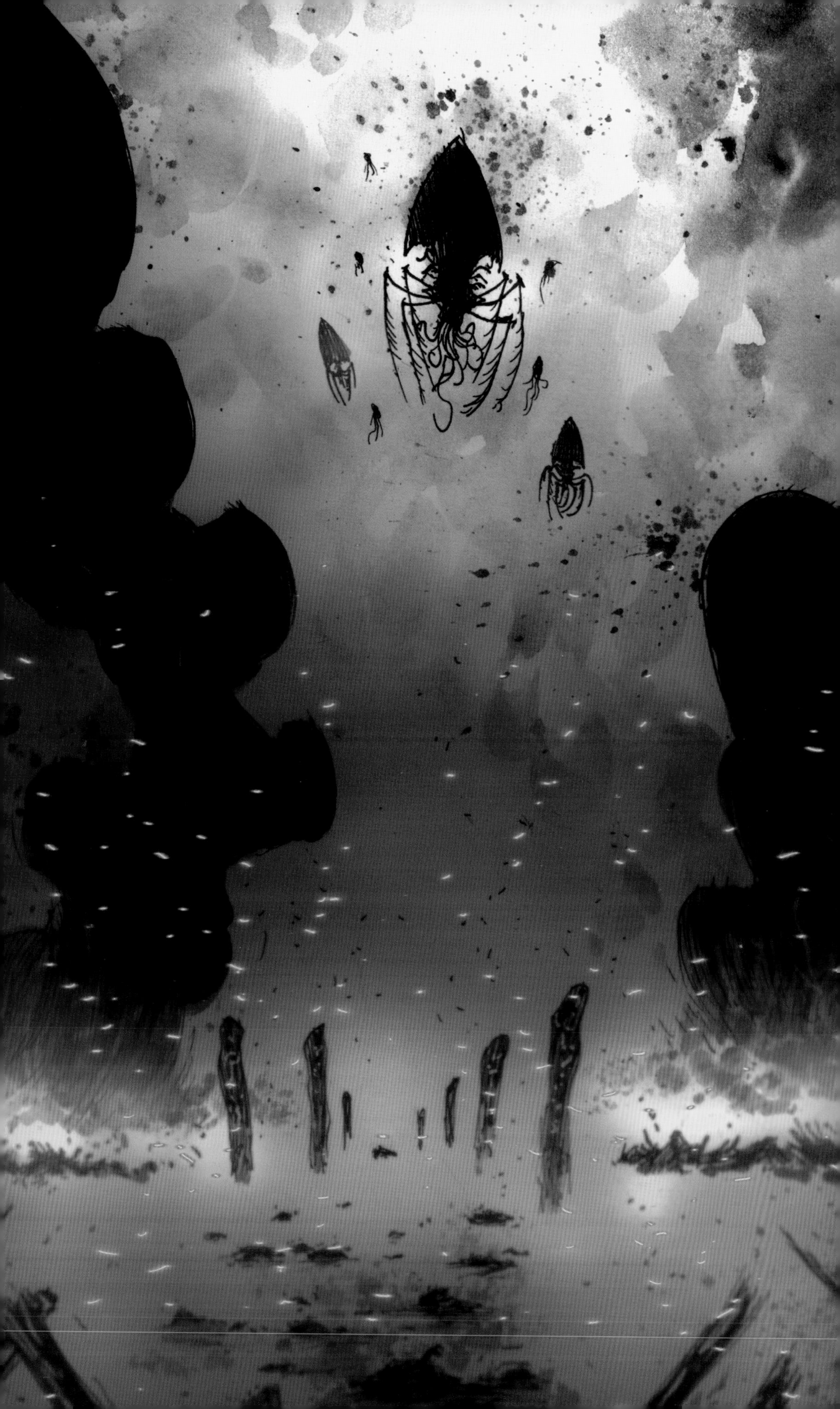

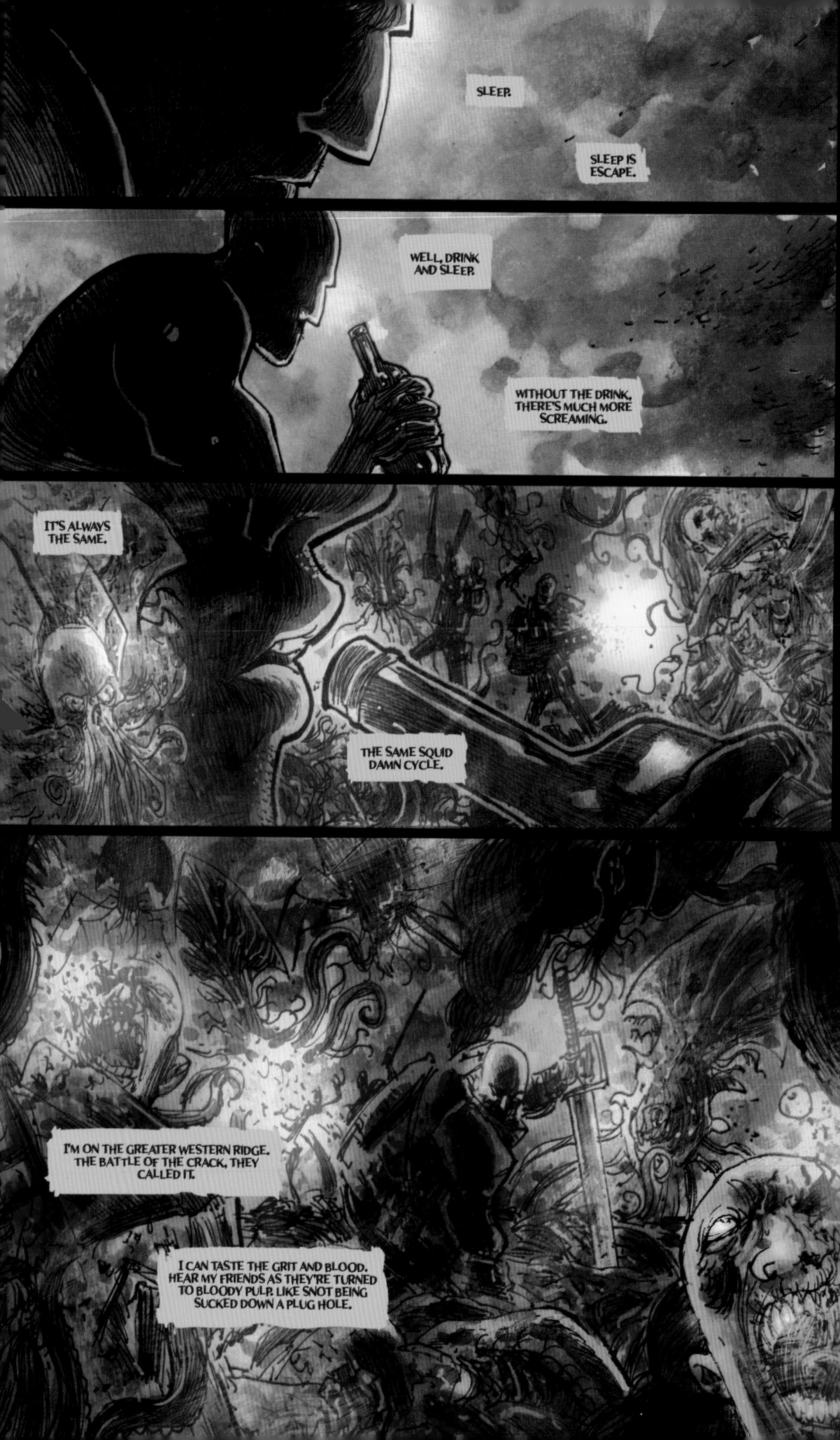

SLEEP.
SLEEP IS ESCAPE.
WELL, DRINK AND SLEEP.
WITHOUT THE DRINK, THERE'S MUCH MORE SCREAMING.
IT'S ALWAYS THE SAME.
THE SAME SQUID DAMN CYCLE.
I'M ON THE GREATER WESTERN RIDGE. THE BATTLE OF THE CRACK, THEY CALLED IT.
I CAN TASTE THE GRIT AND BLOOD. HEAR MY FRIENDS AS THEY'RE TURNED TO BLOODY PULP. LIKE SNOT BEING SUCKED DOWN A PLUG HOLE.

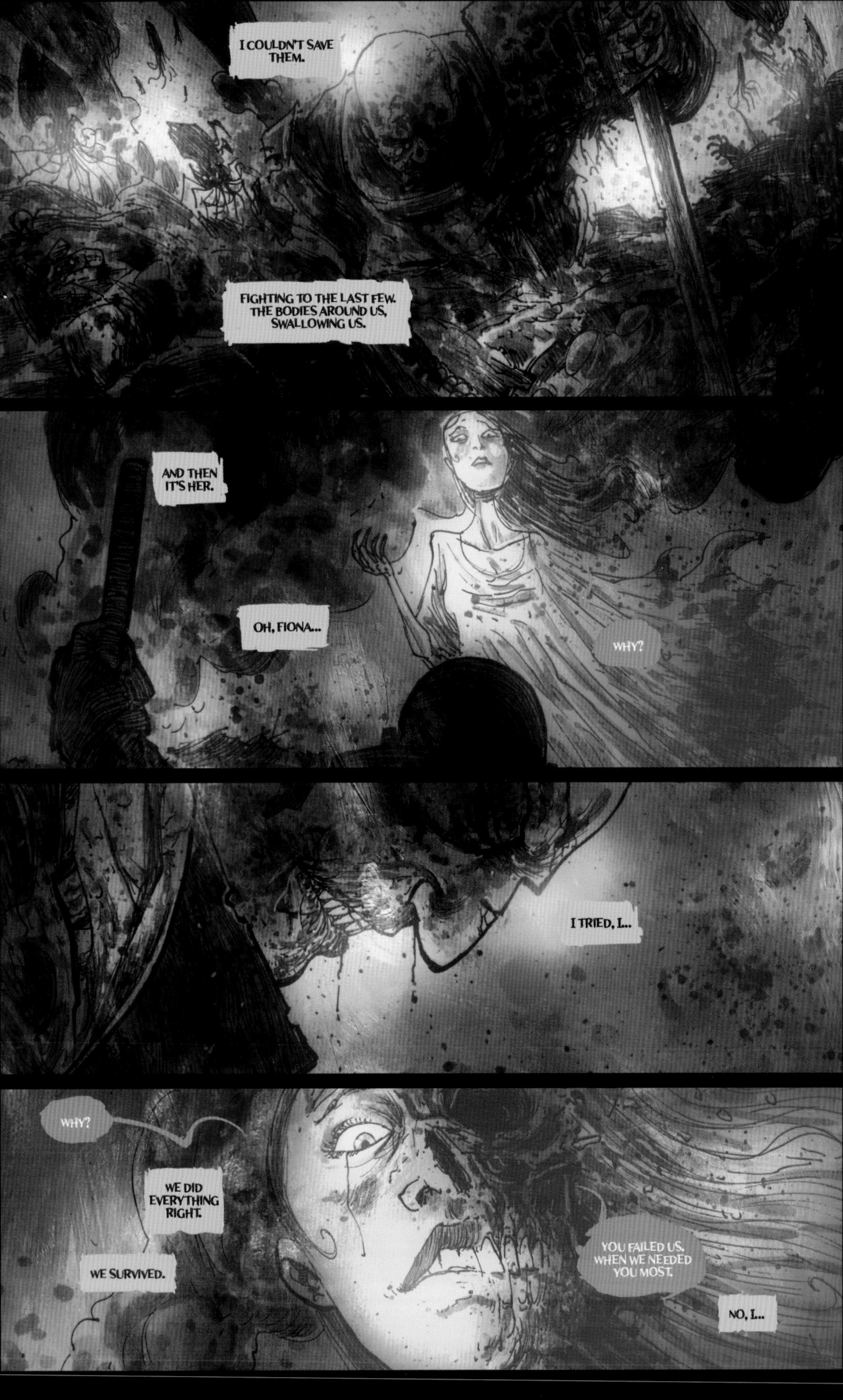
I COULDN'T SAVE THEM.
FIGHTING TO THE LAST FEW. THE BODIES AROUND US, SWALLOWING US.
AND THEN IT'S HER.
OH, FIONA...
WHY?
I TRIED, I...
WHY?
WE DID EVERYTHING RIGHT.
WE SURVIVED.
YOU FAILED US. WHEN WE NEEDED YOU MOST.
NO, I...

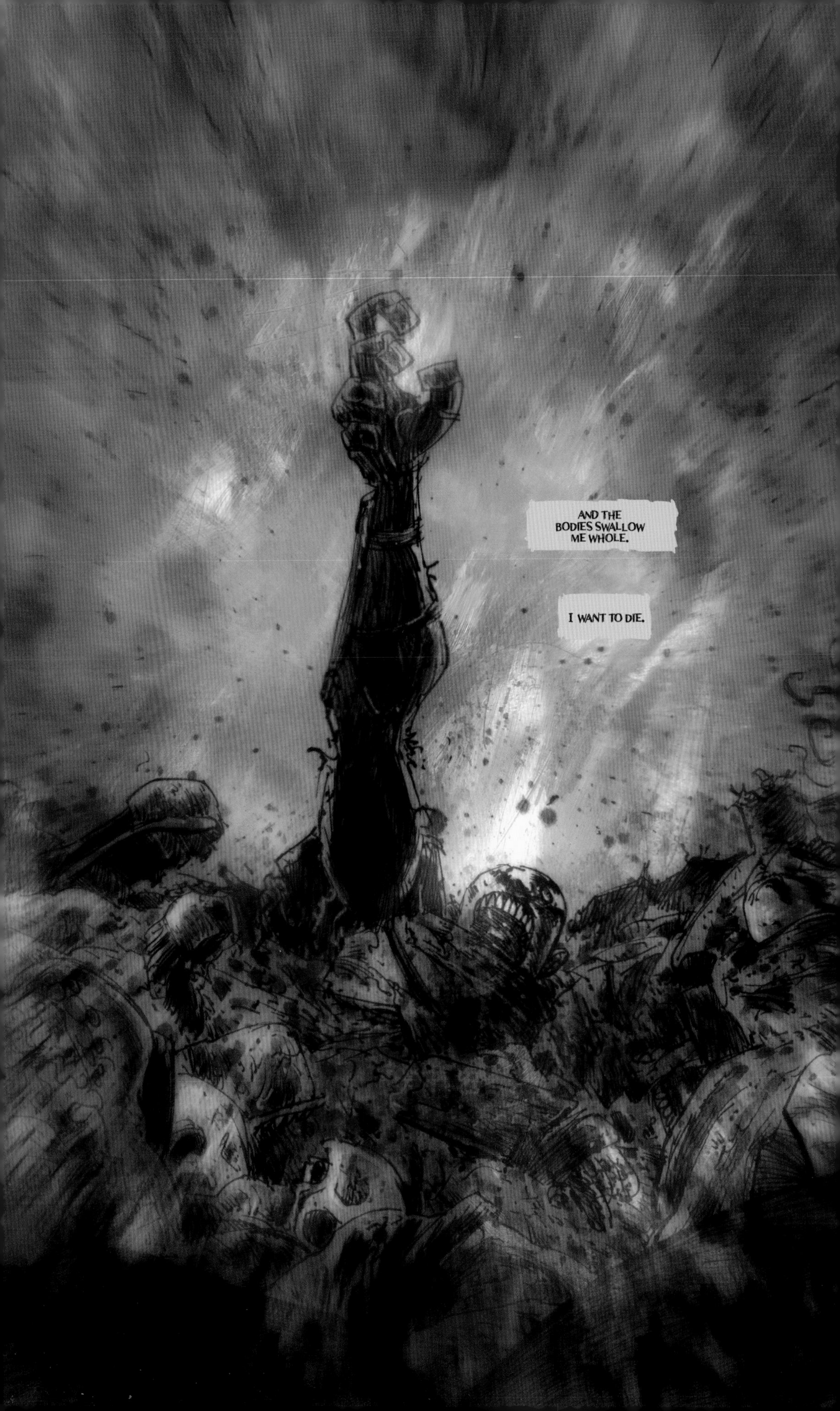
AND THE BODIES SWALLOW ME WHOLE.
I WANT TO DIE.

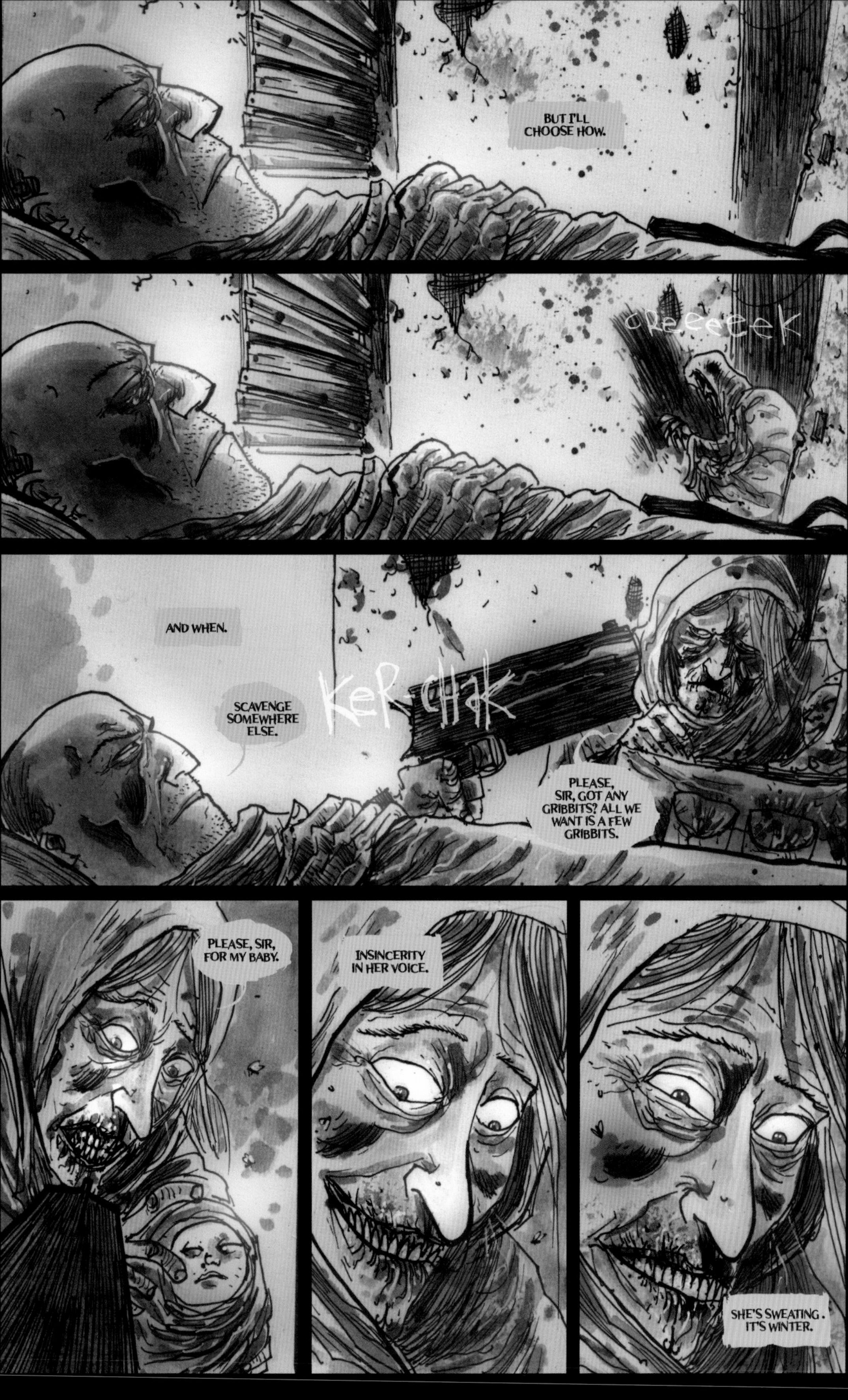
BUT I'LL CHOOSE HOW.
CREEEEEK
AND WHEN.
SCAVENGE SOMEWHERE ELSE.
KER-CHAK
PLEASE, SIR, GOT ANY GRIBBITS? ALL WE WANT IS A FEW GRIBBITS.
PLEASE, SIR, FOR MY BABY.
INSINCERITY IN HER VOICE.
SHE'S SWEATING. IT'S WINTER.

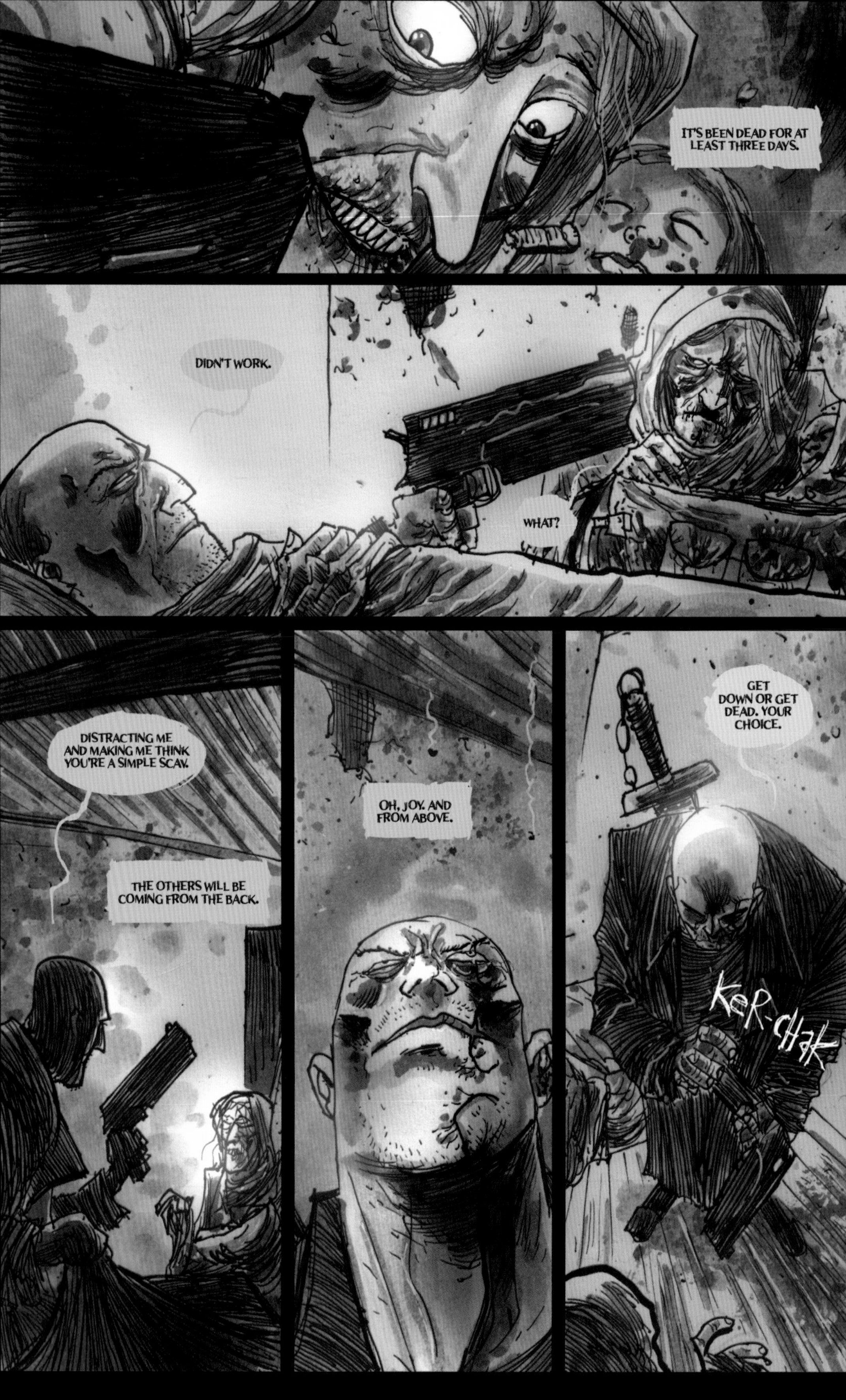
IT'S BEEN DEAD FOR AT LEAST THREE DAYS.
DIDN'T WORK.
WHAT?
DISTRACTING ME AND MAKING ME THINK YOU'RE A SIMPLE SCAV.
THE OTHERS WILL BE COMING FROM THE BACK.
OH, JOY. AND FROM ABOVE.
GET DOWN OR GET DEAD. YOUR CHOICE.
KER-CHAK

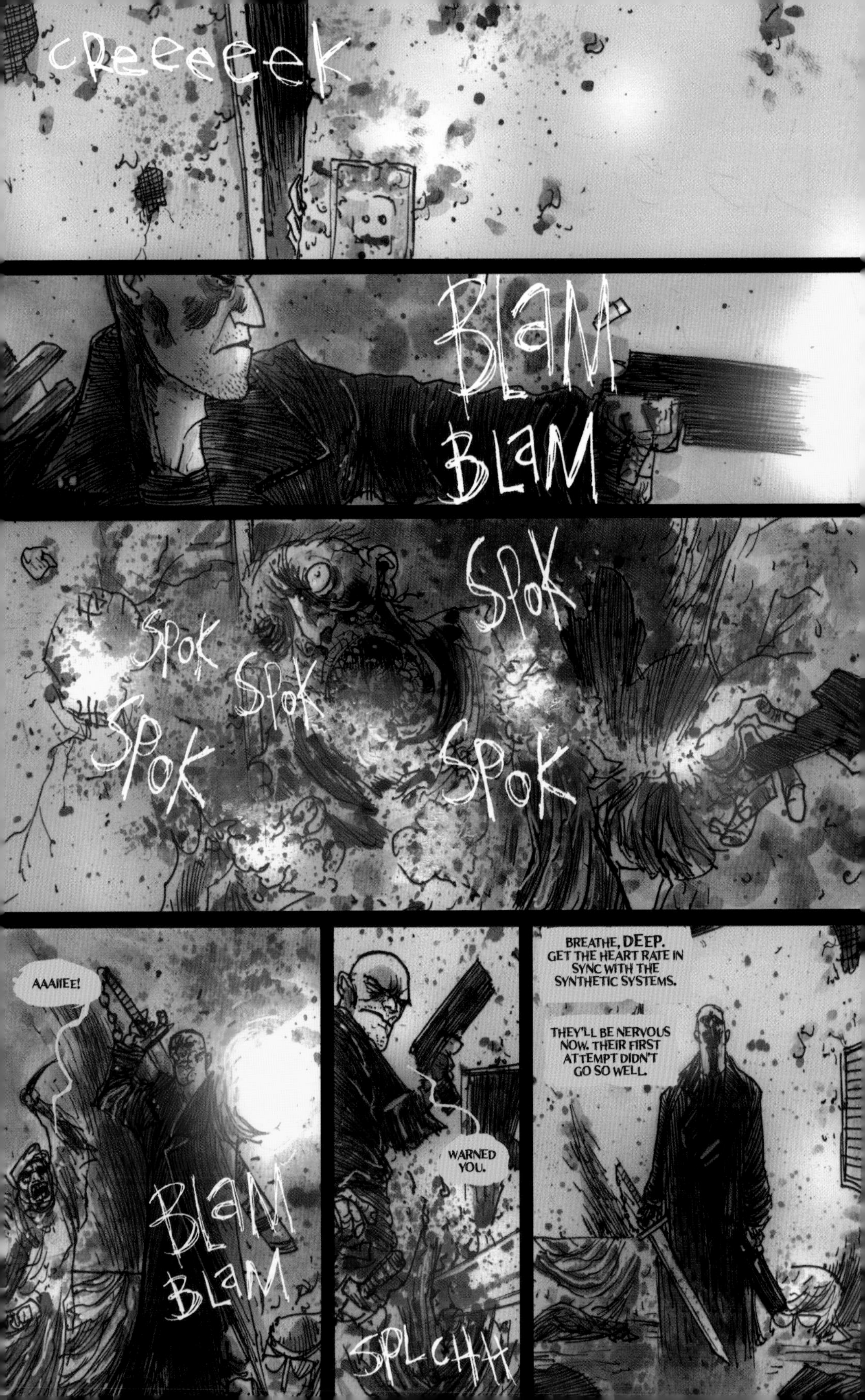
CREEEEEK
BLAM
BLAM
SPOK
SPOK
SPOK
SPOK
SPOK
AAAIIEE!
BLAM
BLAM
WARNED YOU.
SPLCHH
BREATHE, DEEP. GET THE HEART RATE IN SYNC WITH THE SYNTHETIC SYSTEMS.
THEY'LL BE NERVOUS NOW. THEIR FIRST ATTEMPT DIDN'T GO SO WELL.

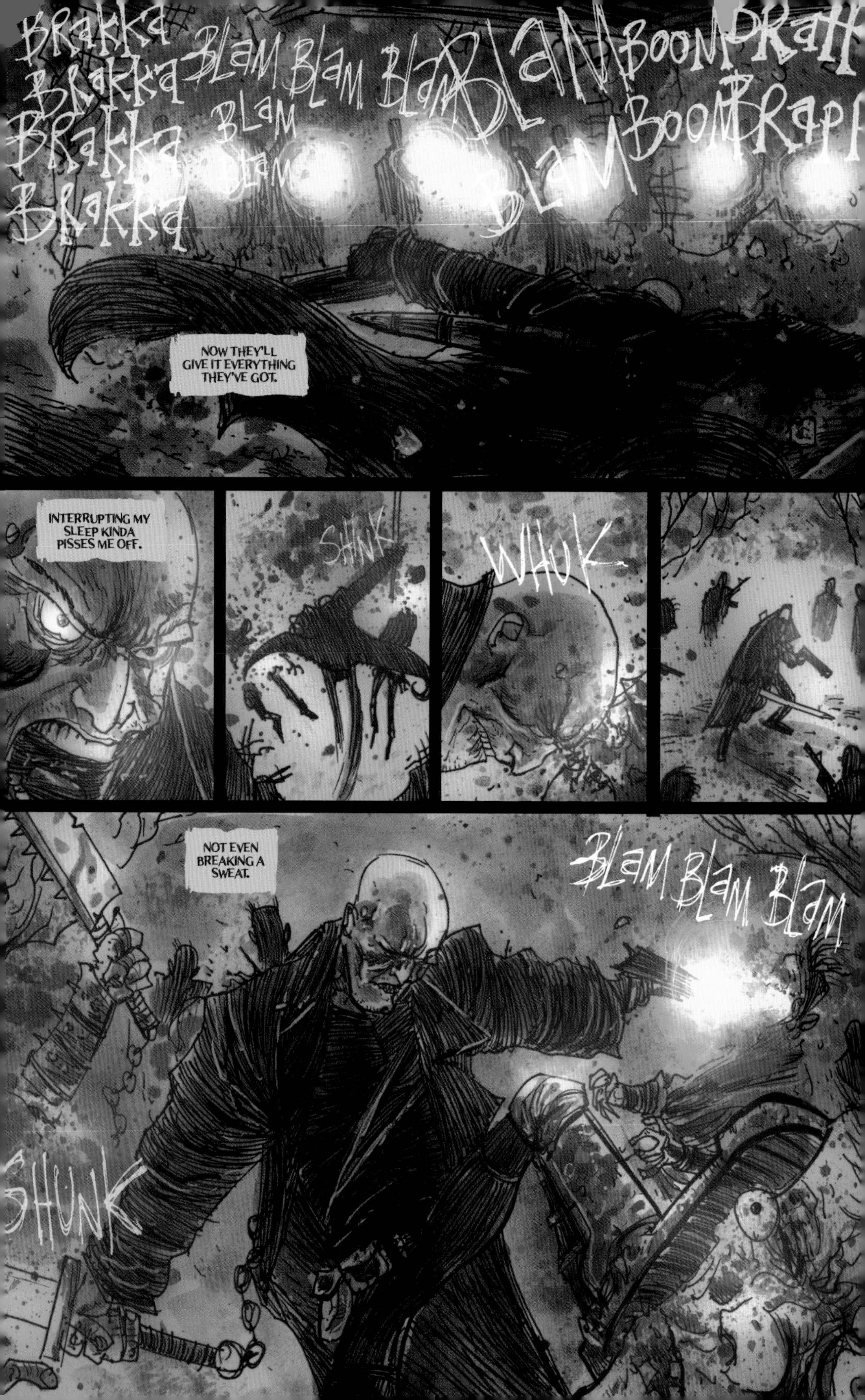
BRAKKA BRAKKA BRAKKA BRAKKA
BLAM BLAM BLAM BLAM BLAM BLAM BLAM BLAM
BOOM BOOM
BRATT BRAP
NOW THEY'LL GIVE IT EVERYTHING THEY'VE GOT.
INTERRUPTING MY SLEEP KINDA PISSES ME OFF.
SHINK
WHUK
NOT EVEN BREAKING A SWEAT.
BLAM BLAM BLAM
SHUNK

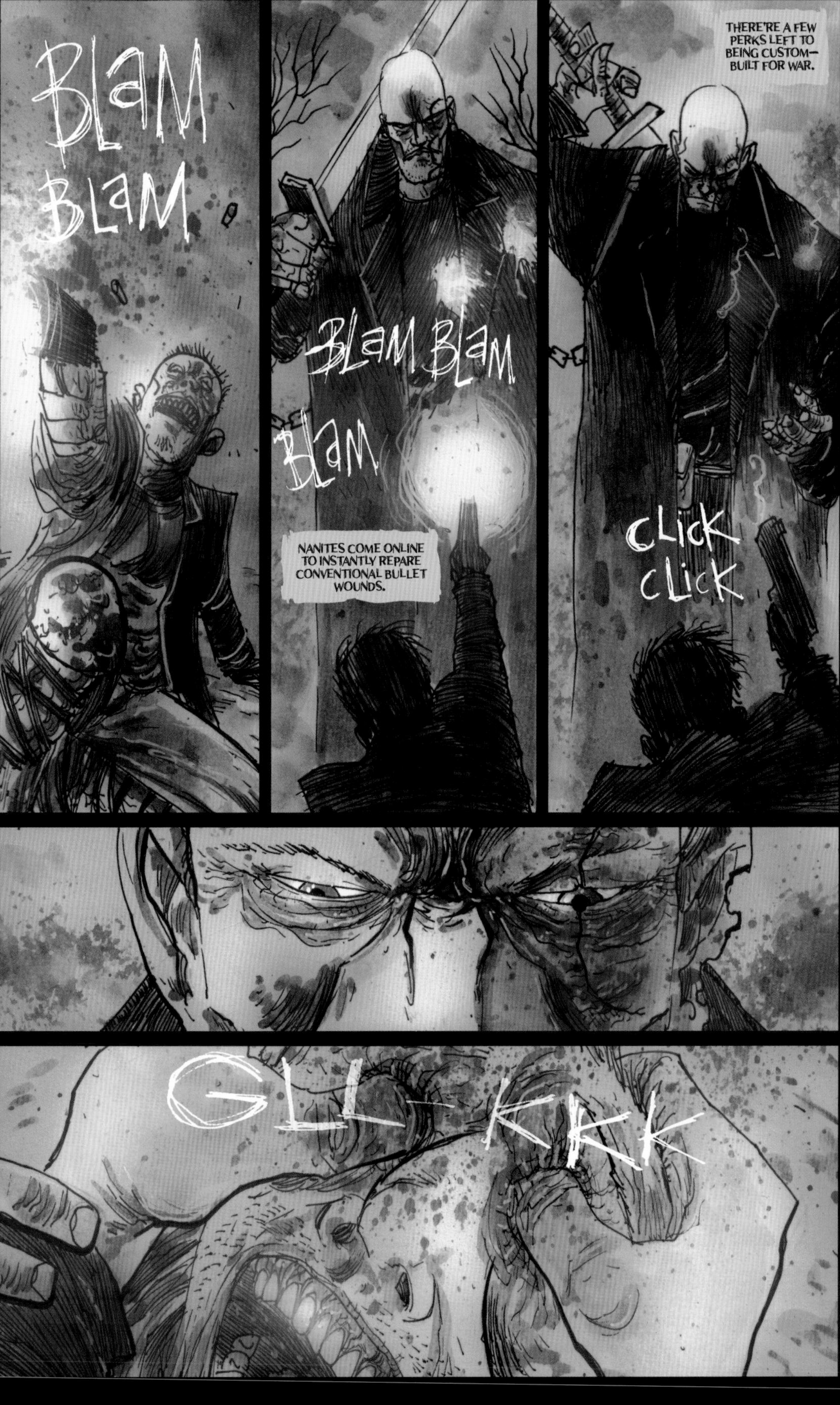
BLAM
BLAM
THERE'RE A FEW PERKS LEFT TO BEING CUSTOM-BUILT FOR WAR.
BLAM BLAM
BLAM
NANITES COME ONLINE TO INSTANTLY REPARE CONVENTIONAL BULLET WOUNDS.
CLICK
CLICK
GLL-KKK

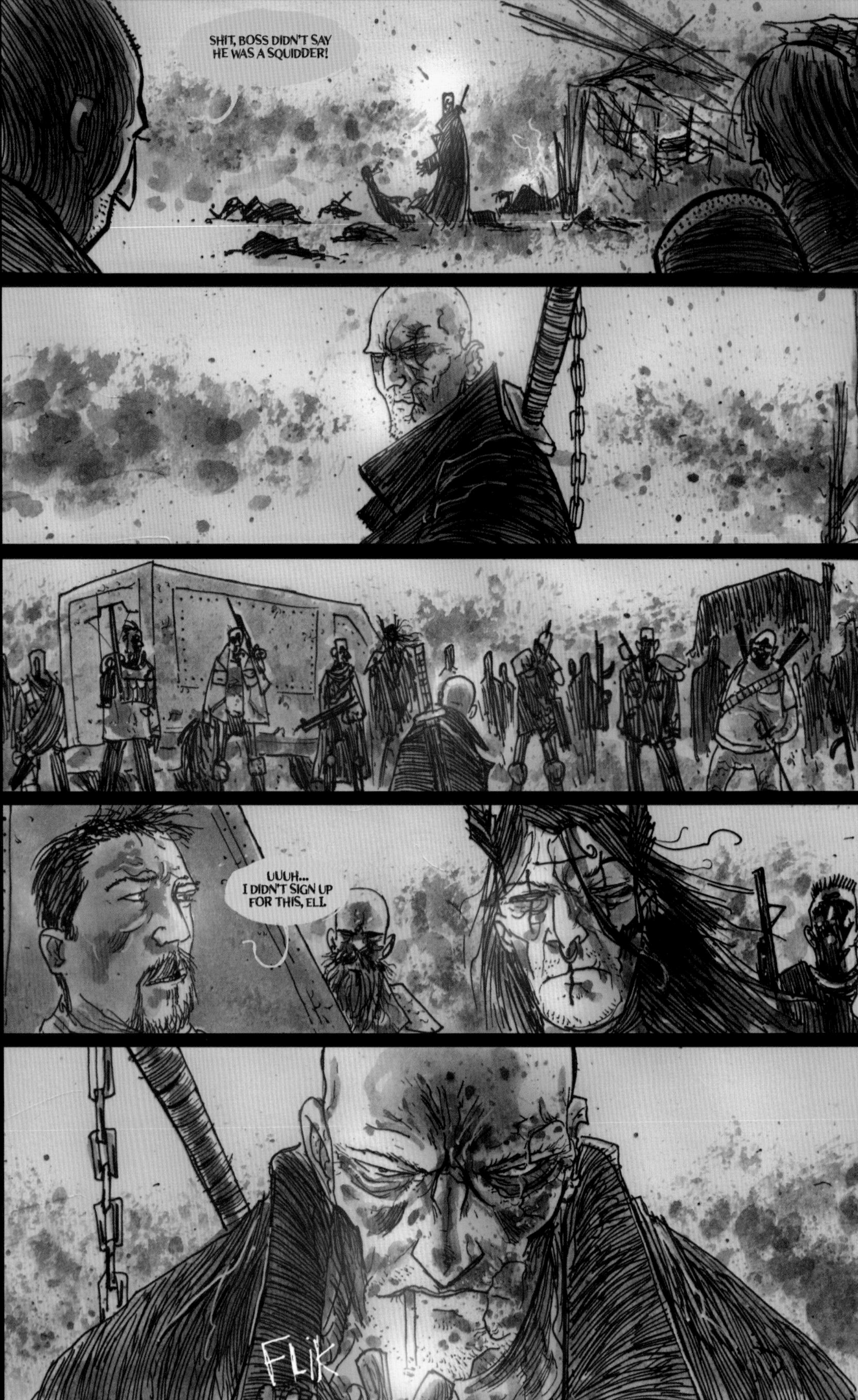
SHIT, BOSS DIDN'T SAY HE WAS A SQUIDDER!
UUUH... I DIDN'T SIGN UP FOR THIS, ELI.
FLIK

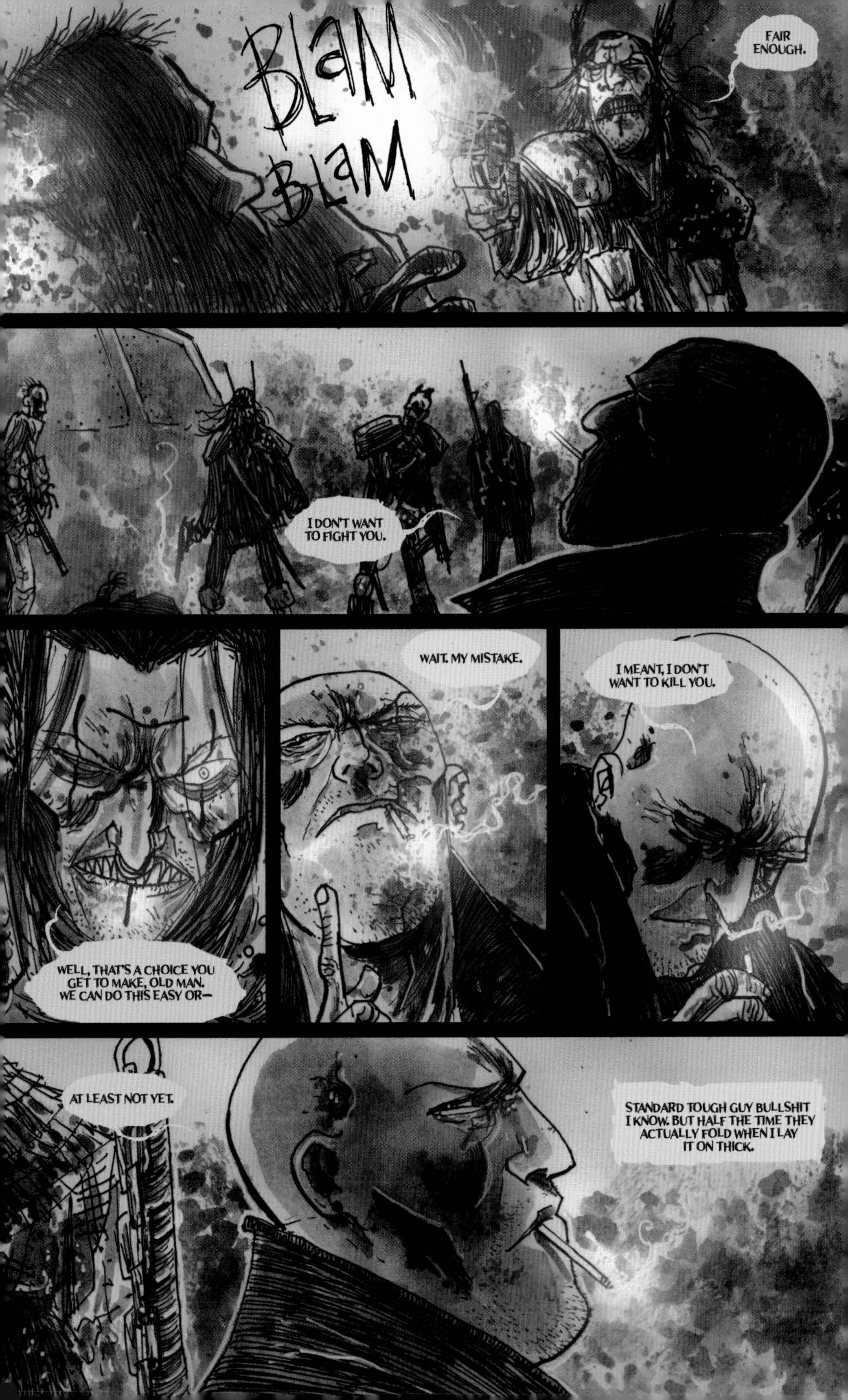
BLAM
BLAM
FAIR ENOUGH.
I DON'T WANT TO FIGHT YOU.
WELL, THAT'S A CHOICE YOU GET TO MAKE, OLD MAN. WE CAN DO THIS EASY OR—
WAIT. MY MISTAKE.
I MEANT, I DON'T WANT TO KILL YOU.
AT LEAST NOT YET.
STANDARD TOUGH GUY BULLSHIT I KNOW. BUT HALF THE TIME THEY ACTUALLY FOLD WHEN I LAY IT ON THICK.

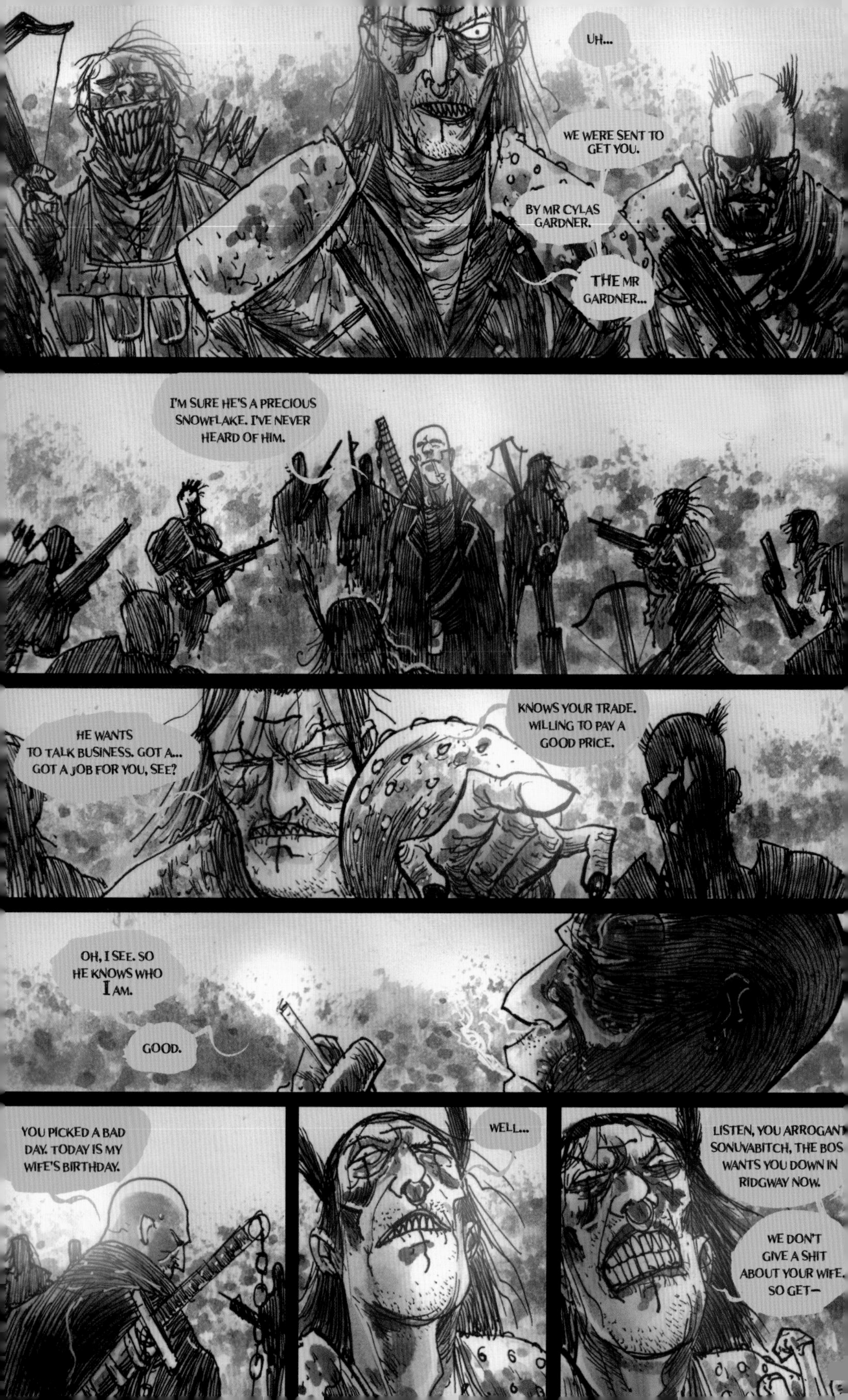
UH...
WE WERE SENT TO GET YOU.
BY MR CYLAS GARDNER.
THE MR GARDNER...
I'M SURE HE'S A PRECIOUS SNOWFLAKE. I'VE NEVER HEARD OF HIM.
HE WANTS TO TALK BUSINESS. GOT A... GOT A JOB FOR YOU, SEE?
KNOWS YOUR TRADE. WILLING TO PAY A GOOD PRICE.
OH, I SEE. SO HE KNOWS WHO I AM.
GOOD.
YOU PICKED A BAD DAY. TODAY IS MY WIFE'S BIRTHDAY.
WELL...
LISTEN, YOU ARROGANT SONUVABITCH, THE BOS WANTS YOU DOWN IN RIDGWAY NOW.
WE DON'T GIVE A SHIT ABOUT YOUR WIFE. SO GET—

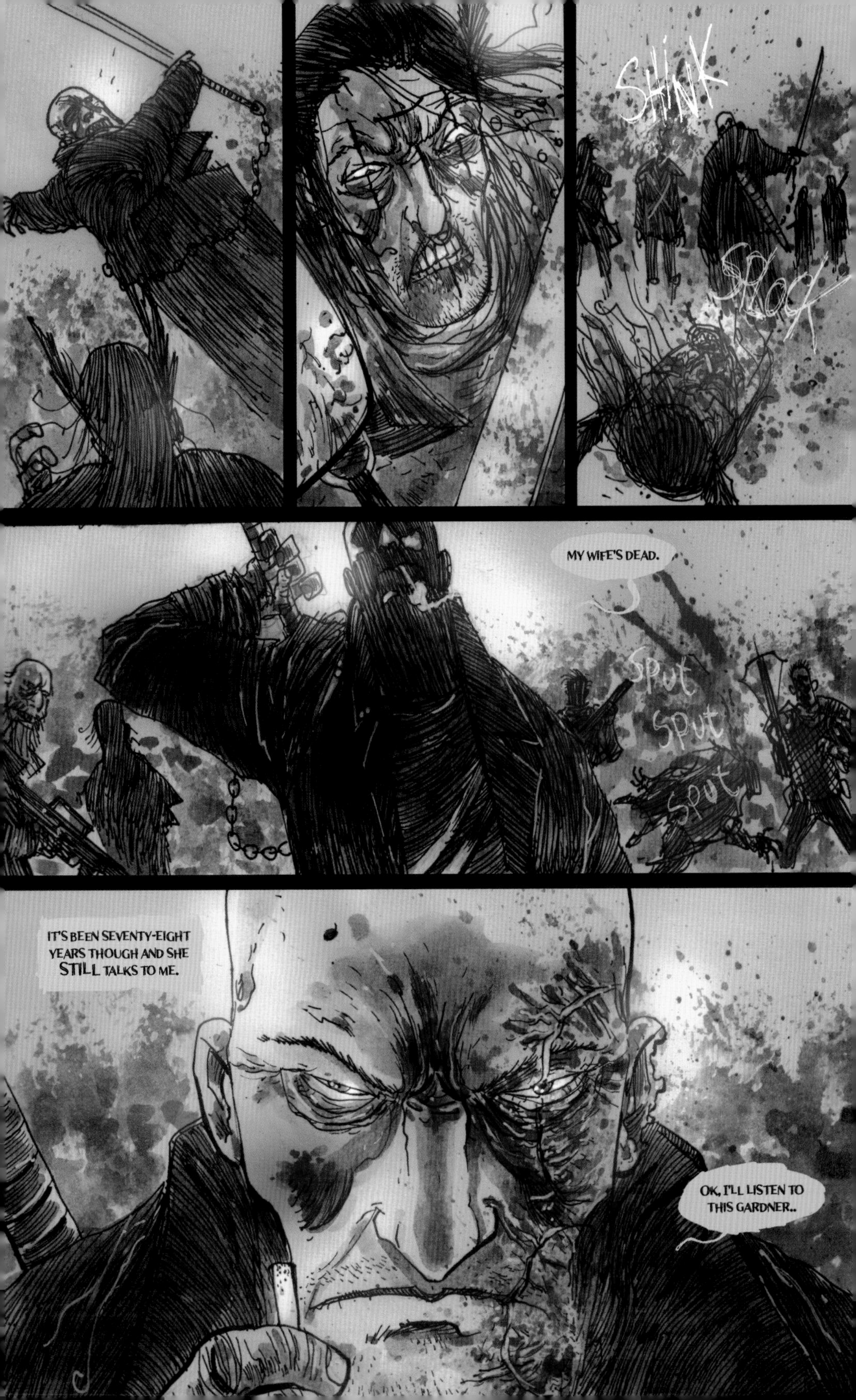
SHINK
SPLOCK
MY WIFE'S DEAD.
SPUT
SPUT
SPUT
IT'S BEEN SEVENTY-EIGHT YEARS THOUGH AND SHE STILL TALKS TO ME.
OK, I'LL LISTEN TO THIS GARDNER..

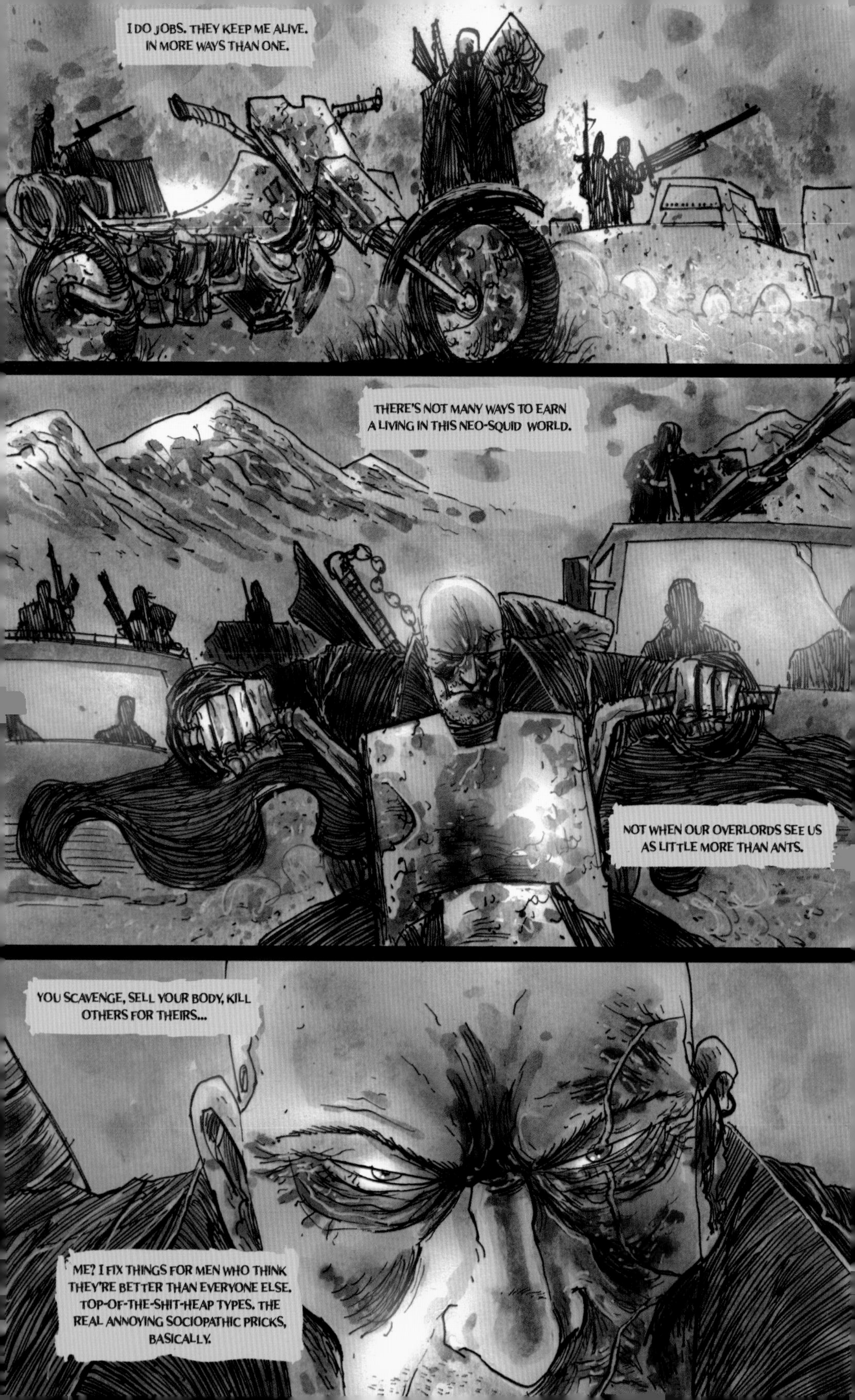
I DO JOBS. THEY KEEP ME ALIVE. IN MORE WAYS THAN ONE.
THERE'S NOT MANY WAYS TO EARN A LIVING IN THIS NEO-SQUID WORLD.
NOT WHEN OUR OVERLORDS SEE US AS LITTLE MORE THAN ANTS.
YOU SCAVENGE, SELL YOUR BODY, KILL OTHERS FOR THEIRS...
ME? I FIX THINGS FOR MEN WHO THINK THEY'RE BETTER THAN EVERYONE ELSE. TOP-OF-THE-SHIT-HEAP TYPES. THE REAL ANNOYING SOCIOPATHIC PRICKS, BASICALLY.

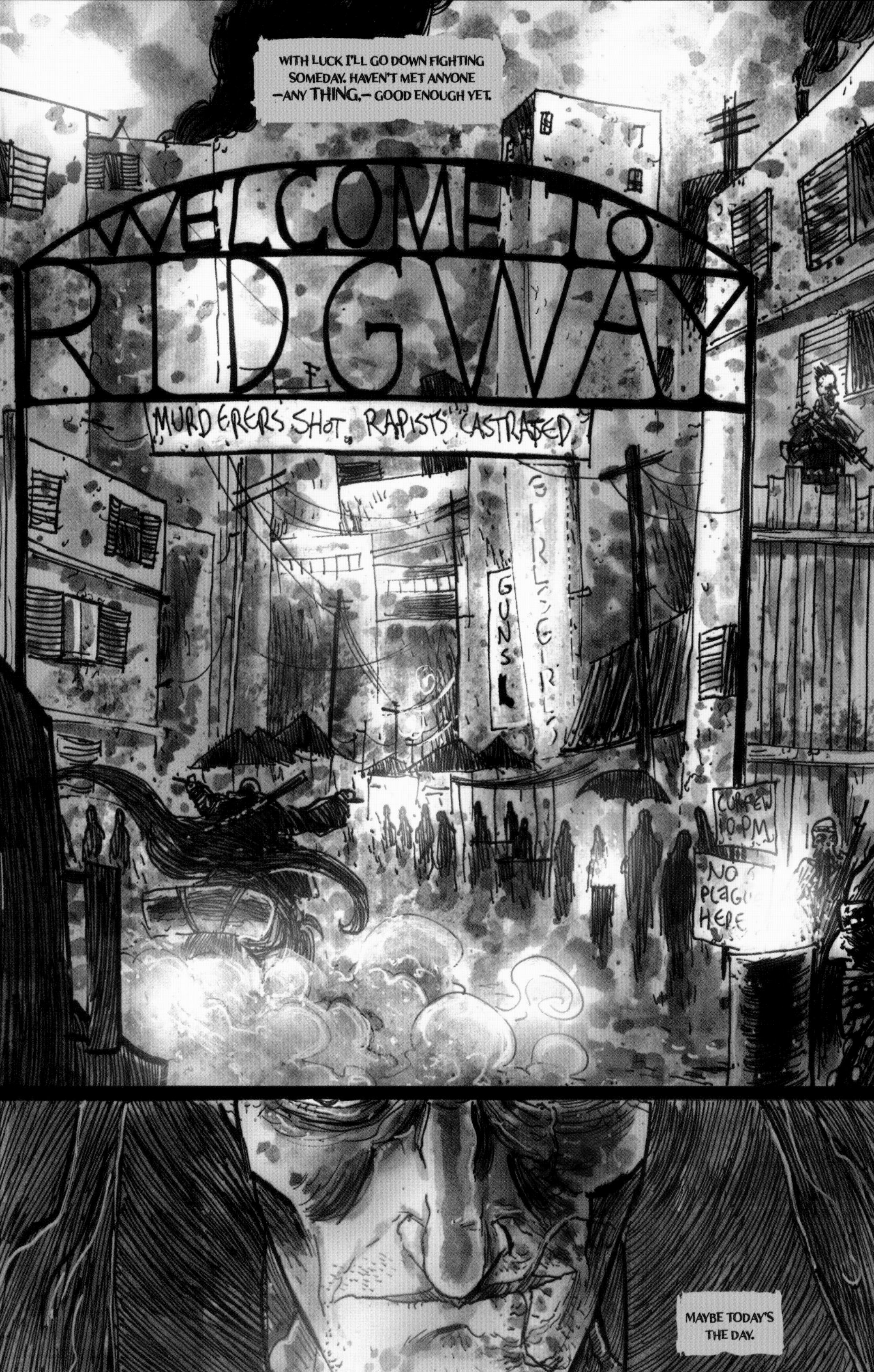
WITH LUCK I'LL GO DOWN FIGHTING SOMEDAY. HAVEN'T MET ANYONE —ANY THING,— GOOD ENOUGH YET.
WELCOME TO
RIDGWAY
MURDERERS SHOT, RAPISTS CASTRATED
GUNS
GIRLS
GIRLS
CURFEW 10 PM
NO PLAGU HERE
MAYBE TODAY'S THE DAY.

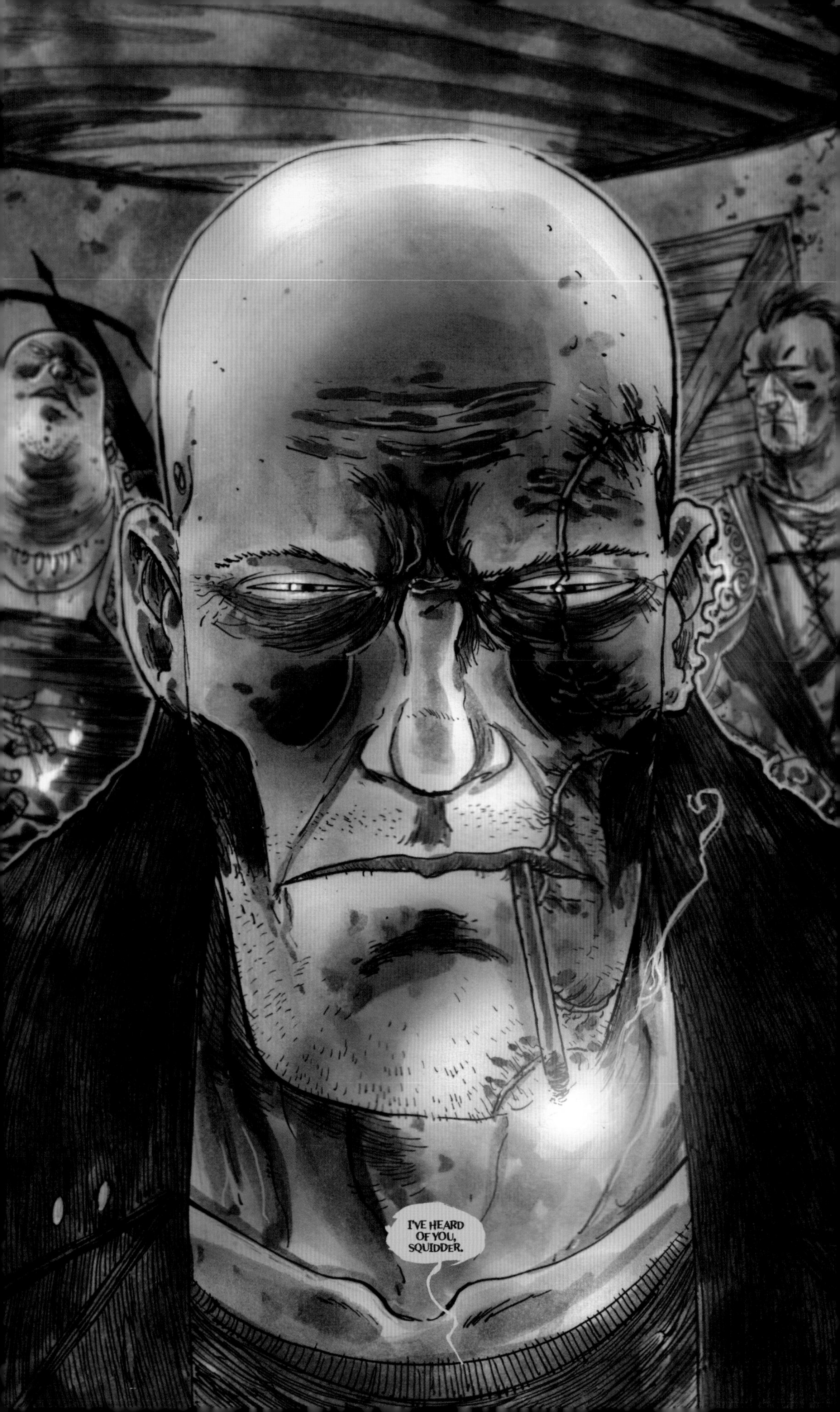
I'VE HEARD OF YOU, SQUIDDER.

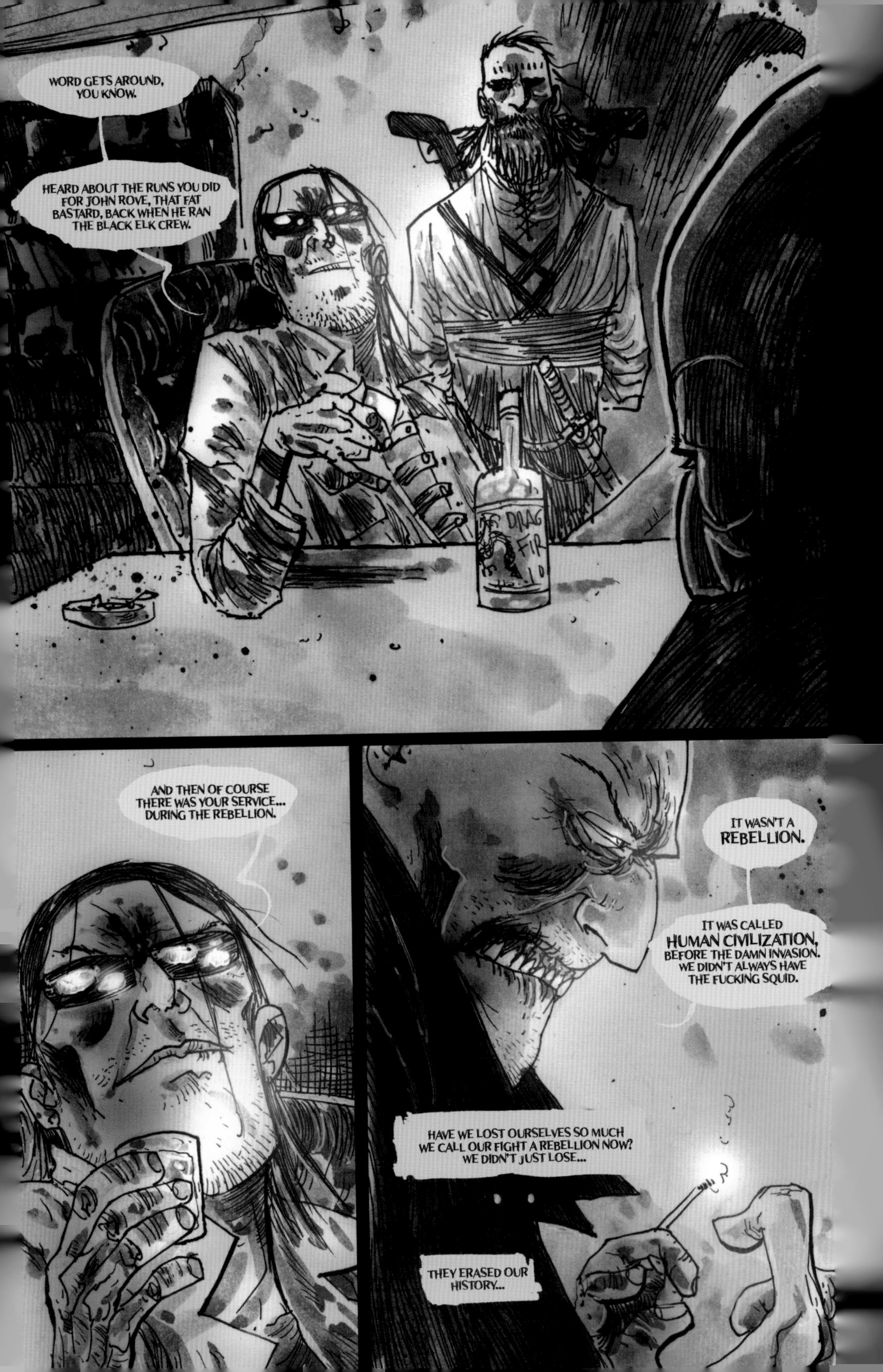
WORD GETS AROUND, YOU KNOW.
HEARD ABOUT THE RUNS YOU DID FOR JOHN ROVE, THAT FAT BASTARD, BACK WHEN HE RAN THE BLACK ELK CREW.
AND THEN OF COURSE THERE WAS YOUR SERVICE... DURING THE REBELLION.
IT WASN'T A REBELLION.
IT WAS CALLED HUMAN CIVILIZATION, BEFORE THE DAMN INVASION. WE DIDN'T ALWAYS HAVE THE FUCKING SQUID.
HAVE WE LOST OURSELVES SO MUCH WE CALL OUR FIGHT A REBELLION NOW? WE DIDN'T JUST LOSE...
THEY ERASED OUR HISTORY...

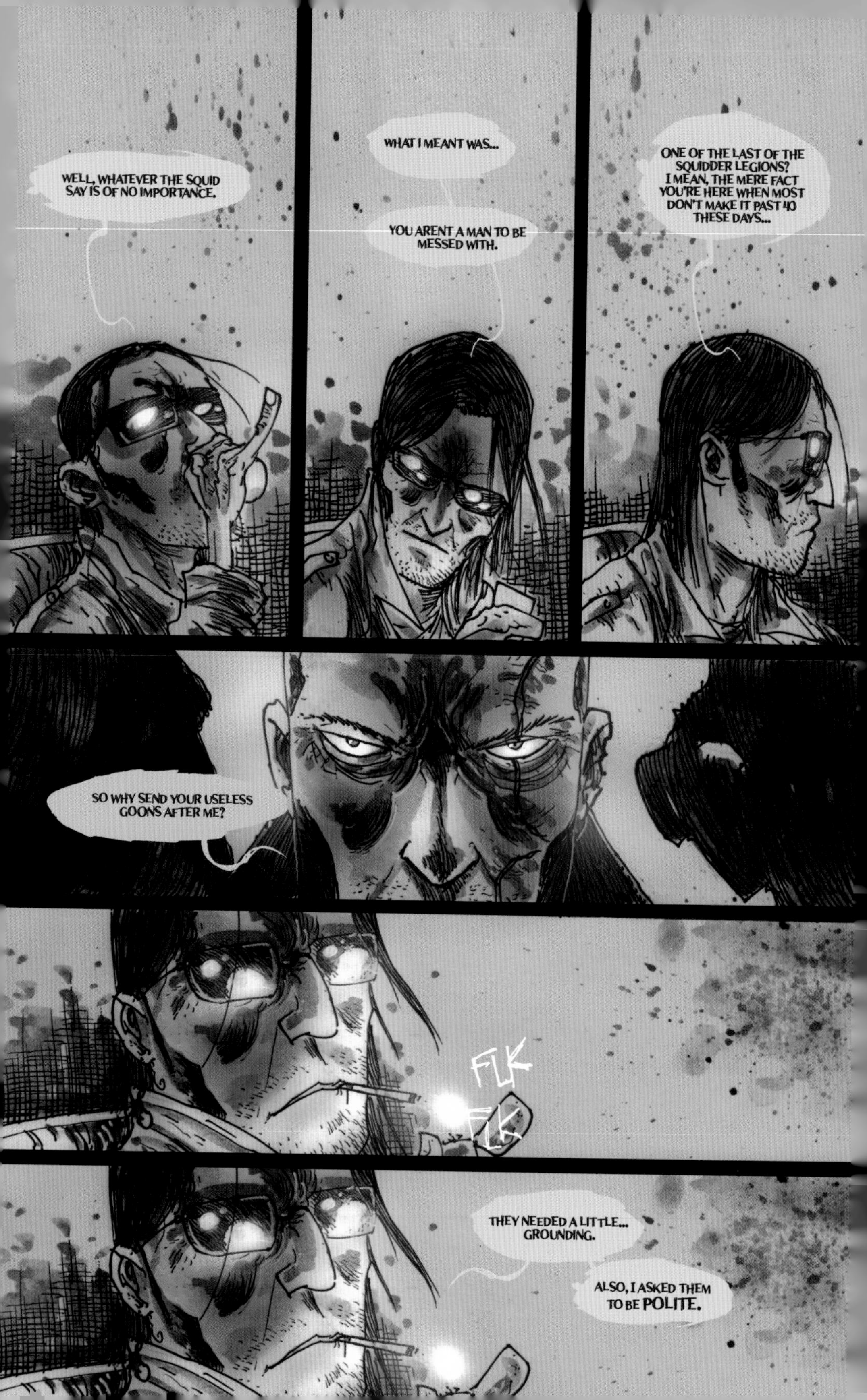
WELL, WHATEVER THE SQUID SAY IS OF NO IMPORTANCE.
WHAT I MEANT WAS...
YOU ARENT A MAN TO BE MESSED WITH.
ONE OF THE LAST OF THE SQUIDDER LEGIONS? I MEAN, THE MERE FACT YOU'RE HERE WHEN MOST DON'T MAKE IT PAST 40 THESE DAYS...
SO WHY SEND YOUR USELESS GOONS AFTER ME?
FLK
FLK
THEY NEEDED A LITTLE... GROUNDING.
ALSO, I ASKED THEM TO BE POLITE.

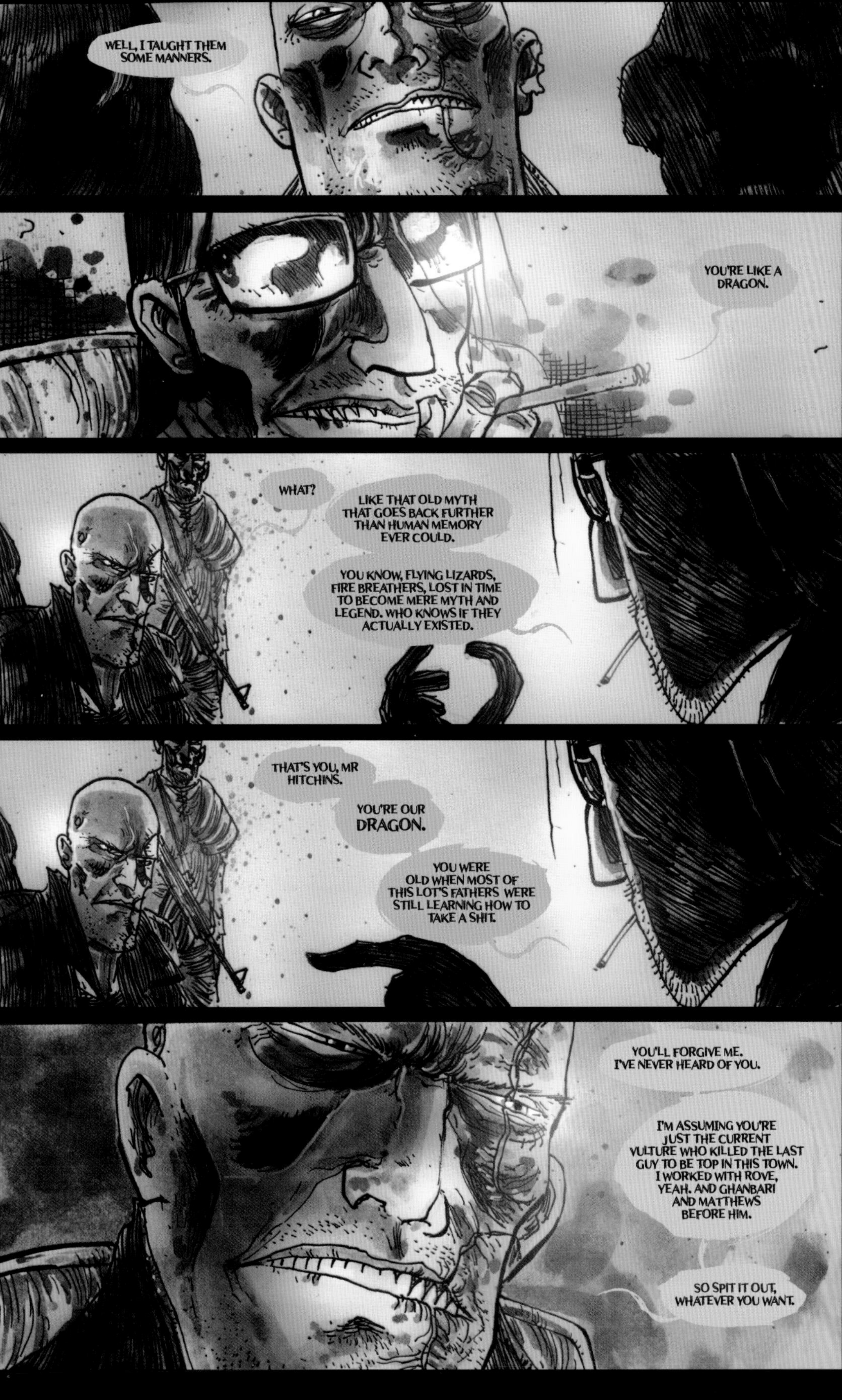
WELL, I TAUGHT THEM SOME MANNERS.
YOU'RE LIKE A DRAGON.
WHAT?
LIKE THAT OLD MYTH THAT GOES BACK FURTHER THAN HUMAN MEMORY EVER COULD.
YOU KNOW, FLYING LIZARDS, FIRE BREATHERS, LOST IN TIME TO BECOME MERE MYTH AND LEGEND. WHO KNOWS IF THEY ACTUALLY EXISTED.
THAT'S YOU, MR HITCHINS.
YOU'RE OUR DRAGON.
YOU WERE OLD WHEN MOST OF THIS LOT'S FATHERS WERE STILL LEARNING HOW TO TAKE A SHIT.
YOU'LL FORGIVE ME. I'VE NEVER HEARD OF YOU.
I'M ASSUMING YOU'RE JUST THE CURRENT VULTURE WHO KILLED THE LAST GUY TO BE TOP IN THIS TOWN. I WORKED WITH ROVE, YEAH. AND GHANBARI AND MATTHEWS BEFORE HIM.
SO SPIT IT OUT, WHATEVER YOU WANT.

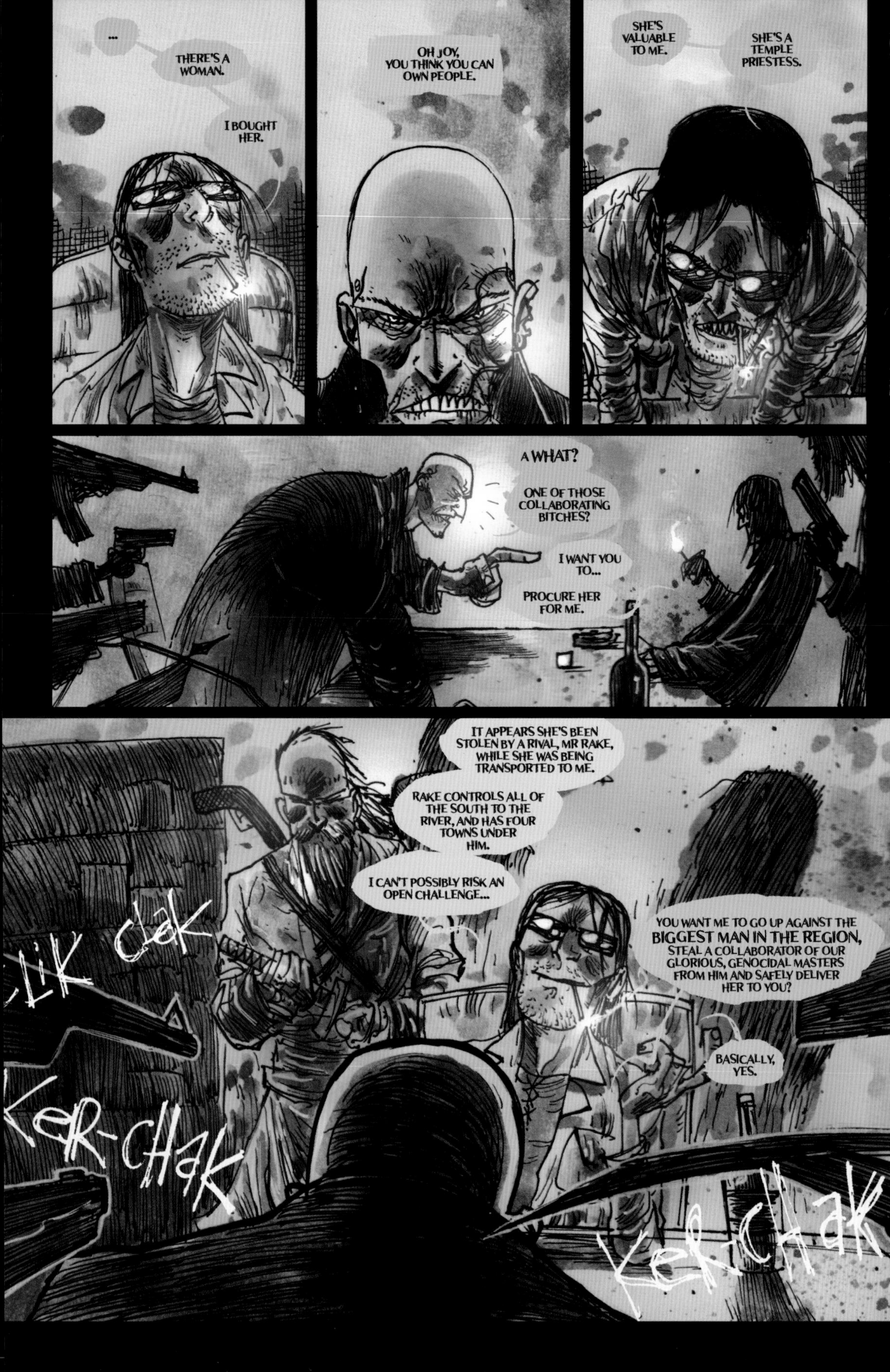
...
THERE'S A WOMAN.
I BOUGHT HER.
OH JOY, YOU THINK YOU CAN OWN PEOPLE.
SHE'S VALUABLE TO ME.
SHE'S A TEMPLE PRIESTESS.
A WHAT?
ONE OF THOSE COLLABORATING BITCHES?
I WANT YOU TO...
PROCURE HER FOR ME.
IT APPEARS SHE'S BEEN STOLEN BY A RIVAL, MR RAKE, WHILE SHE WAS BEING TRANSPORTED TO ME.
RAKE CONTROLS ALL OF THE SOUTH TO THE RIVER, AND HAS FOUR TOWNS UNDER HIM.
I CAN'T POSSIBLY RISK AN OPEN CHALLENGE...
YOU WANT ME TO GO UP AGAINST THE BIGGEST MAN IN THE REGION, STEAL A COLLABORATOR OF OUR GLORIOUS, GENOCIDAL MASTERS FROM HIM AND SAFELY DELIVER HER TO YOU?
BASICALLY, YES.
KER-CHAK
KER-CHAK

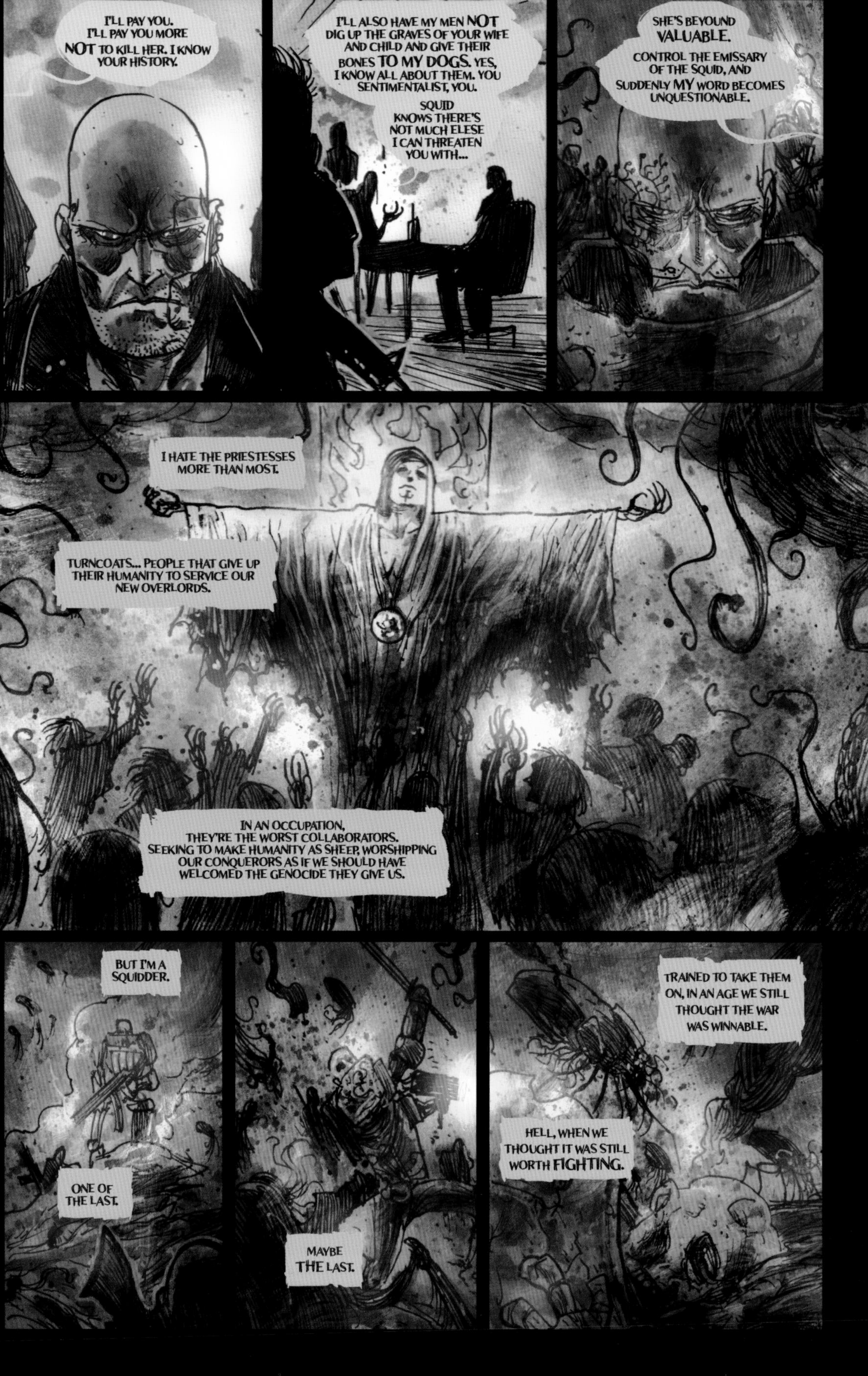
I'LL PAY YOU. I'LL PAY YOU MORE NOT TO KILL HER. I KNOW YOUR HISTORY.
I'LL ALSO HAVE MY MEN NOT DIG UP THE GRAVES OF YOUR WIFE AND CHILD AND GIVE THEIR BONES TO MY DOGS. YES, I KNOW ALL ABOUT THEM. YOU SENTIMENTALIST, YOU.
SQUID KNOWS THERE'S NOT MUCH ELESE I CAN THREATEN YOU WITH...
SHE'S BEYOUND VALUABLE.
CONTROL THE EMISSARY OF THE SQUID, AND SUDDENLY MY WORD BECOMES UNQUESTIONABLE.
I HATE THE PRIESTESSES MORE THAN MOST.
TURNCOATS... PEOPLE THAT GIVE UP THEIR HUMANITY TO SERVICE OUR NEW OVERLORDS.
IN AN OCCUPATION, THEY'RE THE WORST COLLABORATORS. SEEKING TO MAKE HUMANITY AS SHEEP, WORSHIPPING OUR CONQUERORS AS IF WE SHOULD HAVE WELCOMED THE GENOCIDE THEY GIVE US.
BUT I'M A SQUIDDER.
ONE OF THE LAST.
MAYBE THE LAST.
TRAINED TO TAKE THEM ON, IN AN AGE WE STILL THOUGHT THE WAR WAS WINNABLE.
HELL, WHEN WE THOUGHT IT WAS STILL WORTH FIGHTING.

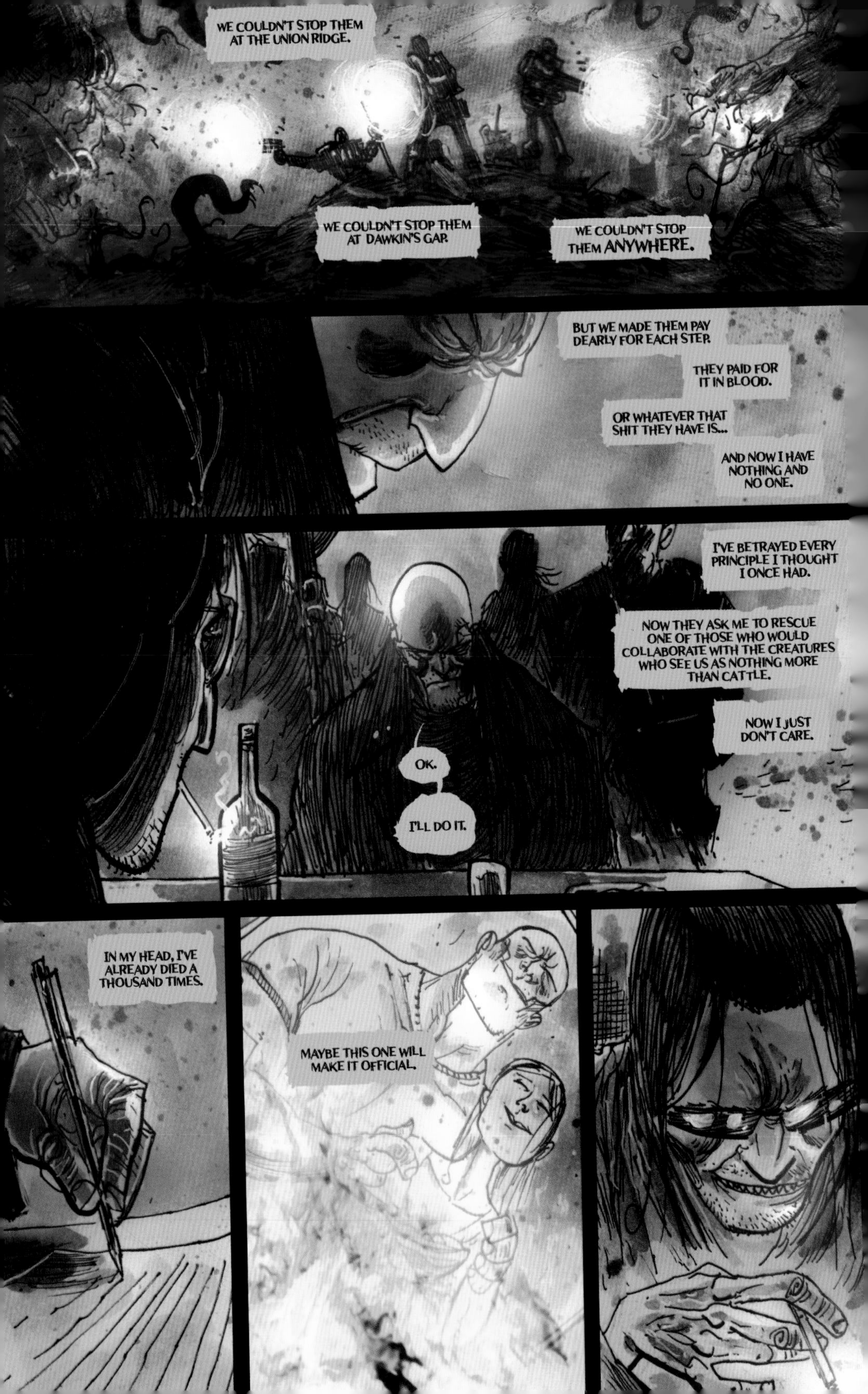
WE COULDN'T STOP THEM AT THE UNION RIDGE.
WE COULDN'T STOP THEM AT DAWKIN'S GAP.
WE COULDN'T STOP THEM ANYWHERE.
BUT WE MADE THEM PAY DEARLY FOR EACH STEP.
THEY PAID FOR IT IN BLOOD.
OR WHATEVER THAT SHIT THEY HAVE IS...
AND NOW I HAVE NOTHING AND NO ONE.
I'VE BETRAYED EVERY PRINCIPLE I THOUGHT I ONCE HAD.
NOW THEY ASK ME TO RESCUE ONE OF THOSE WHO WOULD COLLABORATE WITH THE CREATURES WHO SEE US AS NOTHING MORE THAN CATTLE.
NOW I JUST DON'T CARE.
OK.
I'LL DO IT.
IN MY HEAD, I'VE ALREADY DIED A THOUSAND TIMES.
MAYBE THIS ONE WILL MAKE IT OFFICIAL.

CHAPTER TWO

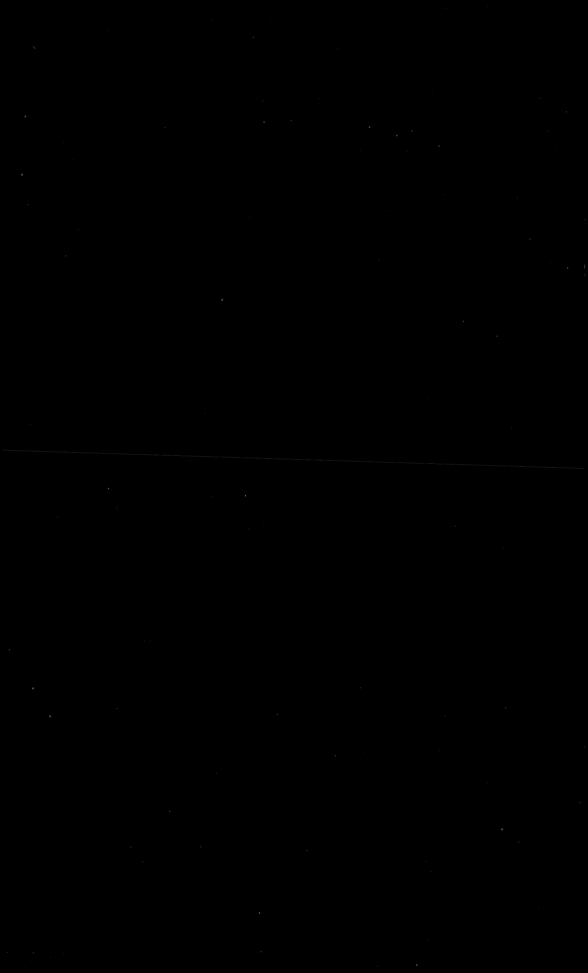

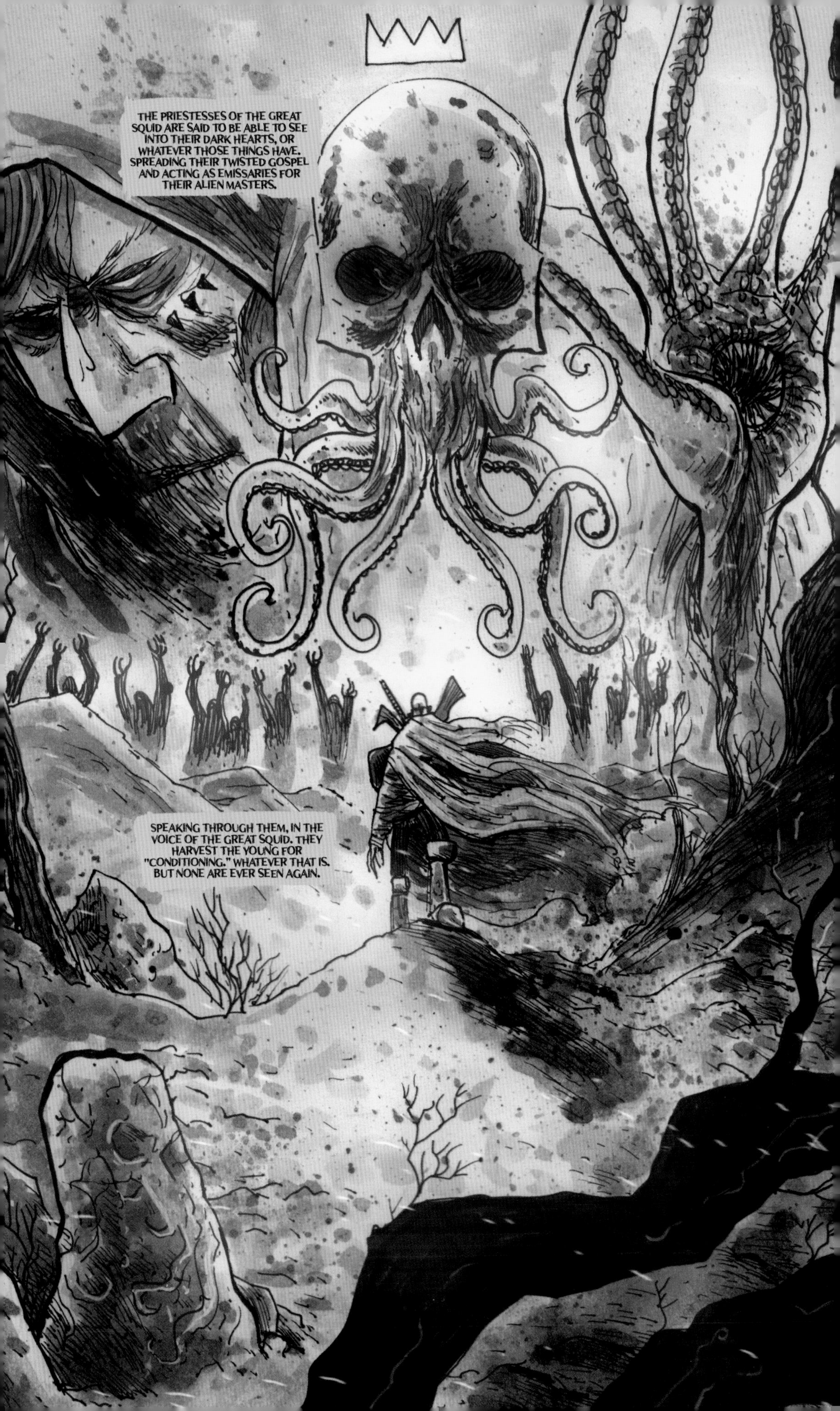

THE PRIESTESSES OF THE GREAT SQUID ARE SAID TO BE ABLE TO SEE INTO THEIR DARK HEARTS, OR WHATEVER THOSE THINGS HAVE. SPREADING THEIR TWISTED GOSPEL AND ACTING AS EMISSARIES FOR THEIR ALIEN MASTERS.
SPEAKING THROUGH THEM, IN THE VOICE OF THE GREAT SQUID. THEY HARVEST THE YOUNG FOR "CONDITIONING." WHATEVER THAT IS. BUT NONE ARE EVER SEEN AGAIN.

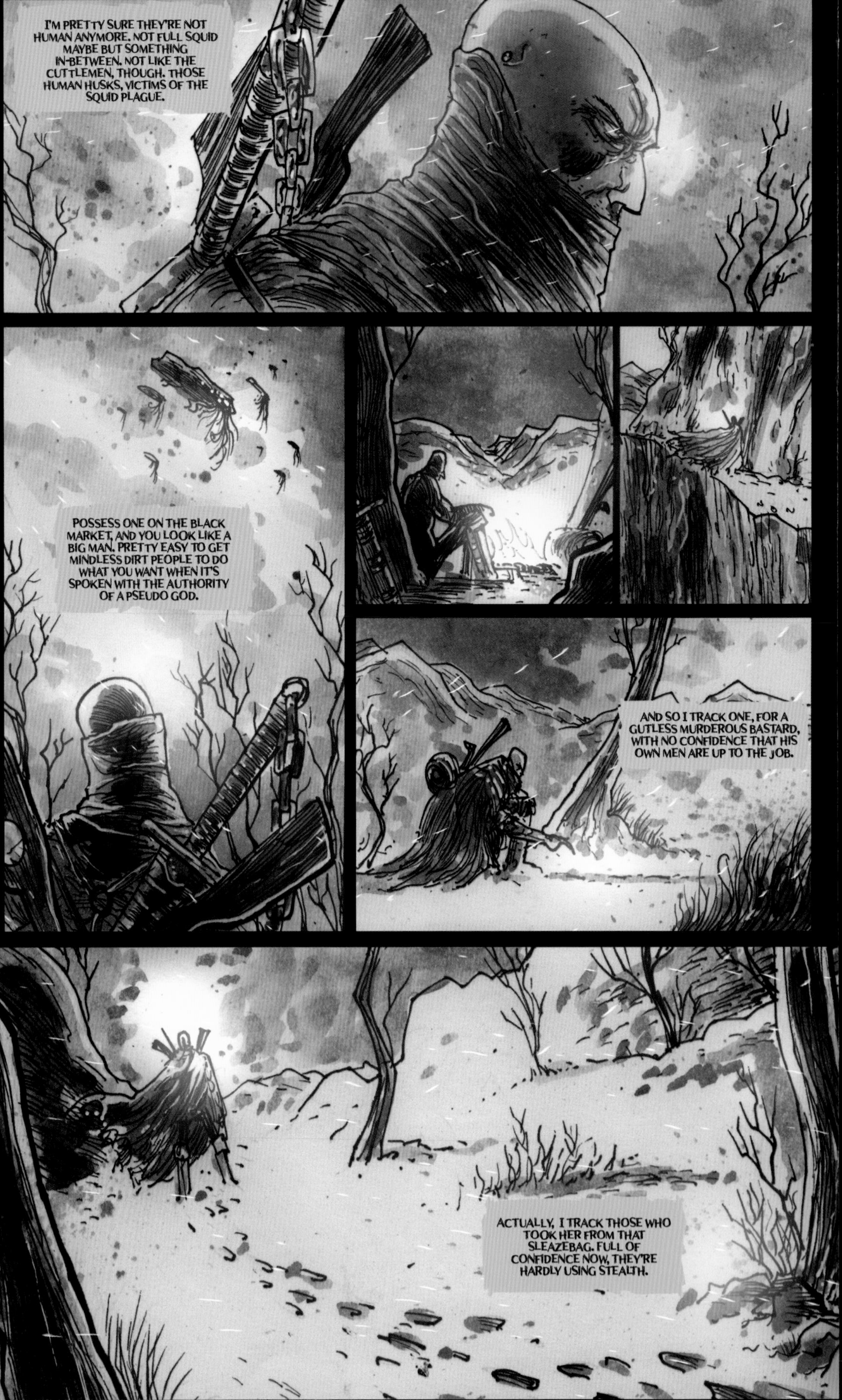
I'M PRETTY SURE THEY'RE NOT HUMAN ANYMORE. NOT FULL SQUID MAYBE BUT SOMETHING IN-BETWEEN. NOT LIKE THE CUTTLEMEN, THOUGH. THOSE HUMAN HUSKS, VICTIMS OF THE SQUID PLAGUE.
POSSESS ONE ON THE BLACK MARKET, AND YOU LOOK LIKE A BIG MAN. PRETTY EASY TO GET MINDLESS DIRT PEOPLE TO DO WHAT YOU WANT WHEN IT'S SPOKEN WITH THE AUTHORITY OF A PSEUDO GOD.
AND SO I TRACK ONE, FOR A GUTLESS MURDEROUS BASTARD, WITH NO CONFIDENCE THAT HIS OWN MEN ARE UP TO THE JOB.
ACTUALLY, I TRACK THOSE WHO TOOK HER FROM THAT SLEAZEBAG. FULL OF CONFIDENCE NOW, THEY'RE HARDLY USING STEALTH.

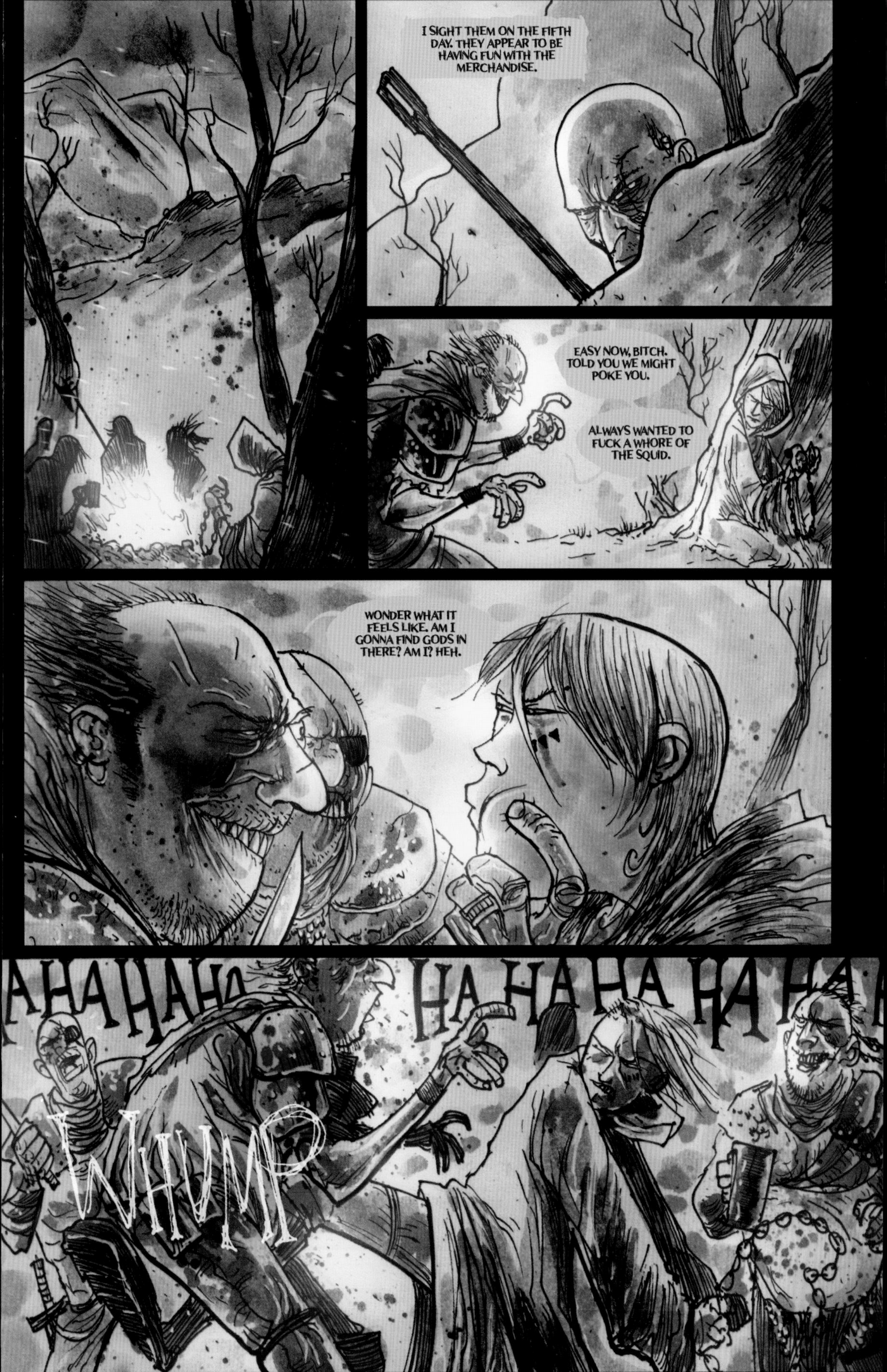
I SIGHT THEM ON THE FIFTH DAY. THEY APPEAR TO BE HAVING FUN WITH THE MERCHANDISE.
EASY NOW, BITCH. TOLD YOU WE MIGHT POKE YOU.
ALWAYS WANTED TO FUCK A WHORE OF THE SQUID.
WONDER WHAT IT FEELS LIKE. AM I GONNA FIND GODS IN THERE? AM I? HEH.
HAHAHAHA
HA HA HA HA HA
WHUMP

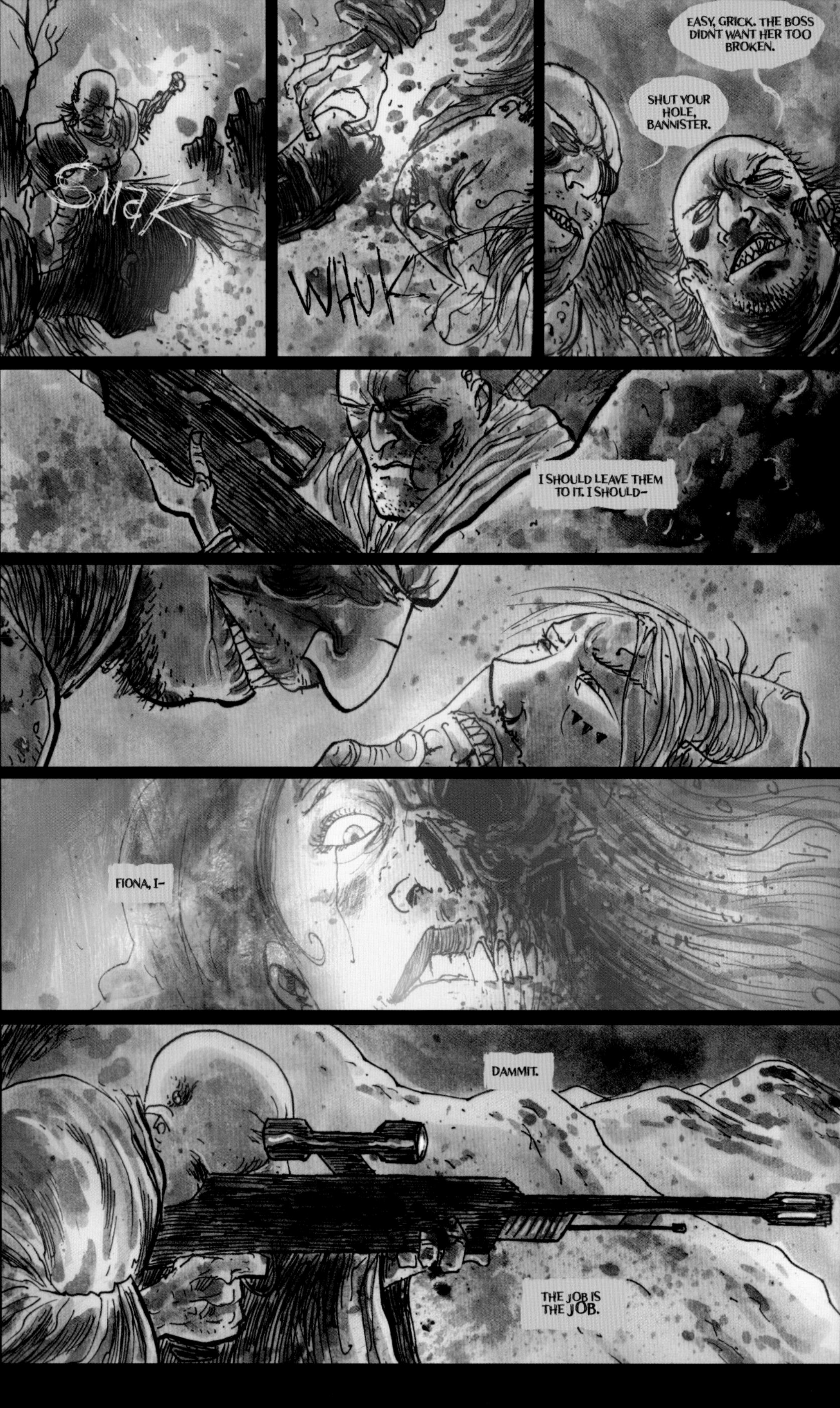
SMAK
WHUK
EASY, GRICK. THE BOSS DIDN'T WANT HER TOO BROKEN.
SHUT YOUR HOLE, BANNISTER.
I SHOULD LEAVE THEM TO IT. I SHOULD–
FIONA, I-
DAMMIT.
THE JOB IS THE JOB.

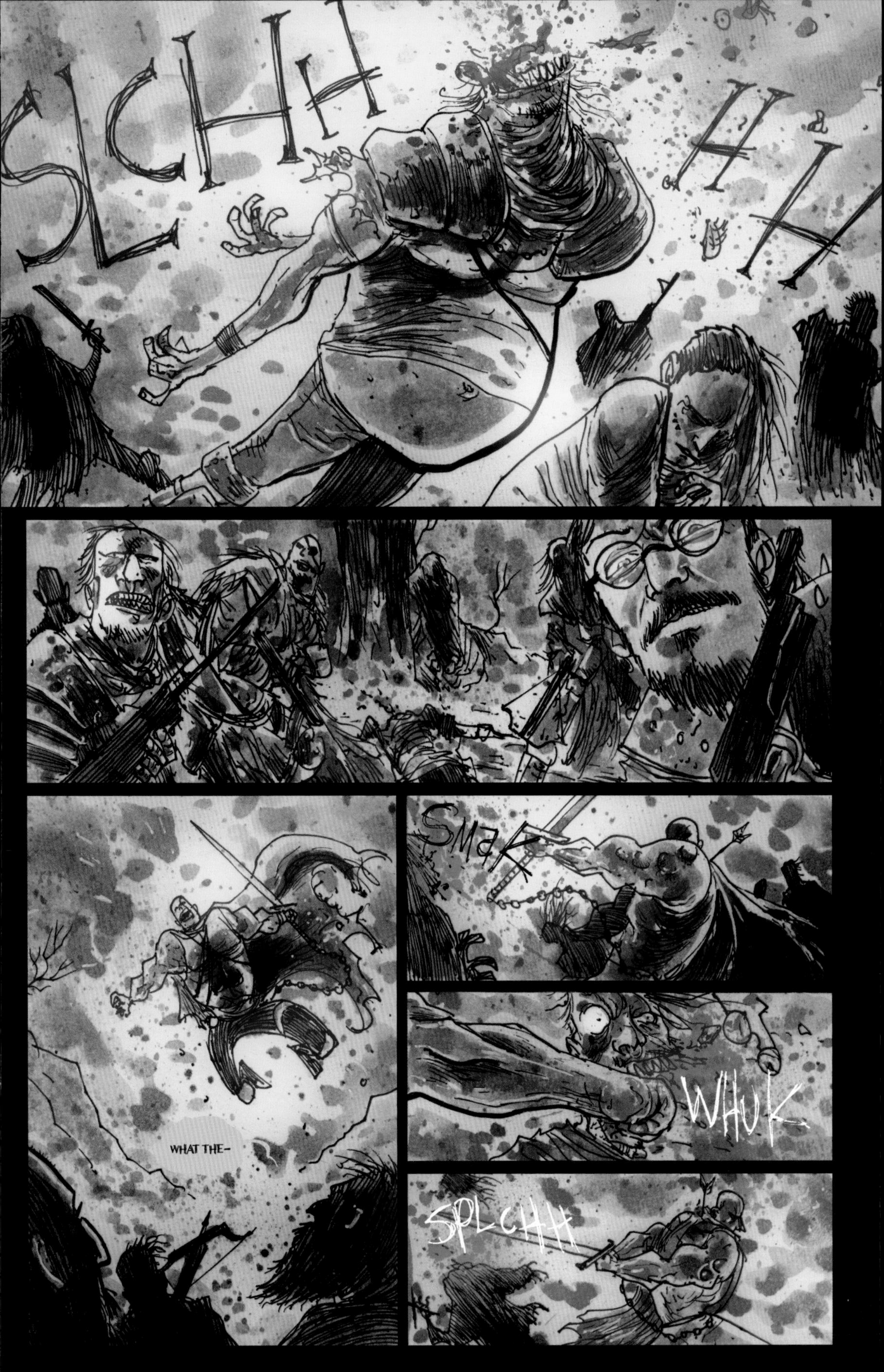
SLCHH
HHH
WHAT THE-
SMAK
WHUK
SPLCHH

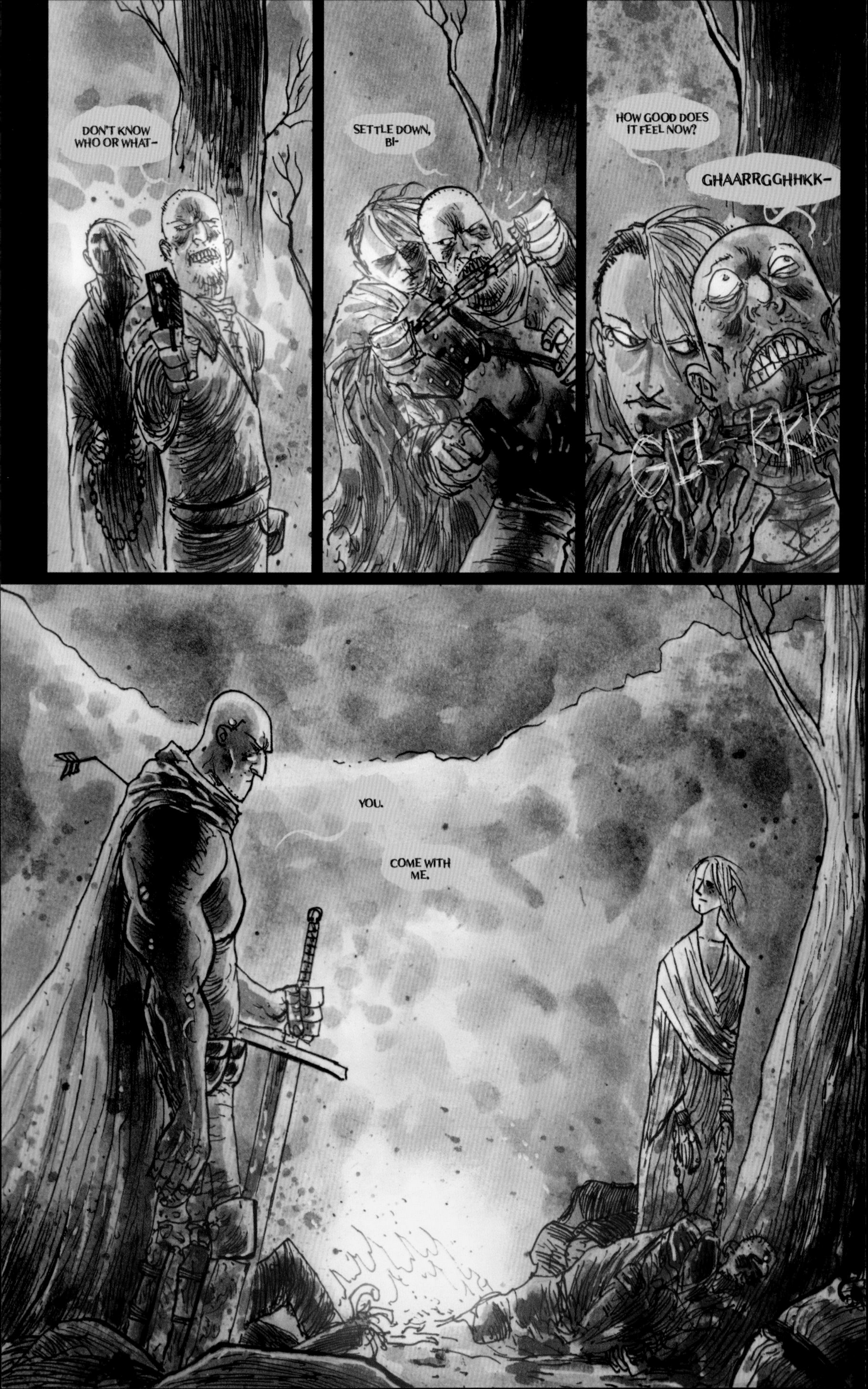
DON'T KNOW WHO OR WHAT-
SETTLE DOWN, BI-
HOW GOOD DOES IT FEEL NOW?
GHAARRGGHHKK-
GLL-KKK
YOU.
COME WITH ME.

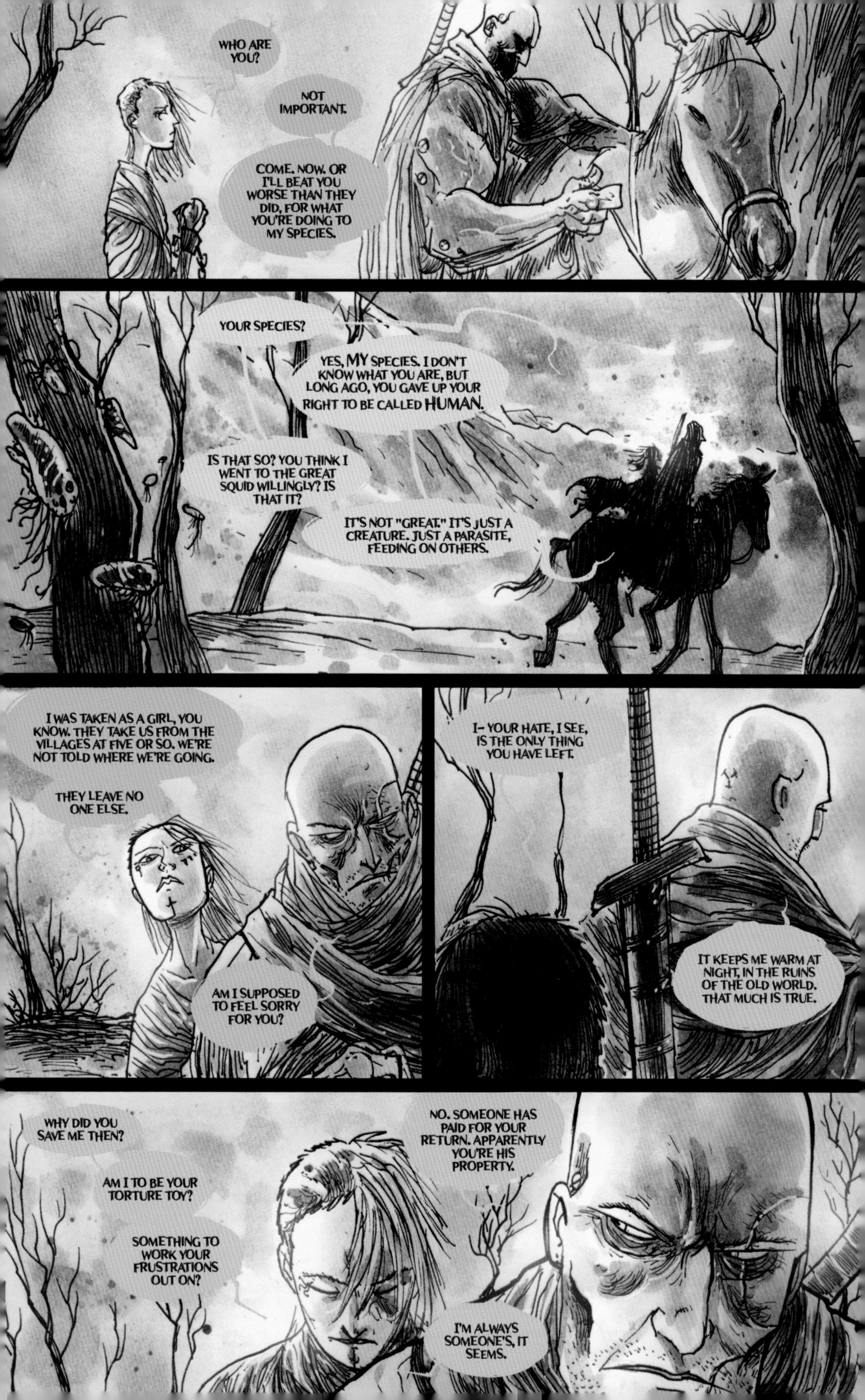
WHO ARE YOU?
NOT IMPORTANT.
COME. NOW. OR I'LL BEAT YOU WORSE THAN THEY DID, FOR WHAT YOU'RE DOING TO MY SPECIES.
YOUR SPECIES?
YES, MY SPECIES. I DON'T KNOW WHAT YOU ARE, BUT LONG AGO, YOU GAVE UP YOUR RIGHT TO BE CALLED HUMAN.
IS THAT SO? YOU THINK I WENT TO THE GREAT SQUID WILLINGLY? IS THAT IT?
IT'S NOT "GREAT." IT'S JUST A CREATURE. JUST A PARASITE, FEEDING ON OTHERS.
I WAS TAKEN AS A GIRL, YOU KNOW. THEY TAKE US FROM THE VILLAGES AT FIVE OR SO. WE'RE NOT TOLD WHERE WE'RE GOING.
THEY LEAVE NO ONE ELSE.
AM I SUPPOSED TO FEEL SORRY FOR YOU?
I- YOUR HATE, I SEE, IS THE ONLY THING YOU HAVE LEFT.
IT KEEPS ME WARM AT NIGHT, IN THE RUINS OF THE OLD WORLD. THAT MUCH IS TRUE.
WHY DID YOU SAVE ME THEN?
AM I TO BE YOUR TORTURE TOY?
SOMETHING TO WORK YOUR FRUSTRATIONS OUT ON?
NO. SOMEONE HAS PAID FOR YOUR RETURN. APPARENTLY YOU'RE HIS PROPERTY.
I'M ALWAYS SOMEONE'S, IT SEEMS.

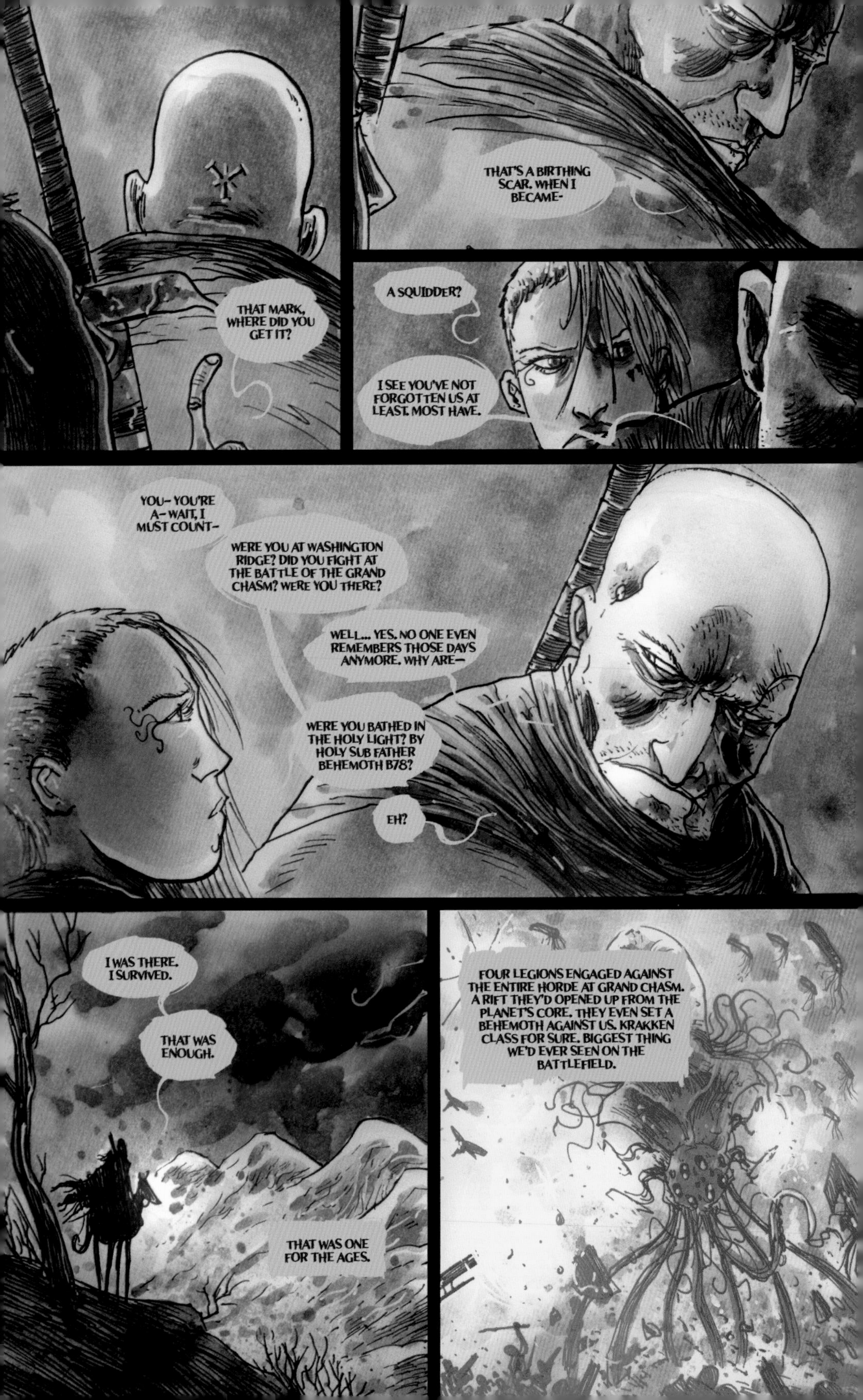
THAT'S A BIRTHING SCAR. WHEN I BECAME-
THAT MARK, WHERE DID YOU GET IT?
A SQUIDDER?
I SEE YOU'VE NOT FORGOTTEN US AT LEAST. MOST HAVE.
YOU- YOU'RE A- WAIT, I MUST COUNT-
WERE YOU AT WASHINGTON RIDGE? DID YOU FIGHT AT THE BATTLE OF THE GRAND CHASM? WERE YOU THERE?
WELL... YES. NO ONE EVEN REMEMBERS THOSE DAYS ANYMORE. WHY ARE-
WERE YOU BATHED IN THE HOLY LIGHT? BY HOLY SUB FATHER BEHEMOTH B78?
EH?
I WAS THERE. I SURVIVED.
THAT WAS ENOUGH.
THAT WAS ONE FOR THE AGES.
FOUR LEGIONS ENGAGED AGAINST THE ENTIRE HORDE AT GRAND CHASM. A RIFT THEY'D OPENED UP FROM THE PLANET'S CORE. THEY EVEN SET A BEHEMOTH AGAINST US. KRAKKEN CLASS FOR SURE. BIGGEST THING WE'D EVER SEEN ON THE BATTLEFIELD.

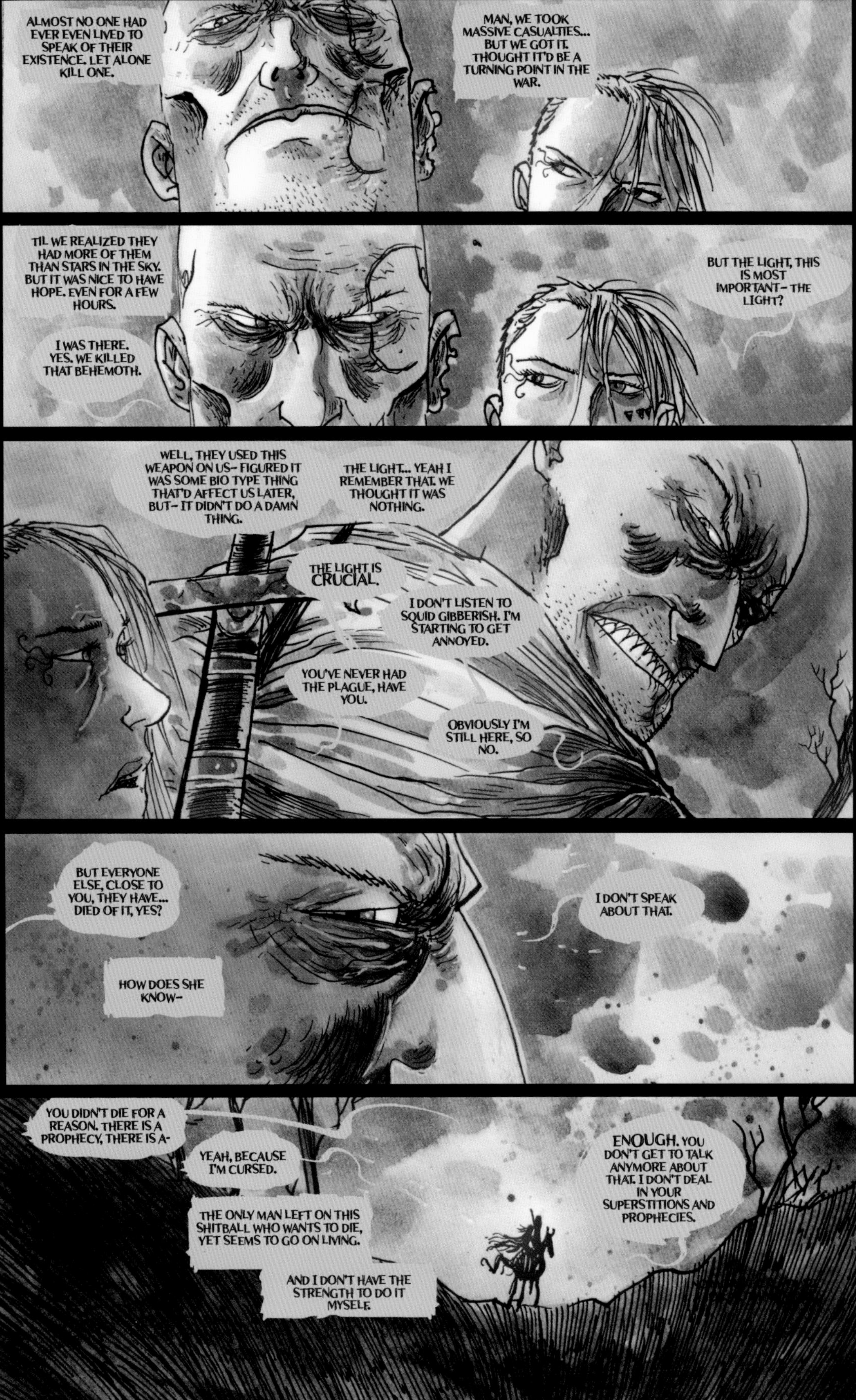
ALMOST NO ONE HAD EVER EVEN LIVED TO SPEAK OF THEIR EXISTENCE. LET ALONE KILL ONE.
MAN, WE TOOK MASSIVE CASUALTIES... BUT WE GOT IT. THOUGHT IT'D BE A TURNING POINT IN THE WAR.
TIL WE REALIZED THEY HAD MORE OF THEM THAN STARS IN THE SKY. BUT IT WAS NICE TO HAVE HOPE. EVEN FOR A FEW HOURS.
I WAS THERE. YES. WE KILLED THAT BEHEMOTH.
BUT THE LIGHT, THIS IS MOST IMPORTANT- THE LIGHT?
WELL, THEY USED THIS WEAPON ON US- FIGURED IT WAS SOME BIO TYPE THING THAT'D AFFECT US LATER, BUT- IT DIDN'T DO A DAMN THING.
THE LIGHT... YEAH I REMEMBER THAT. WE THOUGHT IT WAS NOTHING.
THE LIGHT IS CRUCIAL.
I DON'T LISTEN TO SQUID GIBBERISH. I'M STARTING TO GET ANNOYED.
YOU'VE NEVER HAD THE PLAGUE, HAVE YOU.
OBVIOUSLY I'M STILL HERE, SO NO.
BUT EVERYONE ELSE, CLOSE TO YOU, THEY HAVE... DIED OF IT, YES?
HOW DOES SHE KNOW-
I DON'T SPEAK ABOUT THAT.
YOU DIDN'T DIE FOR A REASON. THERE IS A PROPHECY, THERE IS A-
YEAH, BECAUSE I'M CURSED.
THE ONLY MAN LEFT ON THIS SHITBALL WHO WANTS TO DIE, YET SEEMS TO GO ON LIVING.
AND I DON'T HAVE THE STRENGTH TO DO IT MYSELF.
ENOUGH. YOU DON'T GET TO TALK ANYMORE ABOUT THAT. I DON'T DEAL IN YOUR SUPERSTITIONS AND PROPHECIES.

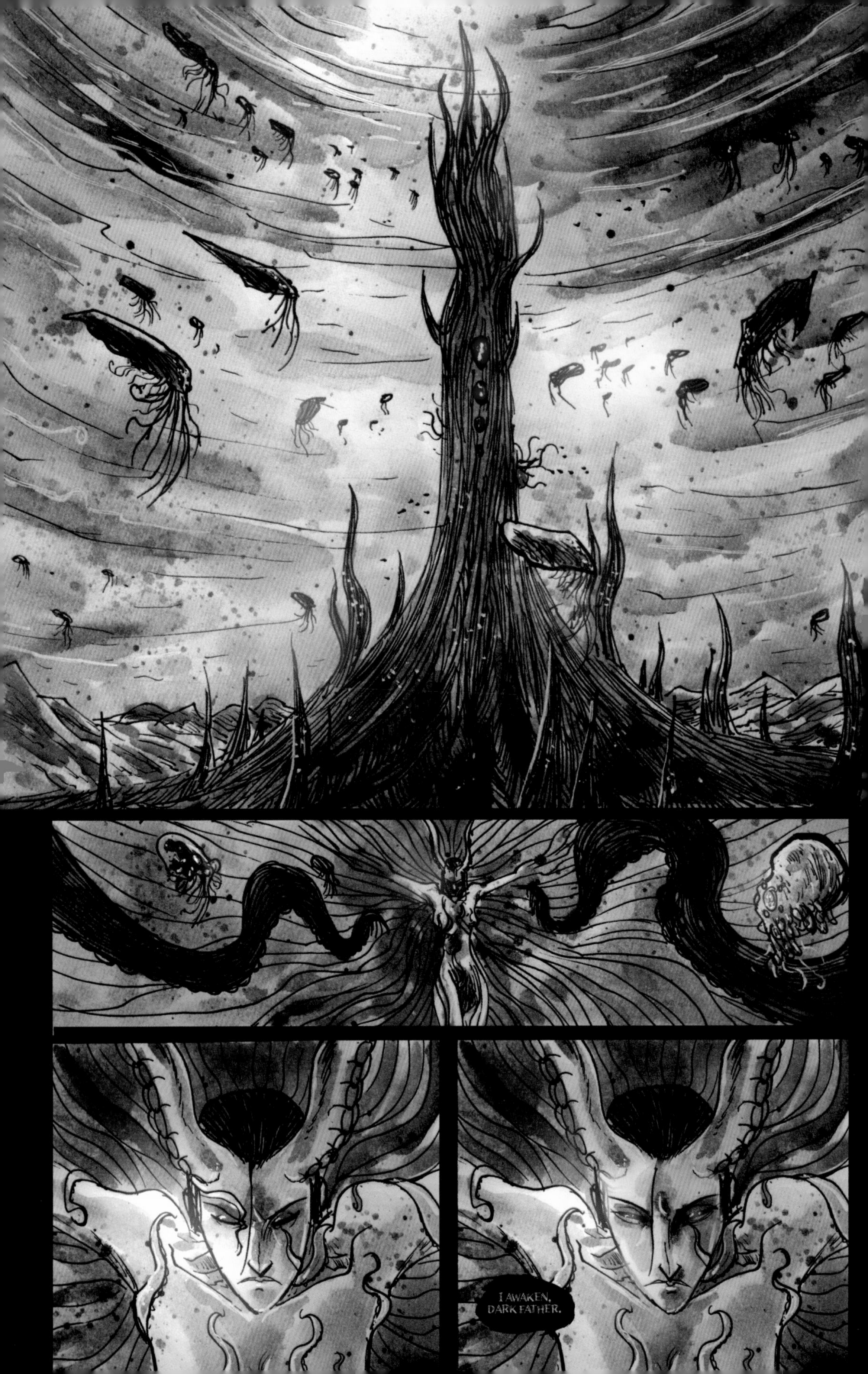
I AWAKEN, DARK FATHER.

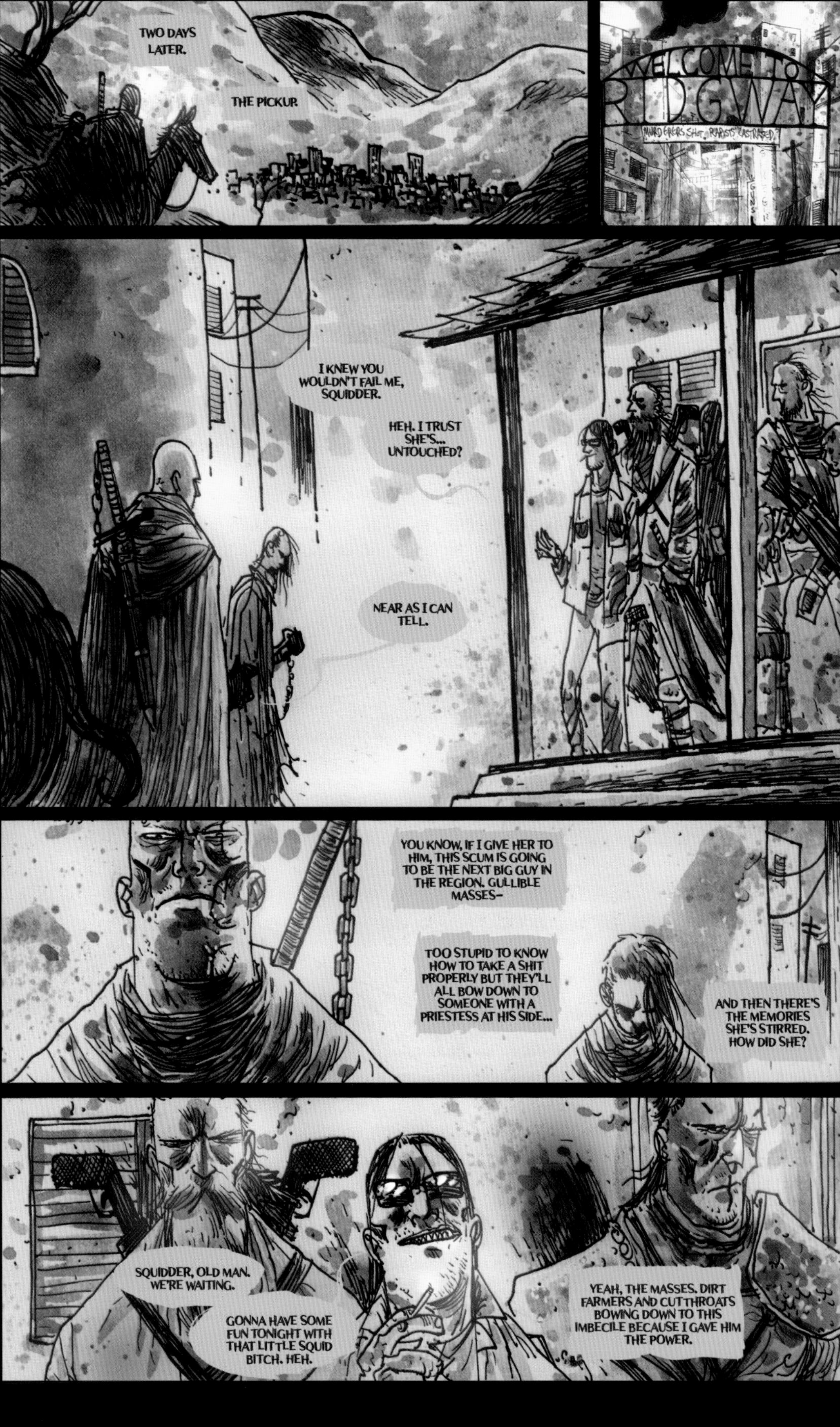
TWO DAYS LATER.
THE PICKUP.
WELCOME TO
I KNEW YOU WOULDN'T FAIL ME, SQUIDDER.
HEH. I TRUST SHE'S... UNTOUCHED?
NEAR AS I CAN TELL.
YOU KNOW, IF I GIVE HER TO HIM, THIS SCUM IS GOING TO BE THE NEXT BIG GUY IN THE REGION. GULLIBLE MASSES–
TOO STUPID TO KNOW HOW TO TAKE A SHIT PROPERLY BUT THEY'LL ALL BOW DOWN TO SOMEONE WITH A PRIESTESS AT HIS SIDE...
AND THEN THERE'S THE MEMORIES SHE'S STIRRED. HOW DID SHE?
SQUIDDER, OLD MAN. WE'RE WAITING.
GONNA HAVE SOME FUN TONIGHT WITH THAT LITTLE SQUID BITCH. HEH.
YEAH, THE MASSES. DIRT FARMERS AND CUTTHROATS BOWING DOWN TO THIS IMBECILE BECAUSE I GAVE HIM THE POWER.

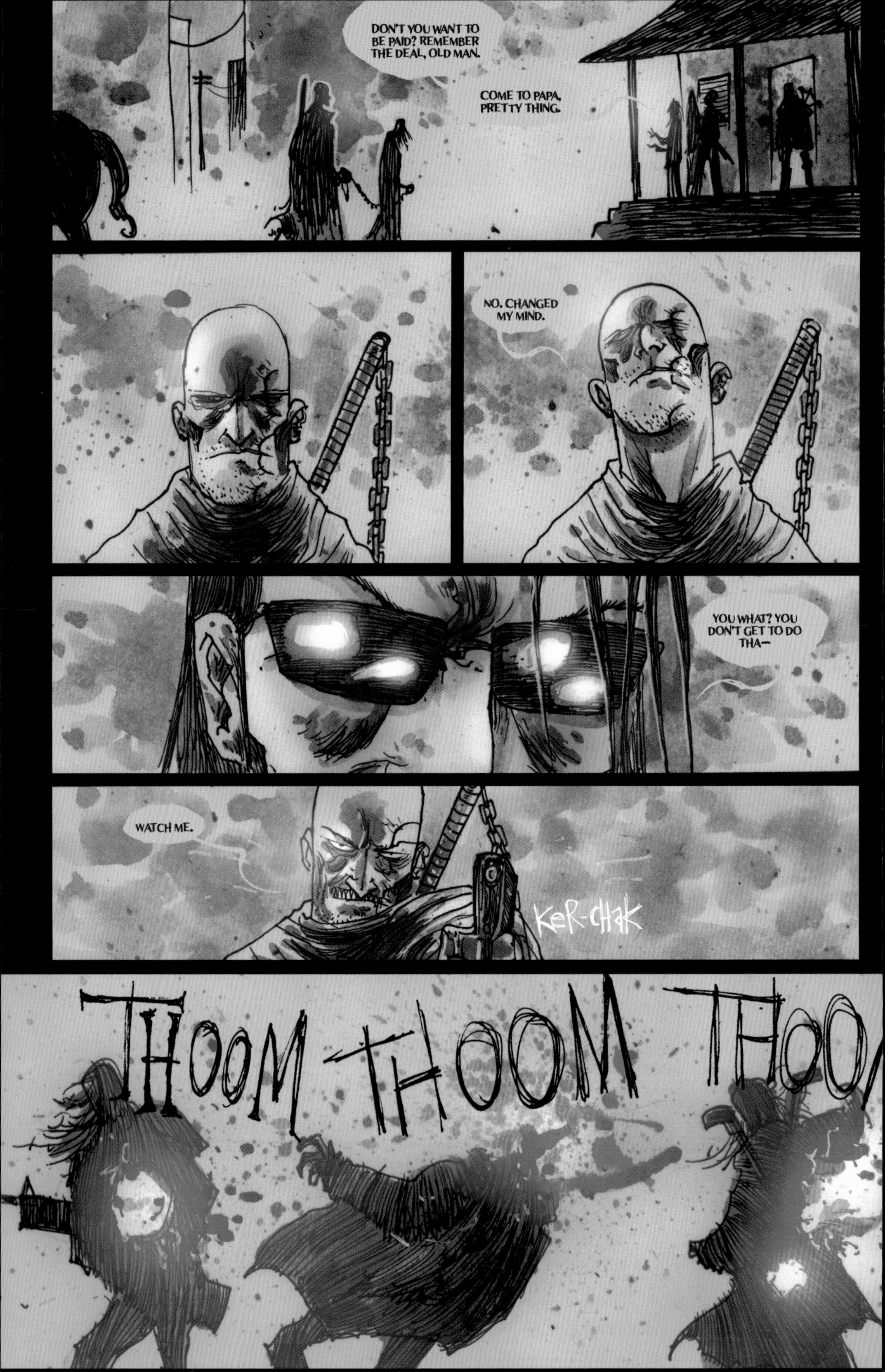
DON'T YOU WANT TO BE PAID? REMEMBER THE DEAL, OLD MAN.
COME TO PAPA, PRETTY THING.
NO. CHANGED MY MIND.
YOU WHAT? YOU DON'T GET TO DO THA—
WATCH ME.
KER-CHAK
THOOM THOOM THOO

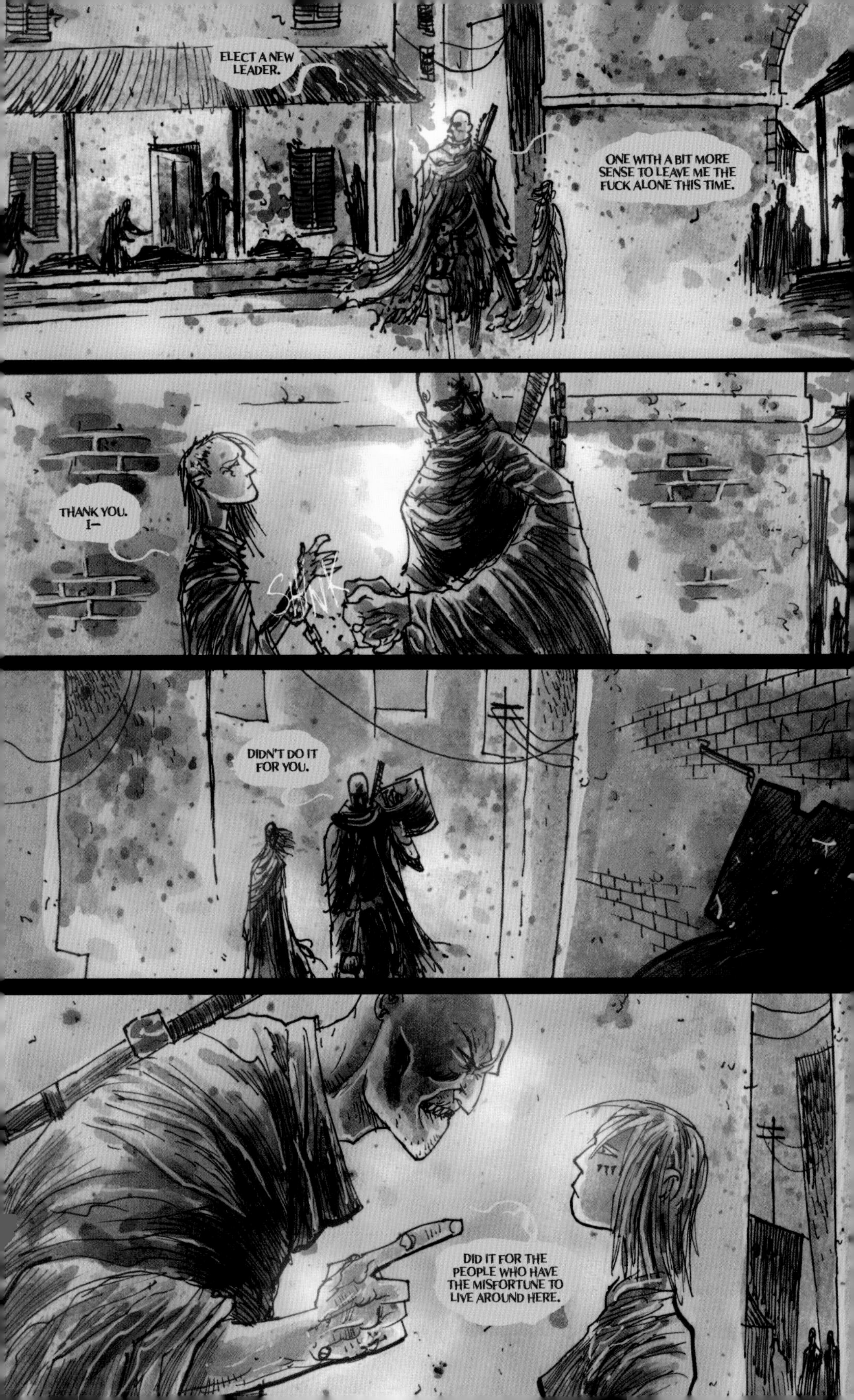
ELECT A NEW LEADER.
ONE WITH A BIT MORE SENSE TO LEAVE ME THE FUCK ALONE THIS TIME.
THANK YOU. I—
SHNK
DIDN'T DO IT FOR YOU.
DID IT FOR THE PEOPLE WHO HAVE THE MISFORTUNE TO LIVE AROUND HERE.

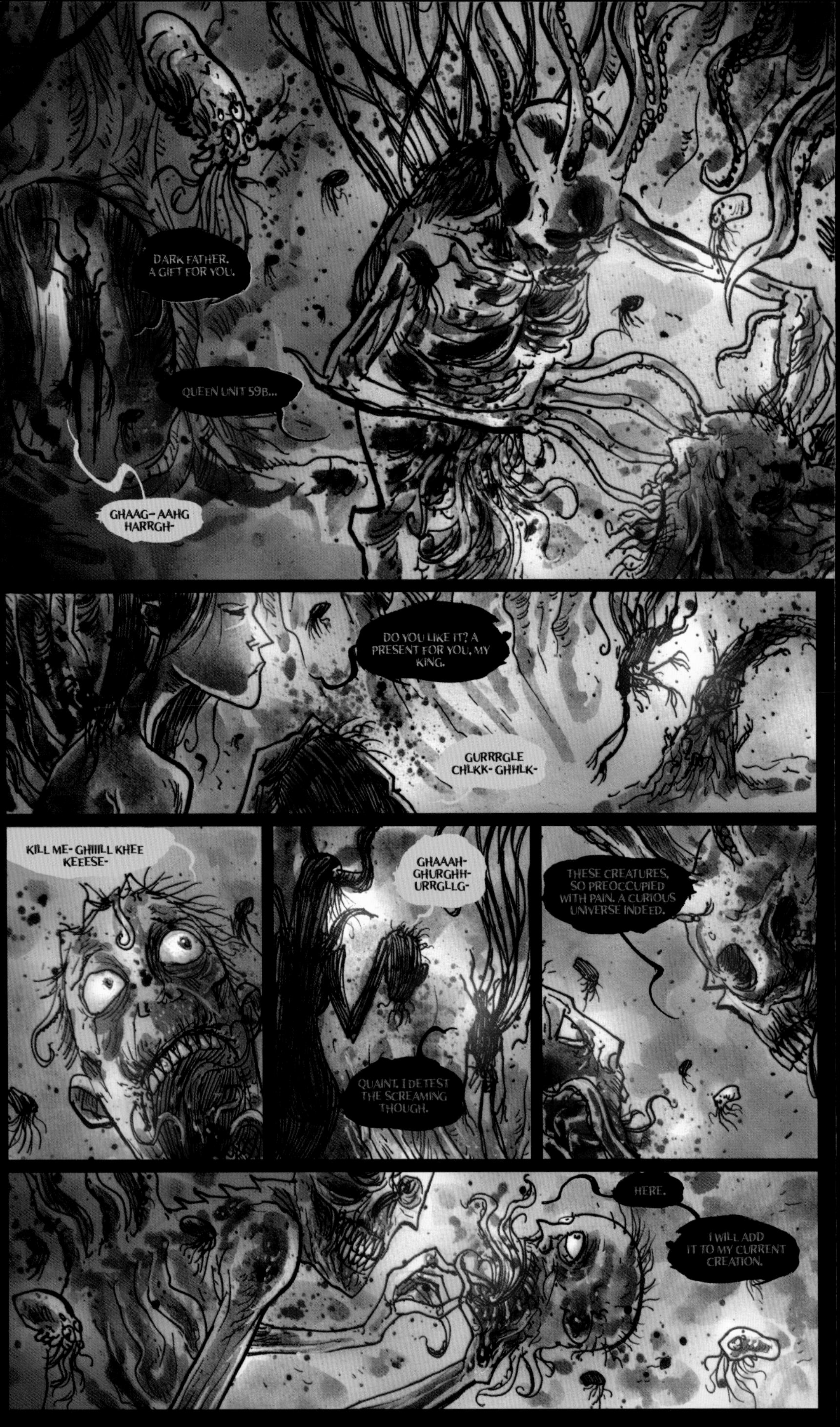
DARK FATHER. A GIFT FOR YOU.
QUEEN UNIT 59B...
GHAAG- AAHG HARRGH-
DO YOU LIKE IT? A PRESENT FOR YOU, MY KING.
GURRRGLE CHLKK- GHHLK-
KILL ME- GHIIILL KHEE KEEESE-
GHAAAH- GHURGHH- URRGLLG-
QUAINT. I DETEST THE SCREAMING THOUGH.
THESE CREATURES, SO PREOCCUPIED WITH PAIN. A CURIOUS UNIVERSE INDEED.
HERE.
I WILL ADD IT TO MY CURRENT CREATION.

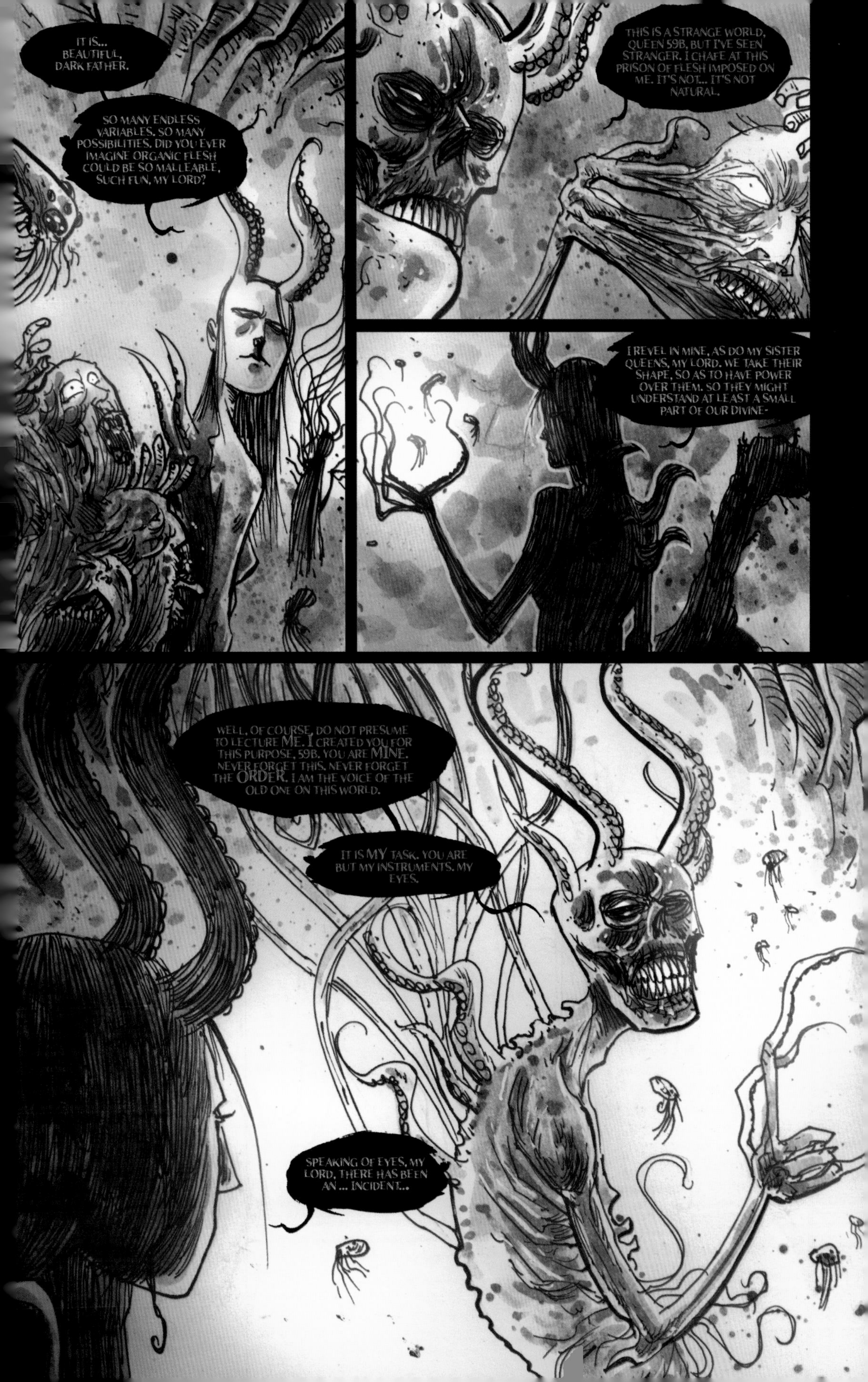
IT IS... BEAUTIFUL, DARK FATHER.
SO MANY ENDLESS VARIABLES. SO MANY POSSIBILITIES. DID YOU EVER IMAGINE ORGANIC FLESH COULD BE SO MALLEABLE, SUCH FUN, MY LORD?
THIS IS A STRANGE WORLD, QUEEN 59B, BUT I'VE SEEN STRANGER. I CHAFE AT THIS PRISON OF FLESH IMPOSED ON ME. IT'S NOT... IT'S NOT NATURAL.
I REVEL IN MINE, AS DO MY SISTER QUEENS, MY LORD. WE TAKE THEIR SHAPE, SO AS TO HAVE POWER OVER THEM. SO THEY MIGHT UNDERSTAND AT LEAST A SMALL PART OF OUR DIVINE-
WELL, OF COURSE. DO NOT PRESUME TO LECTURE ME. I CREATED YOU FOR THIS PURPOSE, 59B. YOU ARE MINE. NEVER FORGET THIS. NEVER FORGET THE ORDER. I AM THE VOICE OF THE OLD ONE ON THIS WORLD.
IT IS MY TASK. YOU ARE BUT MY INSTRUMENTS. MY EYES.
SPEAKING OF EYES, MY LORD, THERE HAS BEEN AN ... INCIDENT...

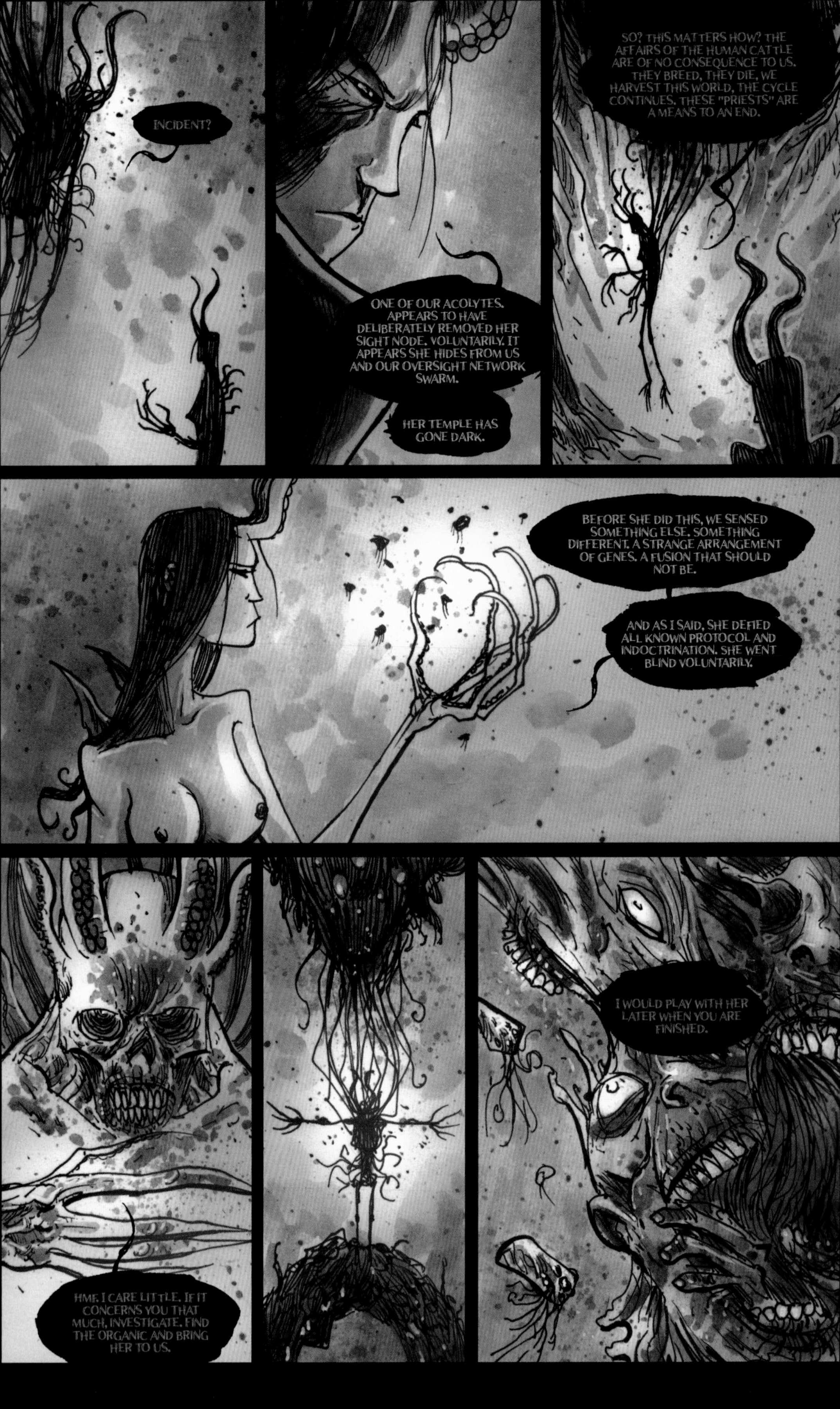
INCIDENT?
ONE OF OUR ACOLYTES. APPEARS TO HAVE DELIBERATELY REMOVED HER SIGHT NODE. VOLUNTARILY. IT APPEARS SHE HIDES FROM US AND OUR OVERSIGHT NETWORK SWARM.
HER TEMPLE HAS GONE DARK.
SO? THIS MATTERS HOW? THE AFFAIRS OF THE HUMAN CATTLE ARE OF NO CONSEQUENCE TO US. THEY BREED, THEY DIE, WE HARVEST THIS WORLD, THE CYCLE CONTINUES. THESE "PRIESTS" ARE A MEANS TO AN END.
BEFORE SHE DID THIS, WE SENSED SOMETHING ELSE. SOMETHING DIFFERENT. A STRANGE ARRANGEMENT OF GENES. A FUSION THAT SHOULD NOT BE.
AND AS I SAID, SHE DEFIED ALL KNOWN PROTOCOL AND INDOCTRINATION. SHE WENT BLIND VOLUNTARILY.
HMF. I CARE LITTLE. IF IT CONCERNS YOU THAT MUCH, INVESTIGATE. FIND THE ORGANIC AND BRING HER TO US.
I WOULD PLAY WITH HER LATER WHEN YOU ARE FINISHED.

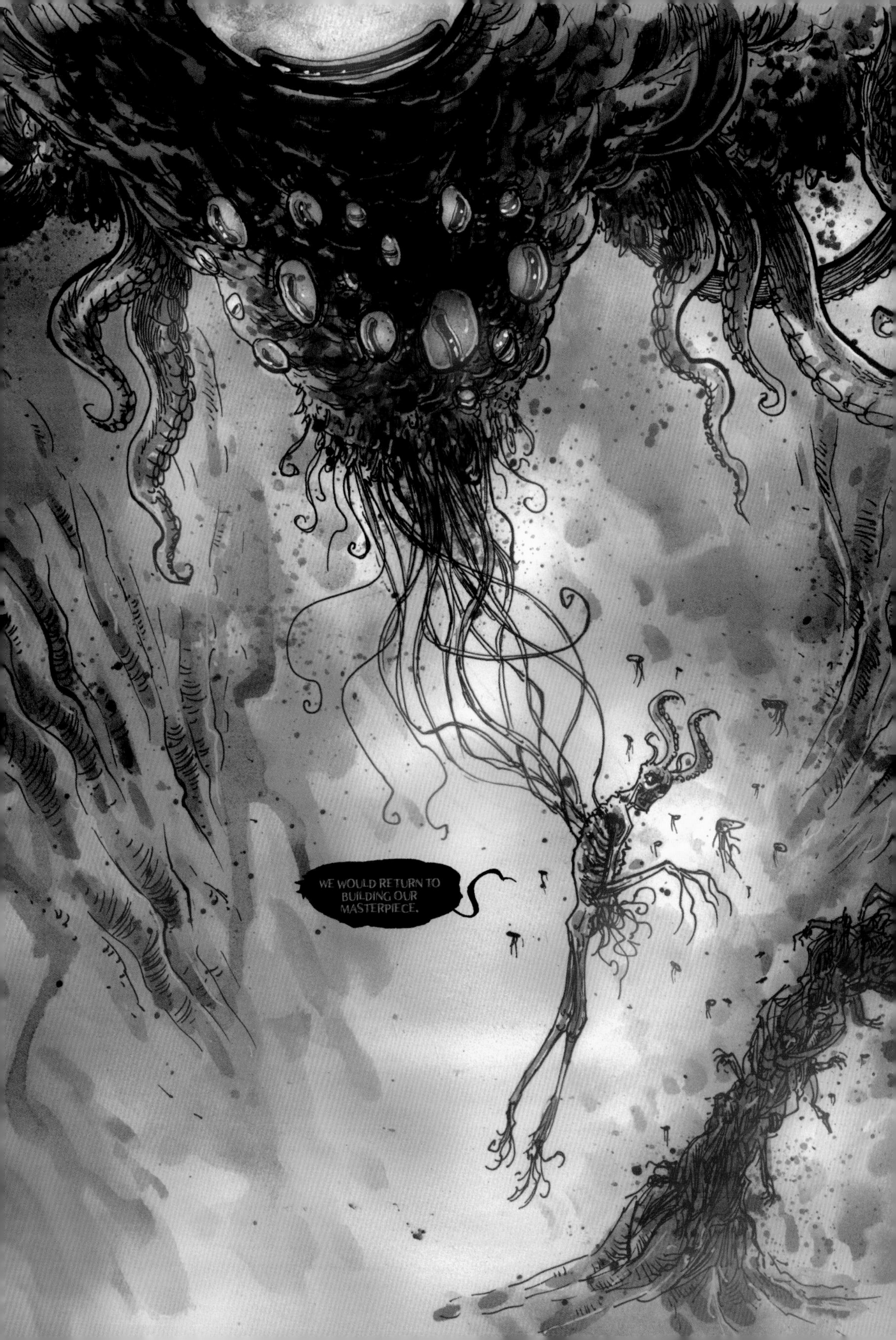
WE WOULD RETURN TO BUILDING OUR MASTERPIECE.

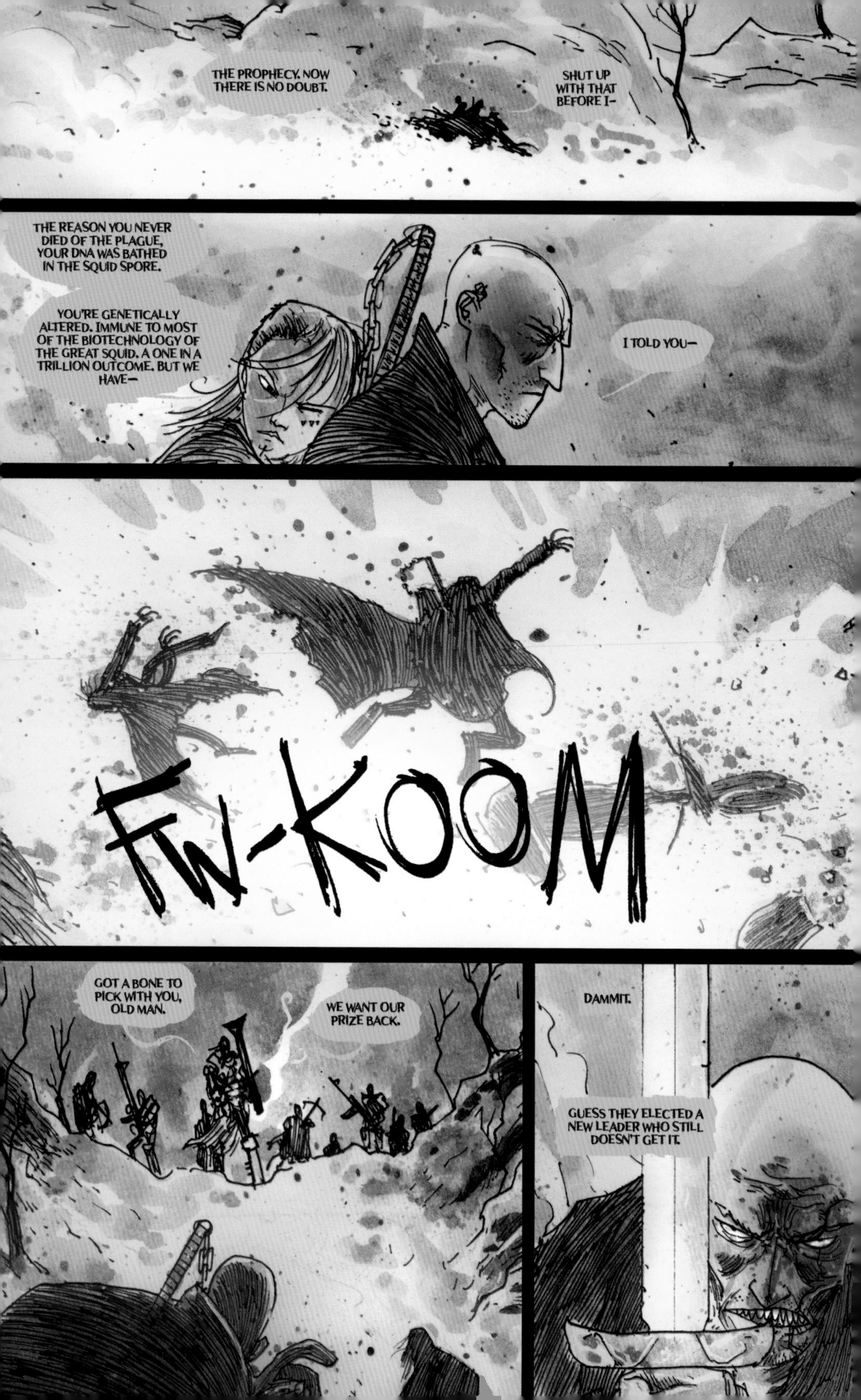
THE PROPHECY. NOW THERE IS NO DOUBT.
SHUT UP WITH THAT BEFORE I–
THE REASON YOU NEVER DIED OF THE PLAGUE, YOUR DNA WAS BATHED IN THE SQUID SPORE.
YOU'RE GENETICALLY ALTERED. IMMUNE TO MOST OF THE BIOTECHNOLOGY OF THE GREAT SQUID. A ONE IN A TRILLION OUTCOME. BUT WE HAVE–
I TOLD YOU–
FW-KOOM
GOT A BONE TO PICK WITH YOU, OLD MAN.
WE WANT OUR PRIZE BACK.
DAMMIT.
GUESS THEY ELECTED A NEW LEADER WHO STILL DOESN'T GET IT.

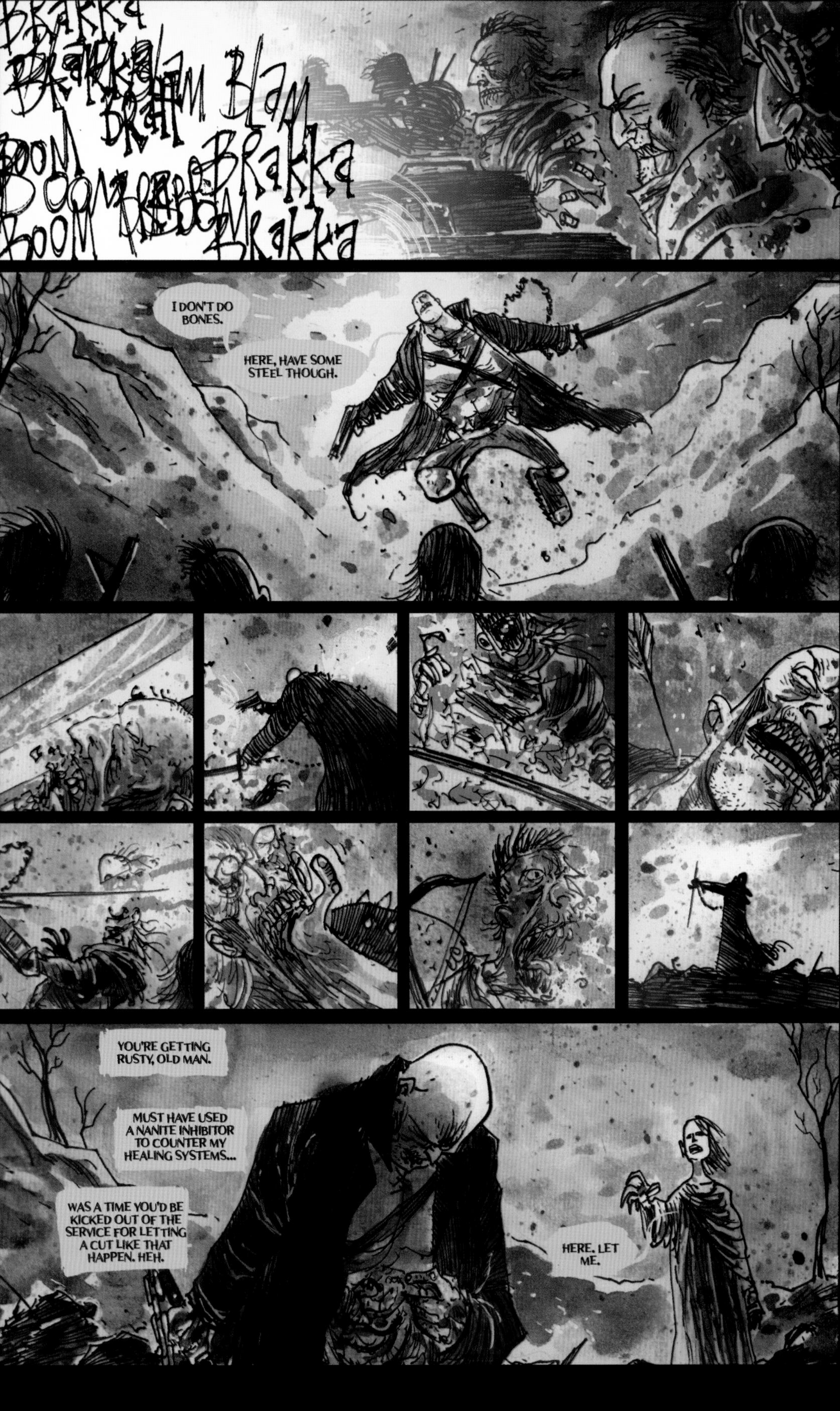
BRAKKA
BLAM
BOOM
BRAKKA
BRAKKA
I DON'T DO BONES.
HERE, HAVE SOME STEEL THOUGH.
YOU'RE GETTING RUSTY, OLD MAN.
MUST HAVE USED A NANITE INHIBITOR TO COUNTER MY HEALING SYSTEMS...
WAS A TIME YOU'D BE KICKED OUT OF THE SERVICE FOR LETTING A CUT LIKE THAT HAPPEN. HEH.
HERE, LET ME.

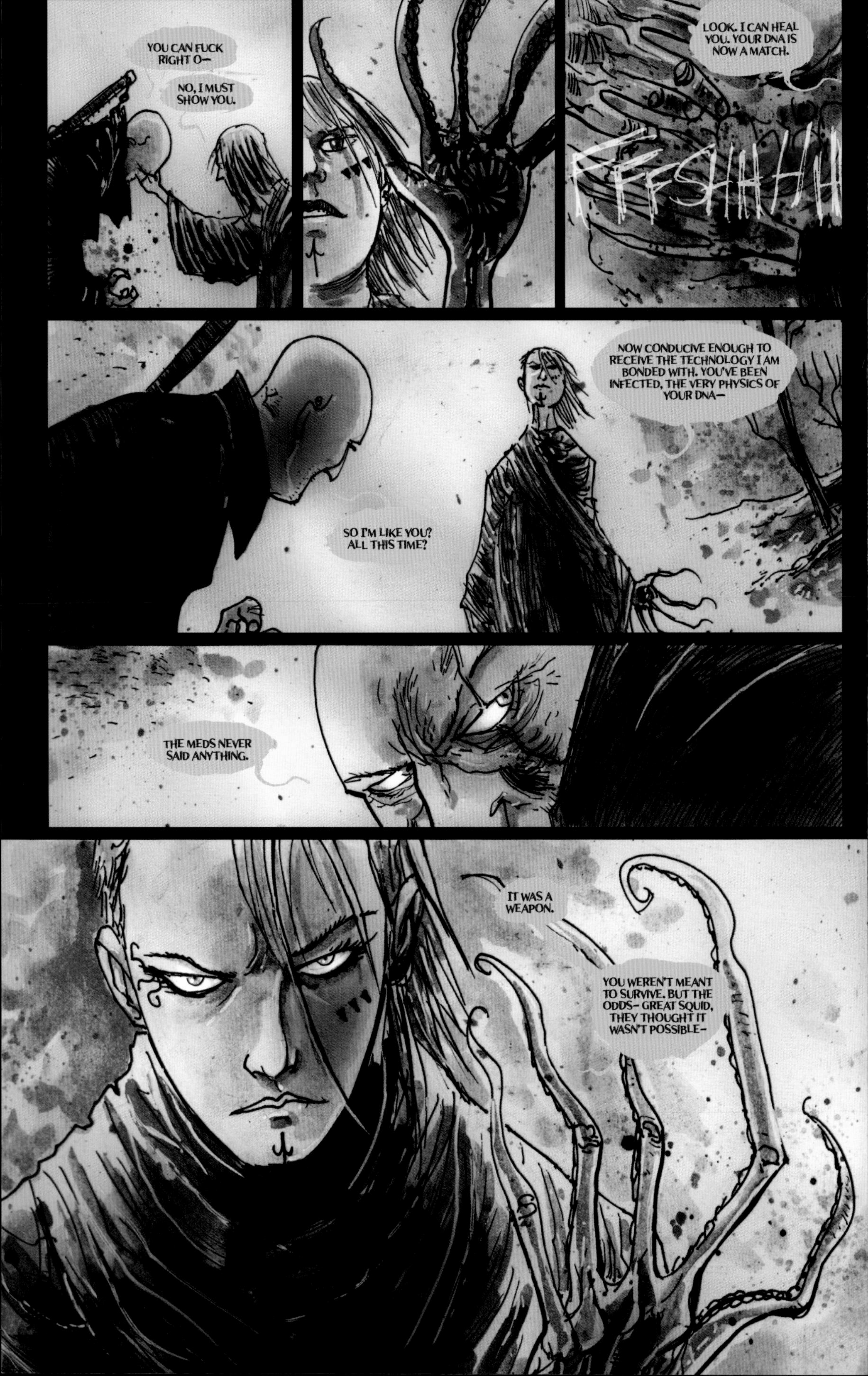
YOU CAN FUCK RIGHT O—
NO, I MUST SHOW YOU.
LOOK. I CAN HEAL YOU. YOUR DNA IS NOW A MATCH.
FFFSHHHH
NOW CONDUCIVE ENOUGH TO RECEIVE THE TECHNOLOGY I AM BONDED WITH. YOU'VE BEEN INFECTED, THE VERY PHYSICS OF YOUR DNA—
SO I'M LIKE YOU? ALL THIS TIME?
THE MEDS NEVER SAID ANYTHING.
IT WAS A WEAPON.
YOU WEREN'T MEANT TO SURVIVE. BUT THE ODDS— GREAT SQUID, THEY THOUGHT IT WASN'T POSSIBLE—

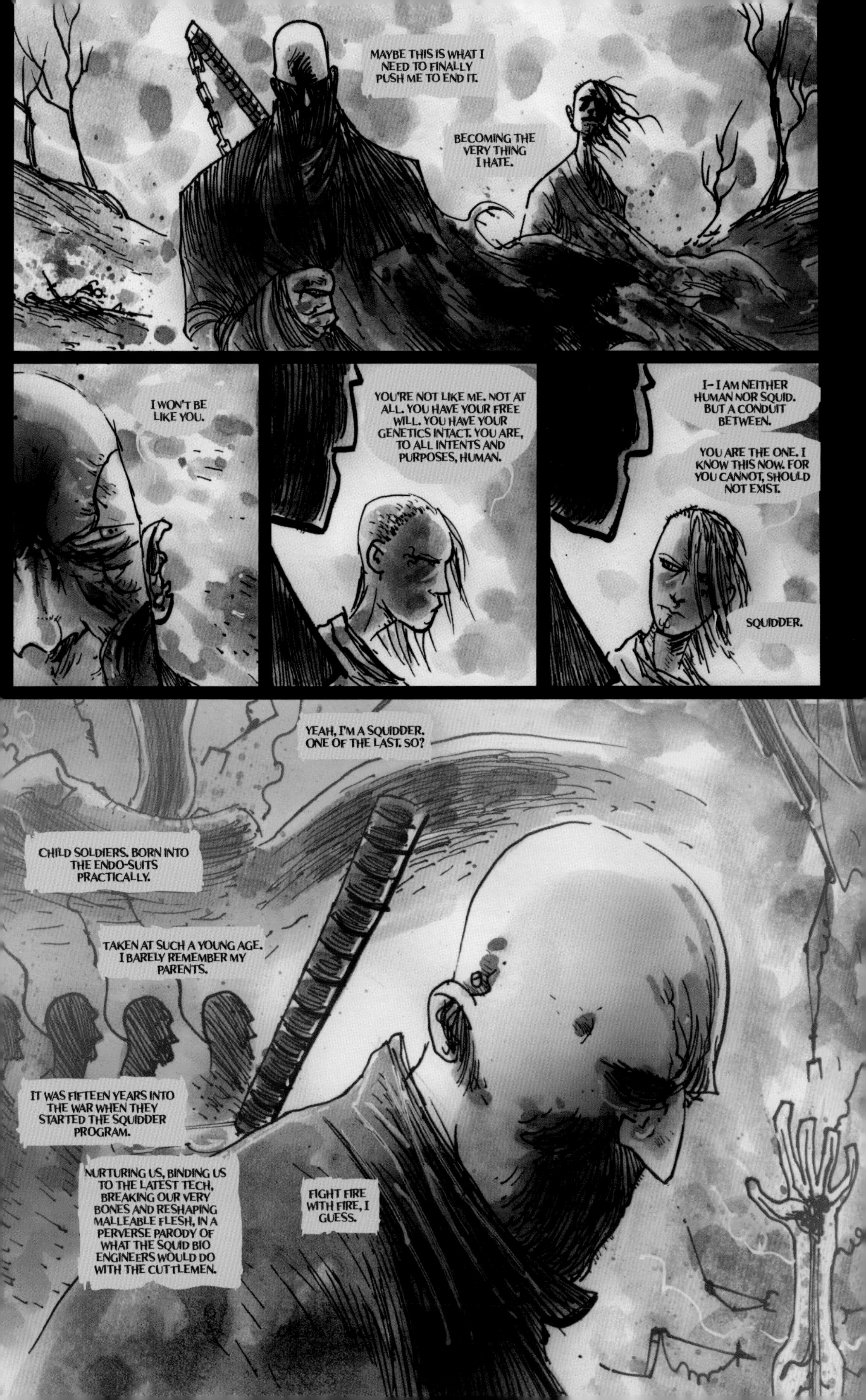
MAYBE THIS IS WHAT I NEED TO FINALLY PUSH ME TO END IT.
BECOMING THE VERY THING I HATE.
I WON'T BE LIKE YOU.
YOU'RE NOT LIKE ME. NOT AT ALL. YOU HAVE YOUR FREE WILL. YOU HAVE YOUR GENETICS INTACT. YOU ARE, TO ALL INTENTS AND PURPOSES, HUMAN.
I- I AM NEITHER HUMAN NOR SQUID. BUT A CONDUIT BETWEEN.
YOU ARE THE ONE. I KNOW THIS NOW. FOR YOU CANNOT, SHOULD NOT EXIST.
SQUIDDER.
YEAH, I'M A SQUIDDER. ONE OF THE LAST. SO?
CHILD SOLDIERS. BORN INTO THE ENDO-SUITS PRACTICALLY.
TAKEN AT SUCH A YOUNG AGE. I BARELY REMEMBER MY PARENTS.
IT WAS FIFTEEN YEARS INTO THE WAR WHEN THEY STARTED THE SQUIDDER PROGRAM.
NURTURING US, BINDING US TO THE LATEST TECH, BREAKING OUR VERY BONES AND RESHAPING MALLEABLE FLESH, IN A PERVERSE PARODY OF WHAT THE SQUID BIO ENGINEERS WOULD DO WITH THE CUTTLEMEN.
FIGHT FIRE WITH FIRE, I GUESS.

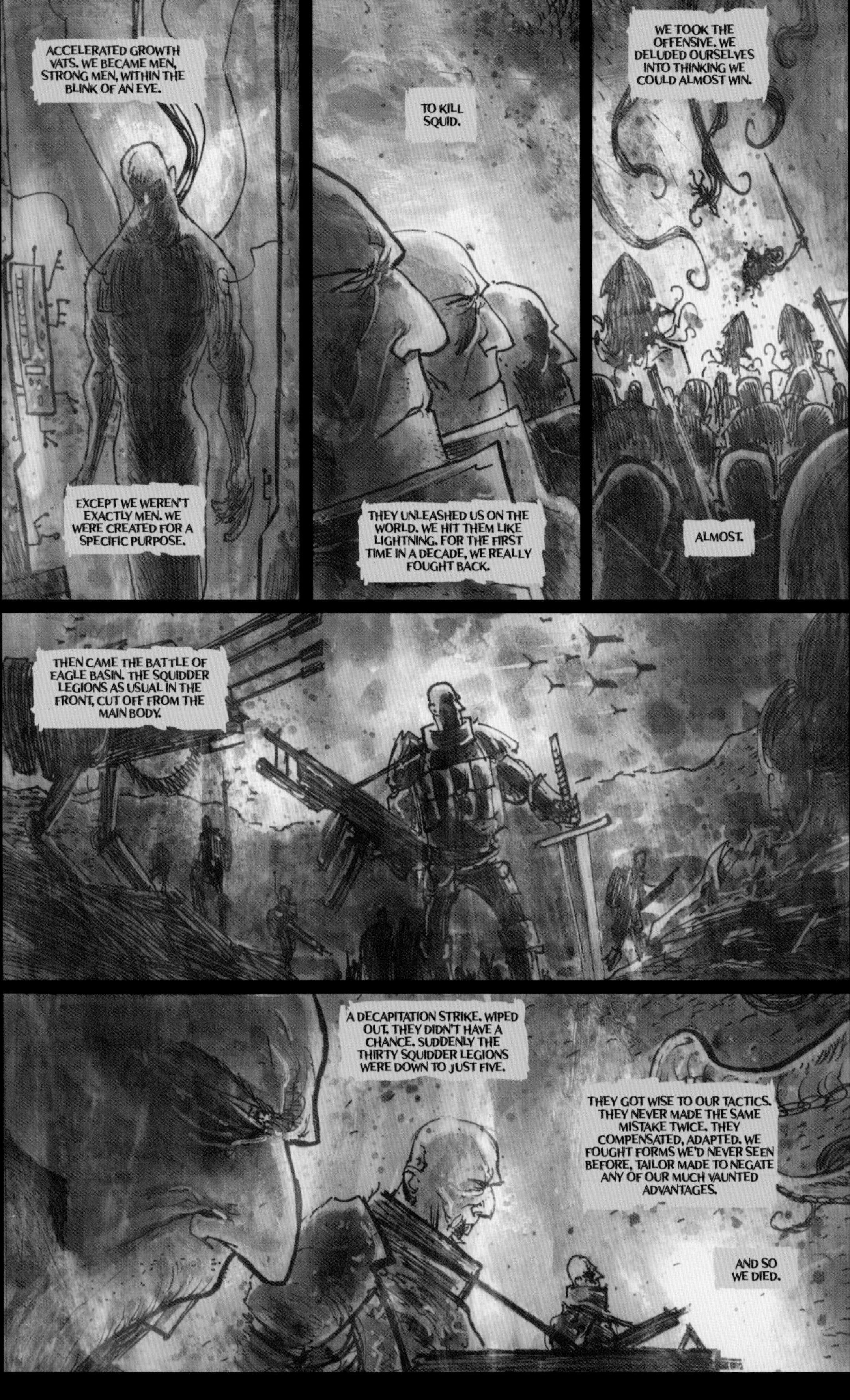
ACCELERATED GROWTH VATS. WE BECAME MEN, STRONG MEN, WITHIN THE BLINK OF AN EYE.
EXCEPT WE WEREN'T EXACTLY MEN. WE WERE CREATED FOR A SPECIFIC PURPOSE.
TO KILL SQUID.
THEY UNLEASHED US ON THE WORLD. WE HIT THEM LIKE LIGHTNING. FOR THE FIRST TIME IN A DECADE, WE REALLY FOUGHT BACK.
WE TOOK THE OFFENSIVE. WE DELUDED OURSELVES INTO THINKING WE COULD ALMOST WIN.
ALMOST.
THEN CAME THE BATTLE OF EAGLE BASIN. THE SQUIDDER LEGIONS AS USUAL IN THE FRONT, CUT OFF FROM THE MAIN BODY.
A DECAPITATION STRIKE. WIPED OUT. THEY DIDN'T HAVE A CHANCE. SUDDENLY THE THIRTY SQUIDDER LEGIONS WERE DOWN TO JUST FIVE.
THEY GOT WISE TO OUR TACTICS. THEY NEVER MADE THE SAME MISTAKE TWICE. THEY COMPENSATED, ADAPTED. WE FOUGHT FORMS WE'D NEVER SEEN BEFORE, TAILOR MADE TO NEGATE ANY OF OUR MUCH VAUNTED ADVANTAGES.
AND SO WE DIED.

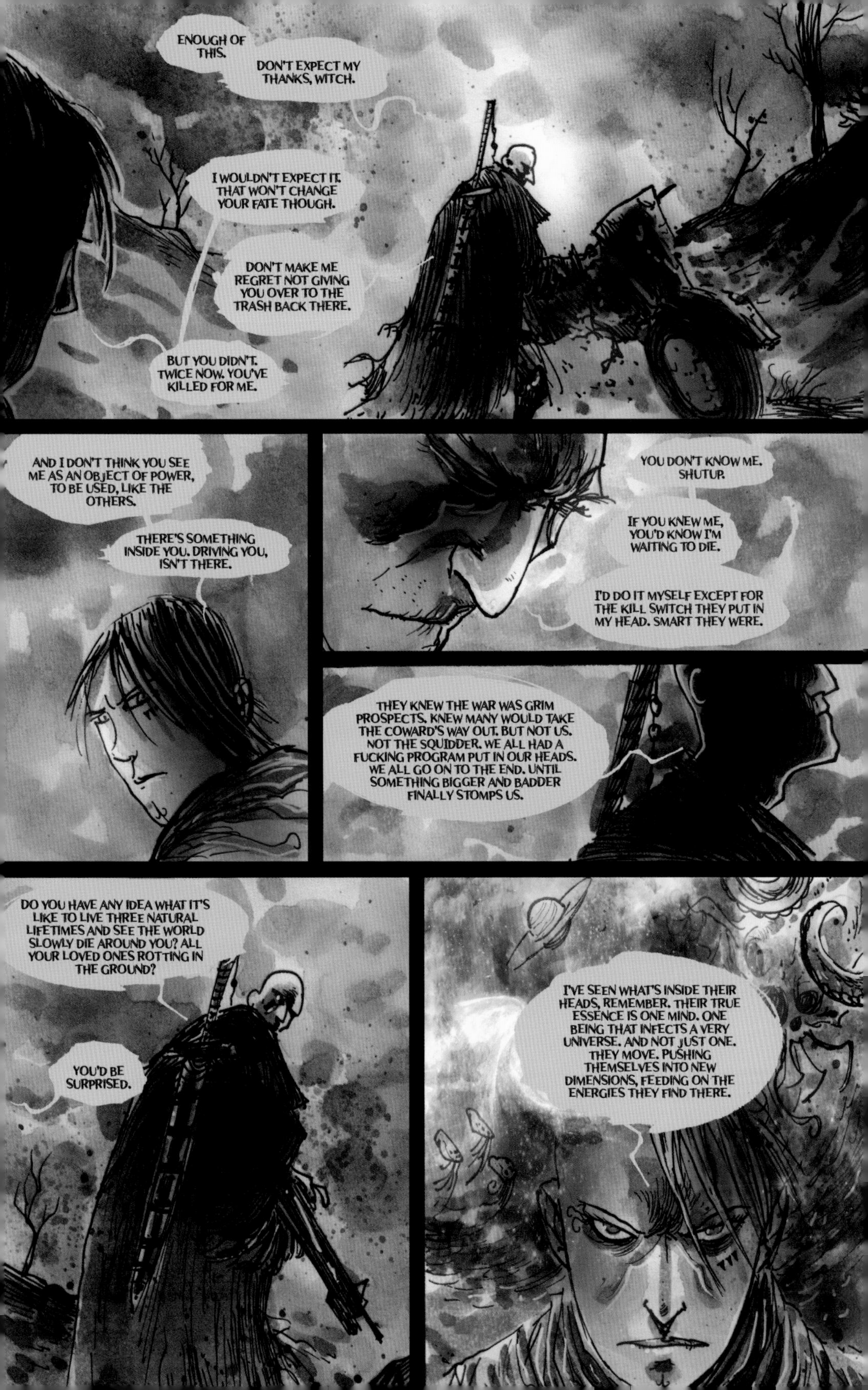
ENOUGH OF THIS.
DON'T EXPECT MY THANKS, WITCH.
I WOULDN'T EXPECT IT. THAT WON'T CHANGE YOUR FATE THOUGH.
DON'T MAKE ME REGRET NOT GIVING YOU OVER TO THE TRASH BACK THERE.
BUT YOU DIDN'T. TWICE NOW. YOU'VE KILLED FOR ME.
AND I DON'T THINK YOU SEE ME AS AN OBJECT OF POWER, TO BE USED, LIKE THE OTHERS.
THERE'S SOMETHING INSIDE YOU. DRIVING YOU, ISN'T THERE.
YOU DON'T KNOW ME. SHUTUP.
IF YOU KNEW ME, YOU'D KNOW I'M WAITING TO DIE.
I'D DO IT MYSELF EXCEPT FOR THE KILL SWITCH THEY PUT IN MY HEAD. SMART THEY WERE.
THEY KNEW THE WAR WAS GRIM PROSPECTS. KNEW MANY WOULD TAKE THE COWARD'S WAY OUT. BUT NOT US. NOT THE SQUIDDER. WE ALL HAD A FUCKING PROGRAM PUT IN OUR HEADS. WE ALL GO ON TO THE END. UNTIL SOMETHING BIGGER AND BADDER FINALLY STOMPS US.
DO YOU HAVE ANY IDEA WHAT IT'S LIKE TO LIVE THREE NATURAL LIFETIMES AND SEE THE WORLD SLOWLY DIE AROUND YOU? ALL YOUR LOVED ONES ROTTING IN THE GROUND?
YOU'D BE SURPRISED.
I'VE SEEN WHAT'S INSIDE THEIR HEADS, REMEMBER. THEIR TRUE ESSENCE IS ONE MIND. ONE BEING THAT INFECTS A VERY UNIVERSE. AND NOT JUST ONE. THEY MOVE. PUSHING THEMSELVES INTO NEW DIMENSIONS, FEEDING ON THE ENERGIES THEY FIND THERE.

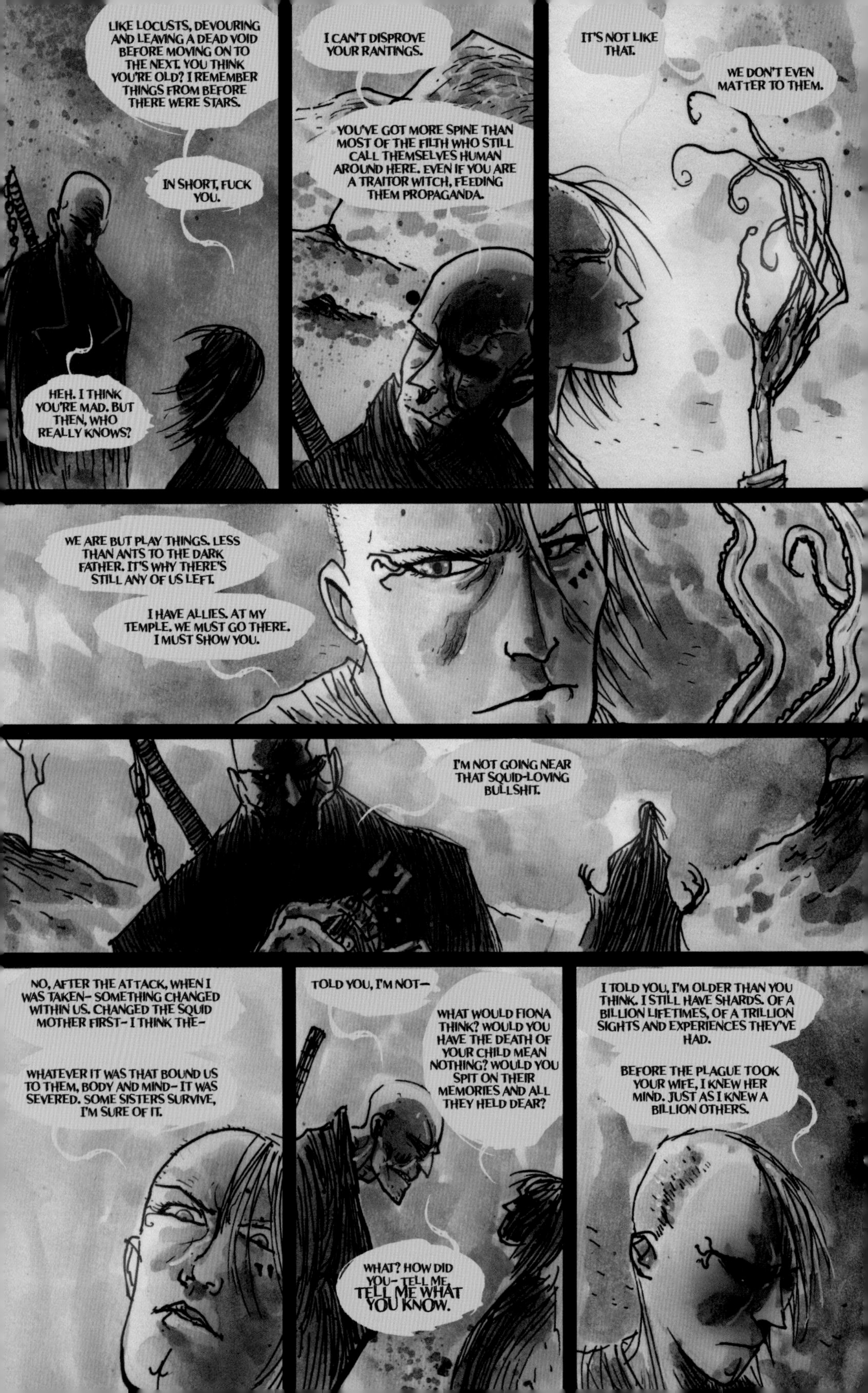
LIKE LOCUSTS, DEVOURING AND LEAVING A DEAD VOID BEFORE MOVING ON TO THE NEXT. YOU THINK YOU'RE OLD? I REMEMBER THINGS FROM BEFORE THERE WERE STARS.
IN SHORT, FUCK YOU.
HEH. I THINK YOU'RE MAD. BUT THEN, WHO REALLY KNOWS?
I CAN'T DISPROVE YOUR RANTINGS.
YOU'VE GOT MORE SPINE THAN MOST OF THE FILTH WHO STILL CALL THEMSELVES HUMAN AROUND HERE. EVEN IF YOU ARE A TRAITOR WITCH, FEEDING THEM PROPAGANDA.
IT'S NOT LIKE THAT.
WE DON'T EVEN MATTER TO THEM.
WE ARE BUT PLAY THINGS. LESS THAN ANTS TO THE DARK FATHER. IT'S WHY THERE'S STILL ANY OF US LEFT.
I HAVE ALLIES. AT MY TEMPLE. WE MUST GO THERE. I MUST SHOW YOU.
I'M NOT GOING NEAR THAT SQUID-LOVING BULLSHIT.
NO, AFTER THE ATTACK, WHEN I WAS TAKEN- SOMETHING CHANGED WITHIN US. CHANGED THE SQUID MOTHER FIRST- I THINK THE-
WHATEVER IT WAS THAT BOUND US TO THEM, BODY AND MIND- IT WAS SEVERED. SOME SISTERS SURVIVE, I'M SURE OF IT.
TOLD YOU, I'M NOT-
WHAT WOULD FIONA THINK? WOULD YOU HAVE THE DEATH OF YOUR CHILD MEAN NOTHING? WOULD YOU SPIT ON THEIR MEMORIES AND ALL THEY HELD DEAR?
WHAT? HOW DID YOU- TELL ME. TELL ME WHAT YOU KNOW.
I TOLD YOU, I'M OLDER THAN YOU THINK. I STILL HAVE SHARDS. OF A BILLION LIFETIMES, OF A TRILLION SIGHTS AND EXPERIENCES THEY'VE HAD.
BEFORE THE PLAGUE TOOK YOUR WIFE, I KNEW HER MIND. JUST AS I KNEW A BILLION OTHERS.

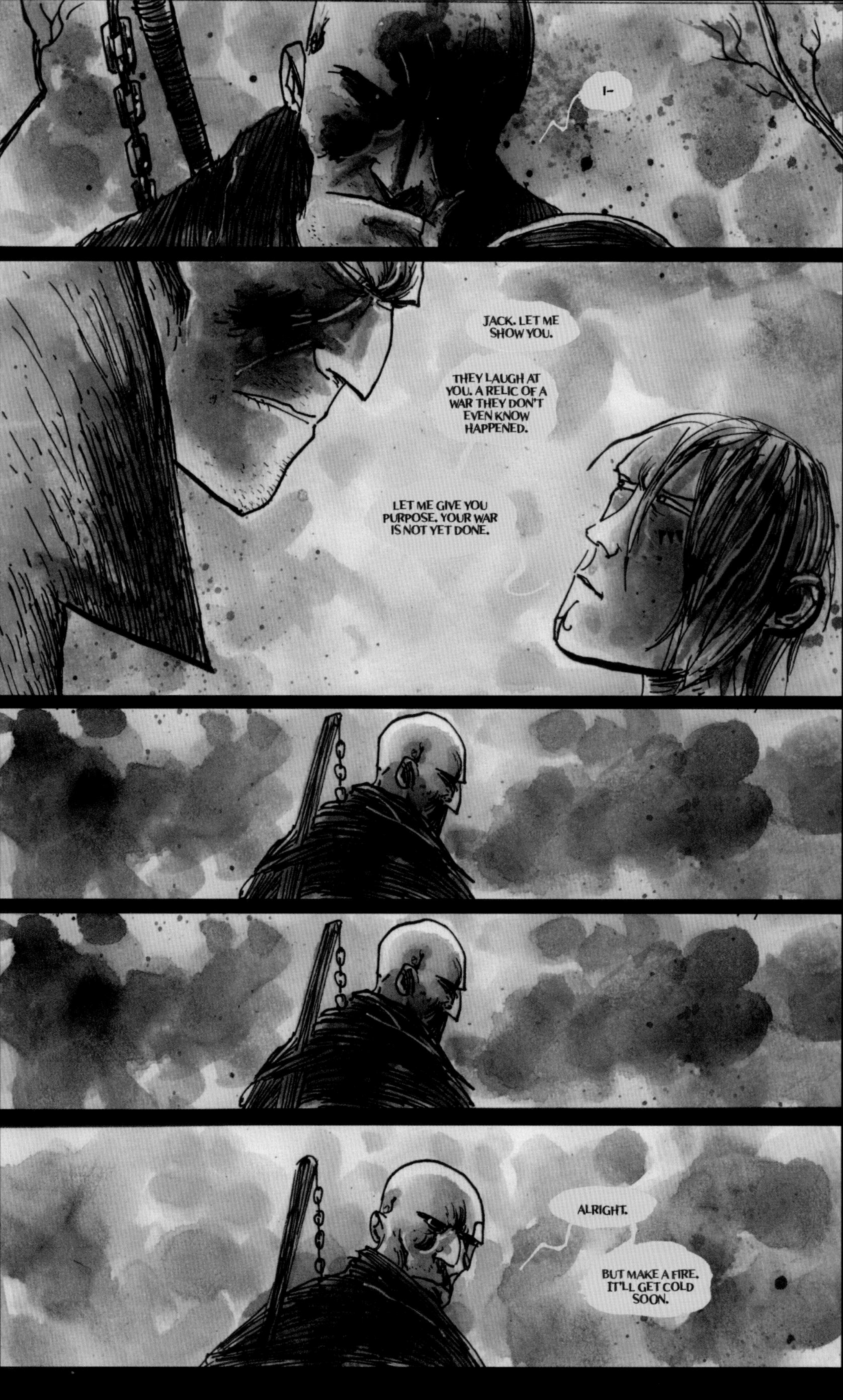
I–
JACK. LET ME SHOW YOU.
THEY LAUGH AT YOU. A RELIC OF A WAR THEY DON'T EVEN KNOW HAPPENED.
LET ME GIVE YOU PURPOSE. YOUR WAR IS NOT YET DONE.
ALRIGHT.
BUT MAKE A FIRE. IT'LL GET COLD SOON.

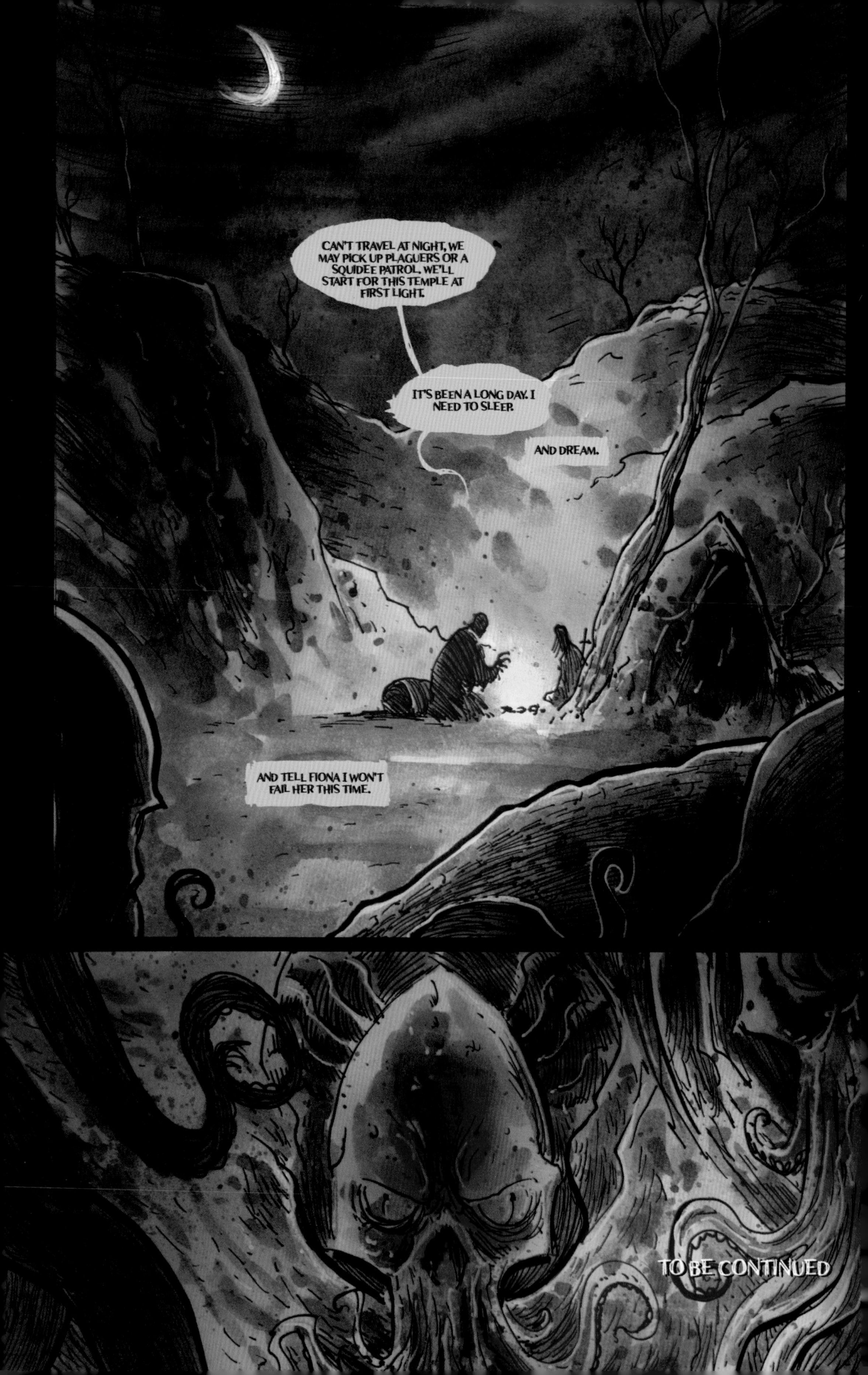
CAN'T TRAVEL AT NIGHT, WE MAY PICK UP PLAGUERS OR A SQUIDEE PATROL. WE'LL START FOR THIS TEMPLE AT FIRST LIGHT.
IT'S BEEN A LONG DAY. I NEED TO SLEEP.
AND DREAM.
AND TELL FIONA I WON'T FAIL HER THIS TIME.
TO BE CONTINUED

CHAPTER THREE

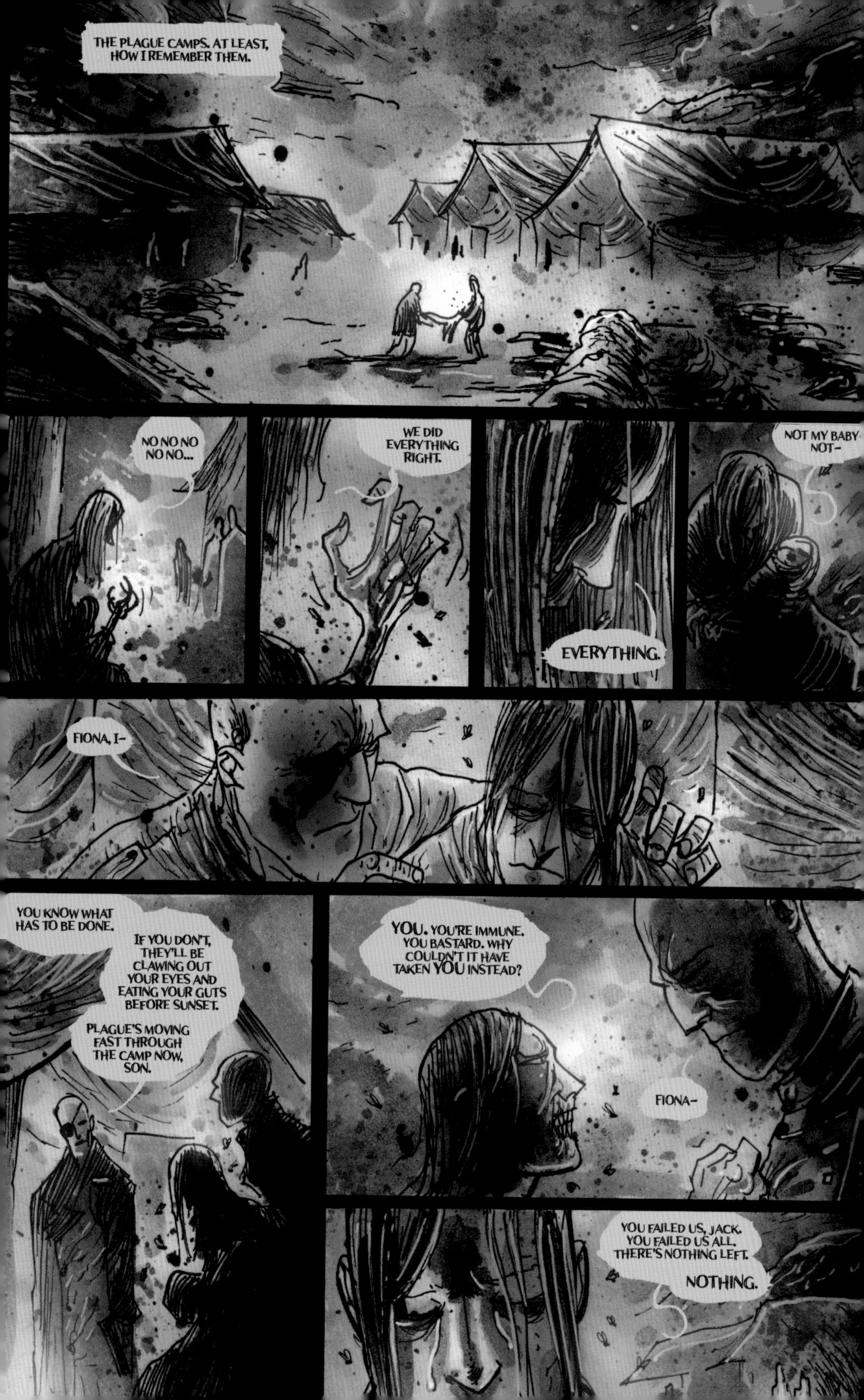
THE PLAGUE CAMPS. AT LEAST, HOW I REMEMBER THEM.
NO NO NO NO NO...
WE DID EVERYTHING RIGHT.
EVERYTHING.
NOT MY BABY NOT-
FIONA, I-
YOU KNOW WHAT HAS TO BE DONE.
IF YOU DON'T, THEY'LL BE CLAWING OUT YOUR EYES AND EATING YOUR GUTS BEFORE SUNSET.
PLAGUE'S MOVING FAST THROUGH THE CAMP NOW, SON.
YOU. YOU'RE IMMUNE. YOU BASTARD. WHY COULDN'T IT HAVE TAKEN YOU INSTEAD?
FIONA-
YOU FAILED US, JACK. YOU FAILED US ALL. THERE'S NOTHING LEFT.
NOTHING.

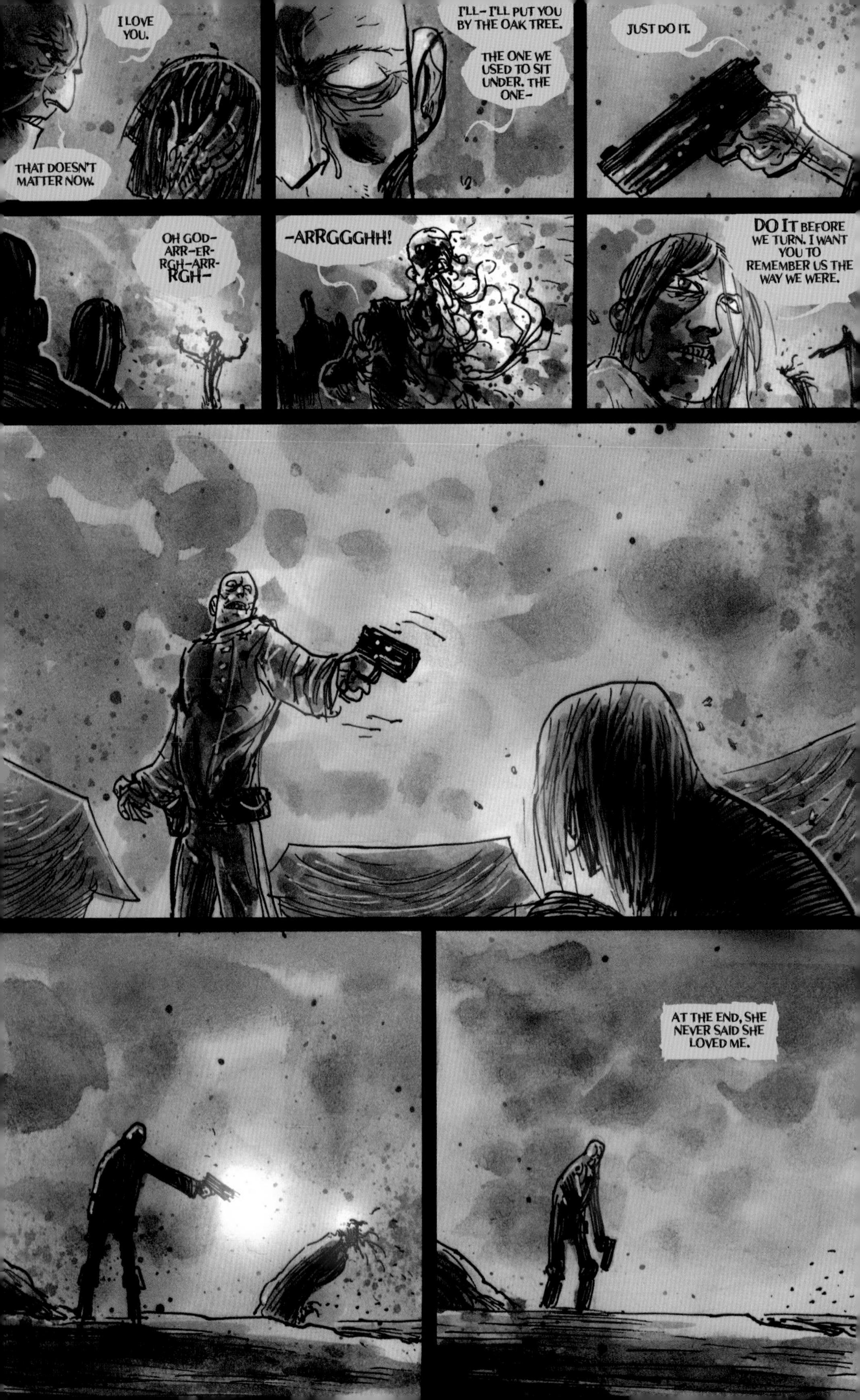
I LOVE YOU.
THAT DOESN'T MATTER NOW.
I'LL- I'LL PUT YOU BY THE OAK TREE.
THE ONE WE USED TO SIT UNDER. THE ONE-
JUST DO IT.
OH GOD- ARR-ER-RGH-ARR-RGH-
-ARRGGGHH!
DO IT BEFORE WE TURN. I WANT YOU TO REMEMBER US THE WAY WE WERE.
AT THE END, SHE NEVER SAID SHE LOVED ME.

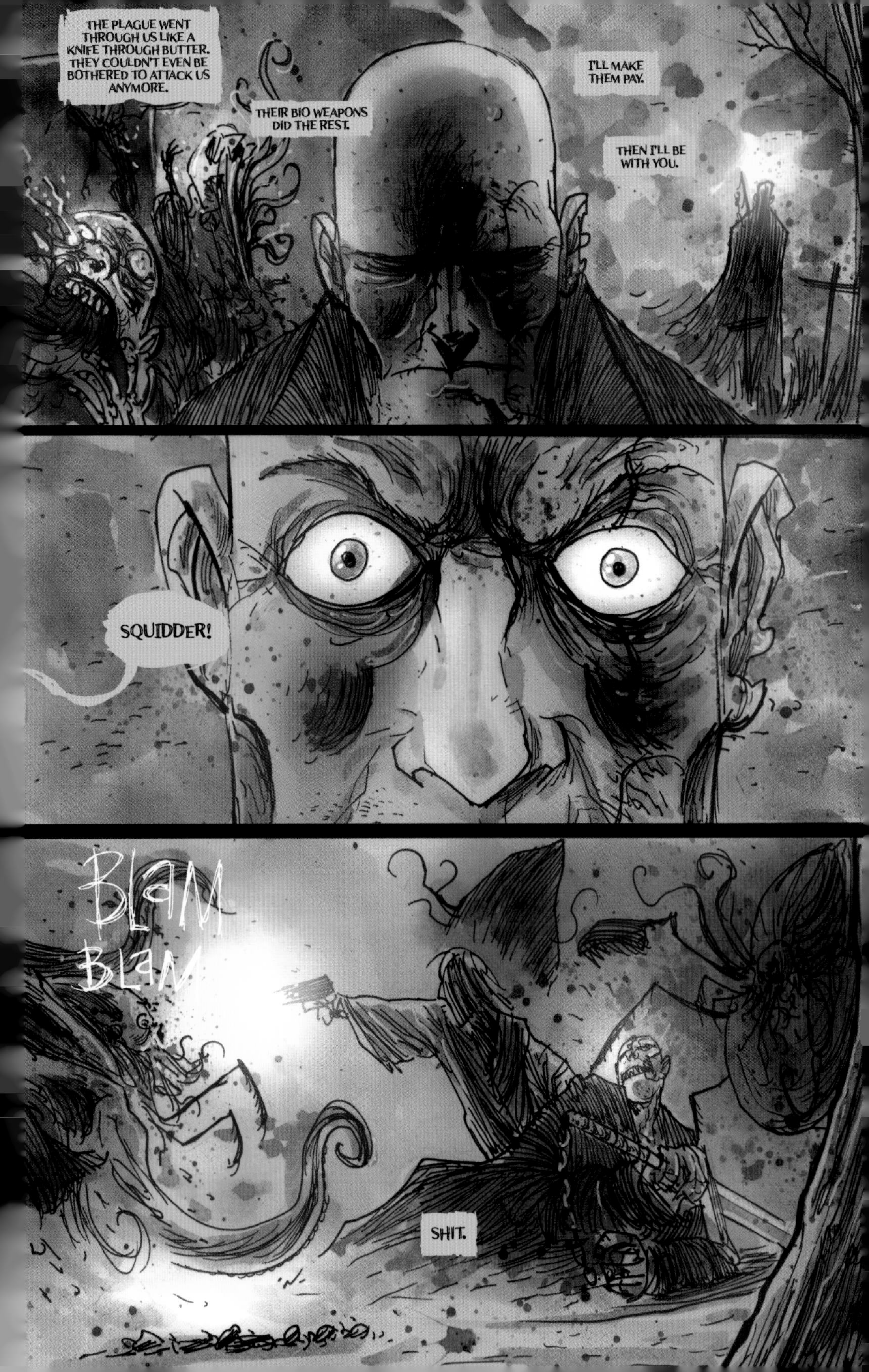
THE PLAGUE WENT THROUGH US LIKE A KNIFE THROUGH BUTTER. THEY COULDN'T EVEN BE BOTHERED TO ATTACK US ANYMORE.
THEIR BIO WEAPONS DID THE REST.
I'LL MAKE THEM PAY.
THEN I'LL BE WITH YOU.
SQUIDDER!
BLAM
BLAM
SHIT.

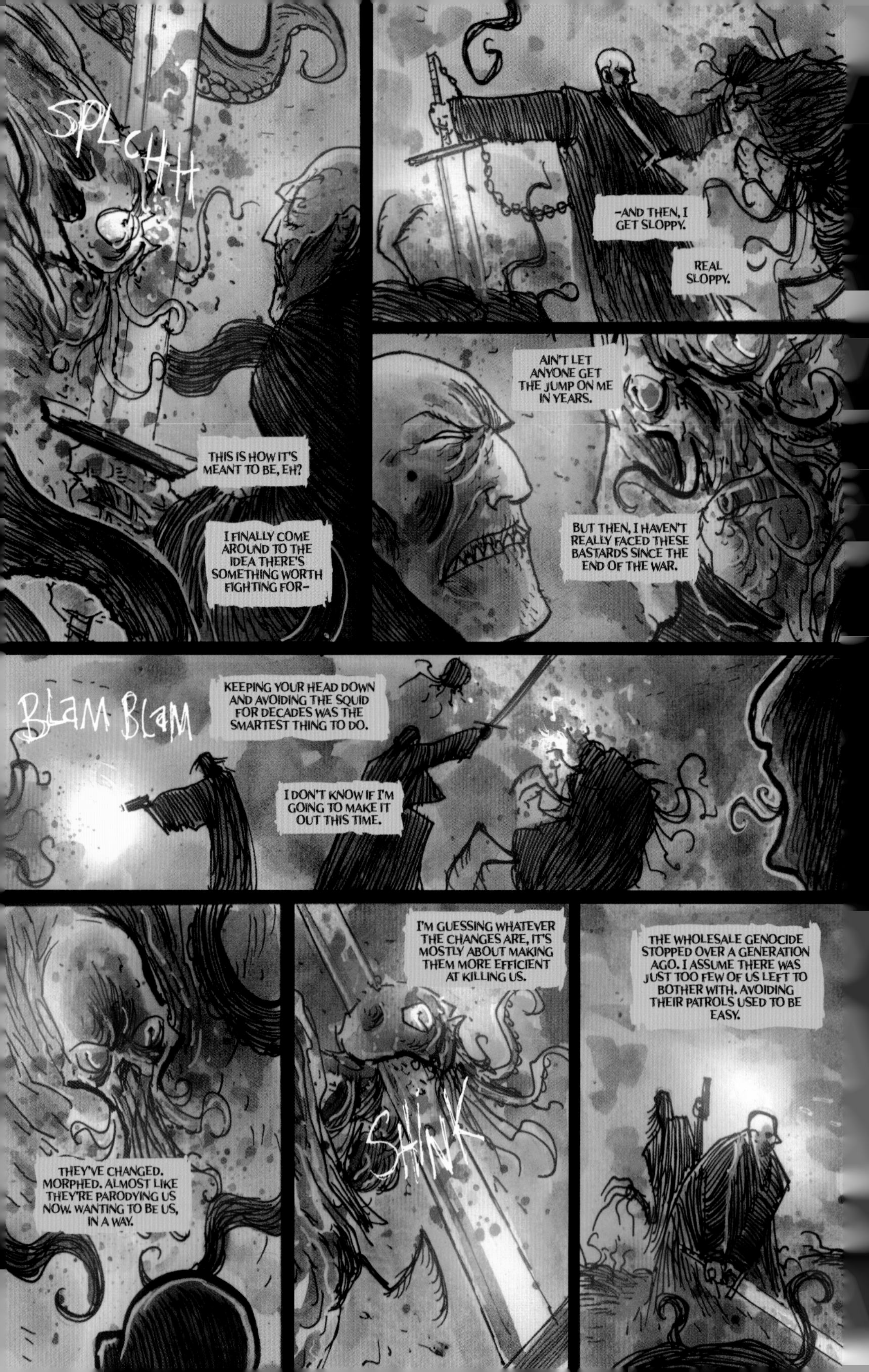
SPLCHH
THIS IS HOW IT'S MEANT TO BE, EH?
I FINALLY COME AROUND TO THE IDEA THERE'S SOMETHING WORTH FIGHTING FOR–
–AND THEN, I GET SLOPPY.
REAL SLOPPY.
AIN'T LET ANYONE GET THE JUMP ON ME IN YEARS.
BUT THEN, I HAVEN'T REALLY FACED THESE BASTARDS SINCE THE END OF THE WAR.
BLAM BLAM
KEEPING YOUR HEAD DOWN AND AVOIDING THE SQUID FOR DECADES WAS THE SMARTEST THING TO DO.
I DON'T KNOW IF I'M GOING TO MAKE IT OUT THIS TIME.
THEY'VE CHANGED. MORPHED. ALMOST LIKE THEY'RE PARODYING US NOW. WANTING TO BE US, IN A WAY.
I'M GUESSING WHATEVER THE CHANGES ARE, IT'S MOSTLY ABOUT MAKING THEM MORE EFFICIENT AT KILLING US.
SHINK
THE WHOLESALE GENOCIDE STOPPED OVER A GENERATION AGO. I ASSUME THERE WAS JUST TOO FEW OF US LEFT TO BOTHER WITH. AVOIDING THEIR PATROLS USED TO BE EASY.

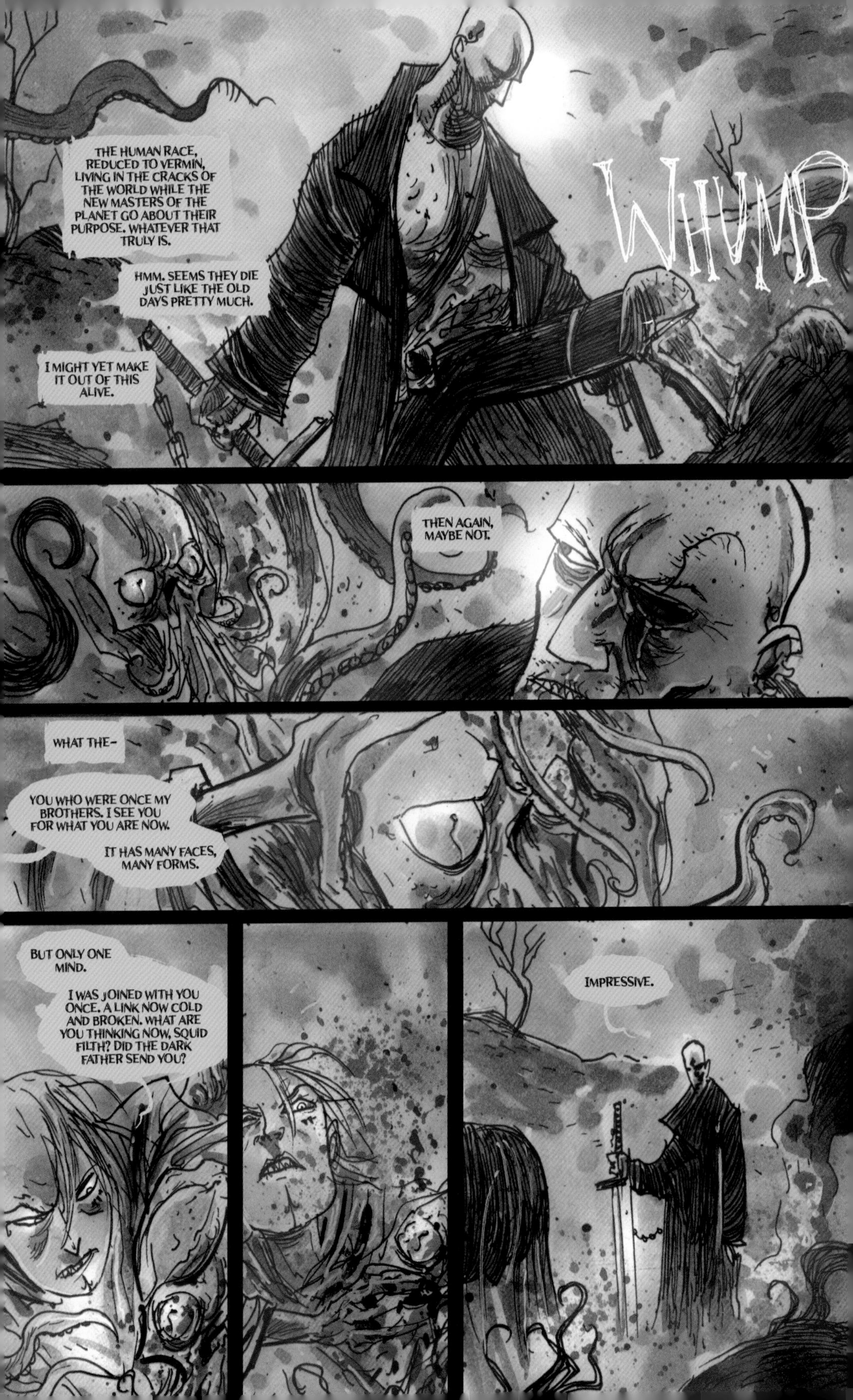
THE HUMAN RACE, REDUCED TO VERMIN, LIVING IN THE CRACKS OF THE WORLD WHILE THE NEW MASTERS OF THE PLANET GO ABOUT THEIR PURPOSE. WHATEVER THAT TRULY IS.
HMM. SEEMS THEY DIE JUST LIKE THE OLD DAYS PRETTY MUCH.
I MIGHT YET MAKE IT OUT OF THIS ALIVE.
WHUMP
THEN AGAIN, MAYBE NOT.
WHAT THE-
YOU WHO WERE ONCE MY BROTHERS. I SEE YOU FOR WHAT YOU ARE NOW.
IT HAS MANY FACES, MANY FORMS.
BUT ONLY ONE MIND.
I WAS JOINED WITH YOU ONCE. A LINK NOW COLD AND BROKEN. WHAT ARE YOU THINKING NOW, SQUID FILTH? DID THE DARK FATHER SEND YOU?
IMPRESSIVE.

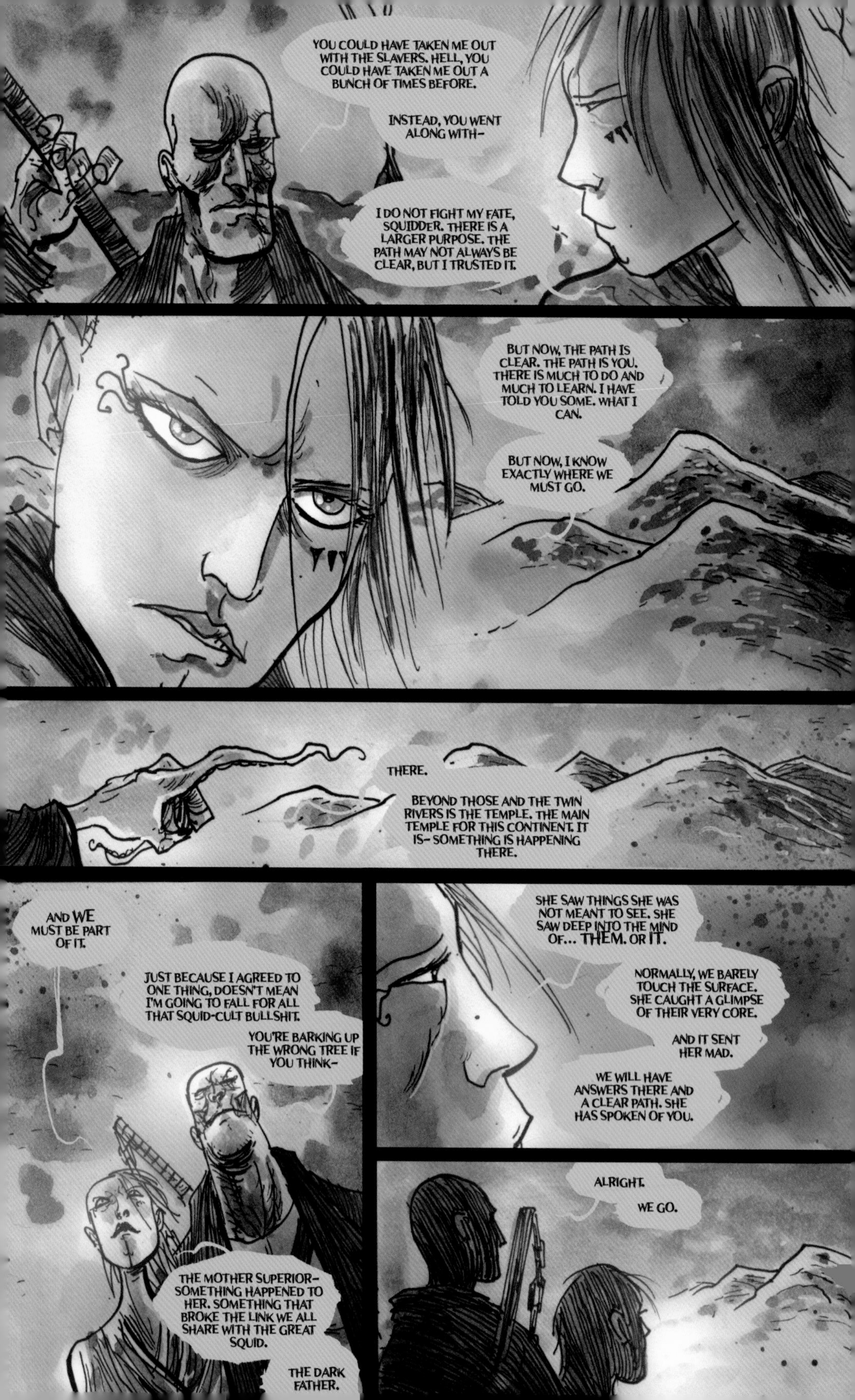

YOU COULD HAVE TAKEN ME OUT WITH THE SLAVERS. HELL, YOU COULD HAVE TAKEN ME OUT A BUNCH OF TIMES BEFORE.
INSTEAD, YOU WENT ALONG WITH-
I DO NOT FIGHT MY FATE, SQUIDDER. THERE IS A LARGER PURPOSE. THE PATH MAY NOT ALWAYS BE CLEAR, BUT I TRUSTED IT.
BUT NOW, THE PATH IS CLEAR. THE PATH IS YOU. THERE IS MUCH TO DO AND MUCH TO LEARN. I HAVE TOLD YOU SOME. WHAT I CAN.
BUT NOW, I KNOW EXACTLY WHERE WE MUST GO.
THERE.
BEYOND THOSE AND THE TWIN RIVERS IS THE TEMPLE. THE MAIN TEMPLE FOR THIS CONTINENT. IT IS- SOMETHING IS HAPPENING THERE.
AND WE MUST BE PART OF IT.
JUST BECAUSE I AGREED TO ONE THING, DOESN'T MEAN I'M GOING TO FALL FOR ALL THAT SQUID-CULT BULLSHIT.
YOU'RE BARKING UP THE WRONG TREE IF YOU THINK-
THE MOTHER SUPERIOR- SOMETHING HAPPENED TO HER. SOMETHING THAT BROKE THE LINK WE ALL SHARE WITH THE GREAT SQUID.
THE DARK FATHER.
SHE SAW THINGS SHE WAS NOT MEANT TO SEE. SHE SAW DEEP INTO THE MIND OF... THEM. OR IT.
NORMALLY, WE BARELY TOUCH THE SURFACE. SHE CAUGHT A GLIMPSE OF THEIR VERY CORE.
AND IT SENT HER MAD.
WE WILL HAVE ANSWERS THERE AND A CLEAR PATH. SHE HAS SPOKEN OF YOU.
ALRIGHT.
WE GO.

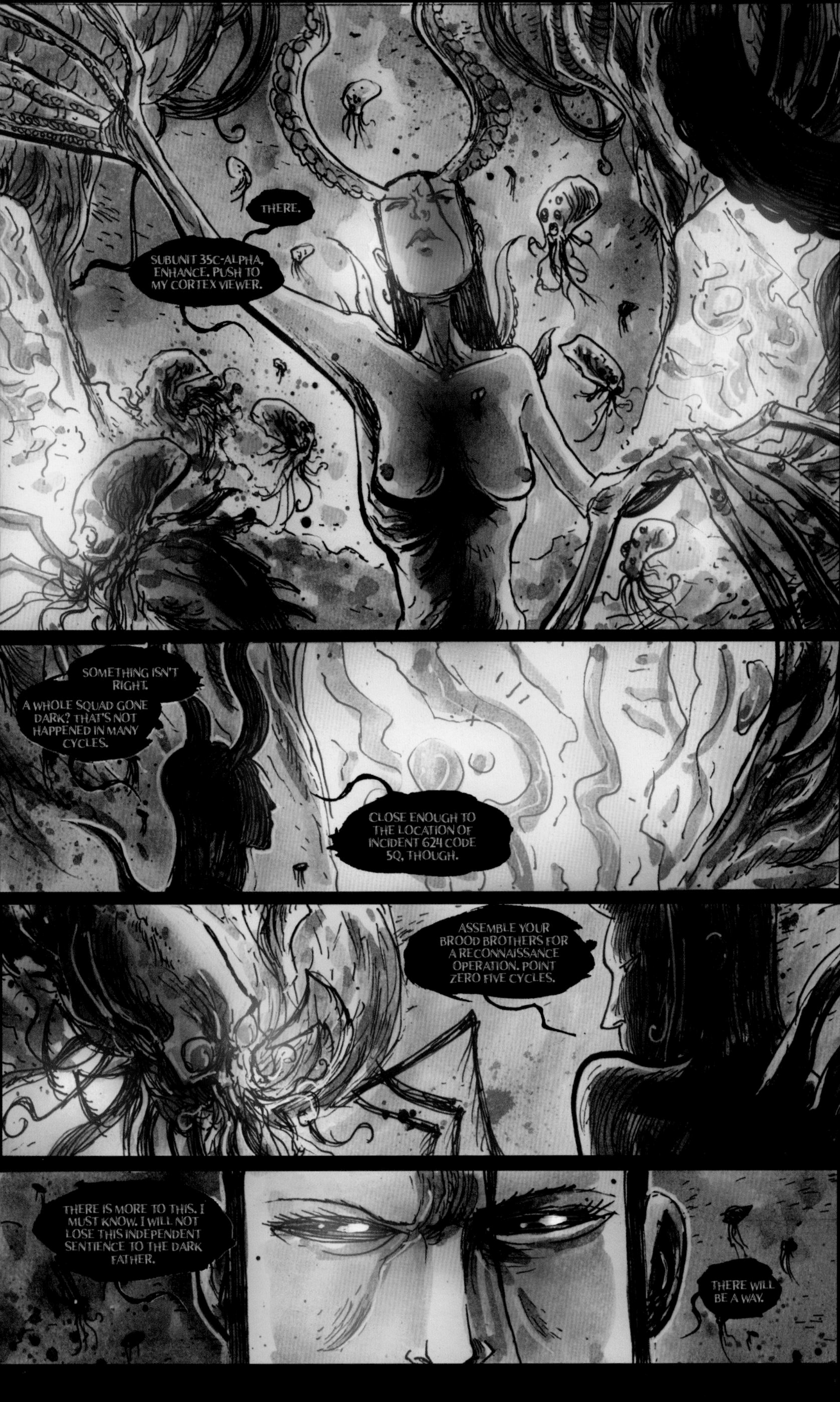
THERE.
SUBUNIT 35C-ALPHA, ENHANCE. PUSH TO MY CORTEX VIEWER.
SOMETHING ISN'T RIGHT.
A WHOLE SQUAD GONE DARK? THAT'S NOT HAPPENED IN MANY CYCLES.
CLOSE ENOUGH TO THE LOCATION OF INCIDENT 624 CODE 5Q, THOUGH.
ASSEMBLE YOUR BROOD BROTHERS FOR A RECONNAISSANCE OPERATION. POINT ZERO FIVE CYCLES.
THERE IS MORE TO THIS. I MUST KNOW. I WILL NOT LOSE THIS INDEPENDENT SENTIENCE TO THE DARK FATHER.
THERE WILL BE A WAY.

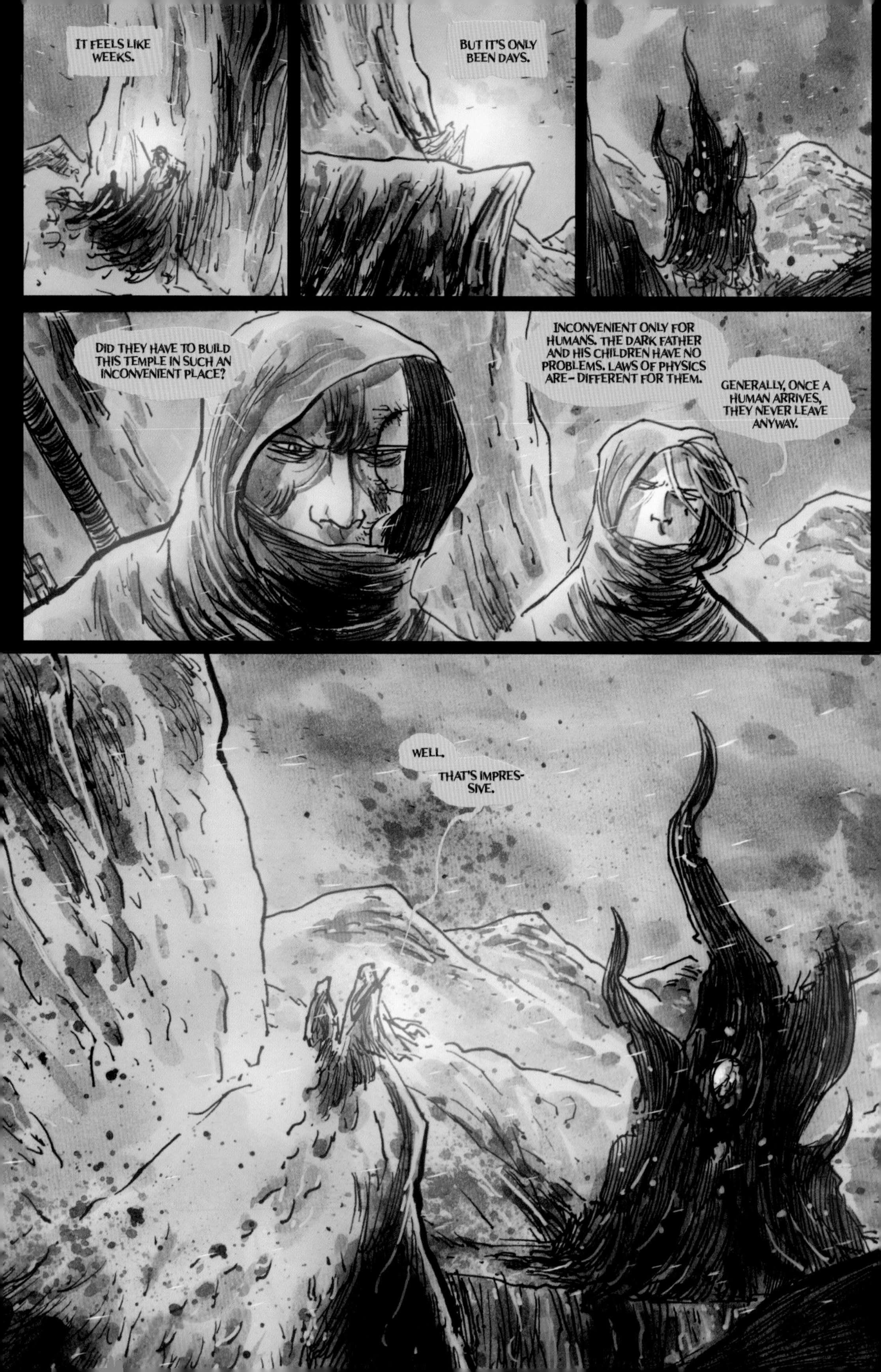
IT FEELS LIKE WEEKS.
BUT IT'S ONLY BEEN DAYS.
DID THEY HAVE TO BUILD THIS TEMPLE IN SUCH AN INCONVENIENT PLACE?
INCONVENIENT ONLY FOR HUMANS. THE DARK FATHER AND HIS CHILDREN HAVE NO PROBLEMS. LAWS OF PHYSICS ARE– DIFFERENT FOR THEM.
GENERALLY, ONCE A HUMAN ARRIVES, THEY NEVER LEAVE ANYWAY.
WELL,
THAT'S IMPRES-SIVE.

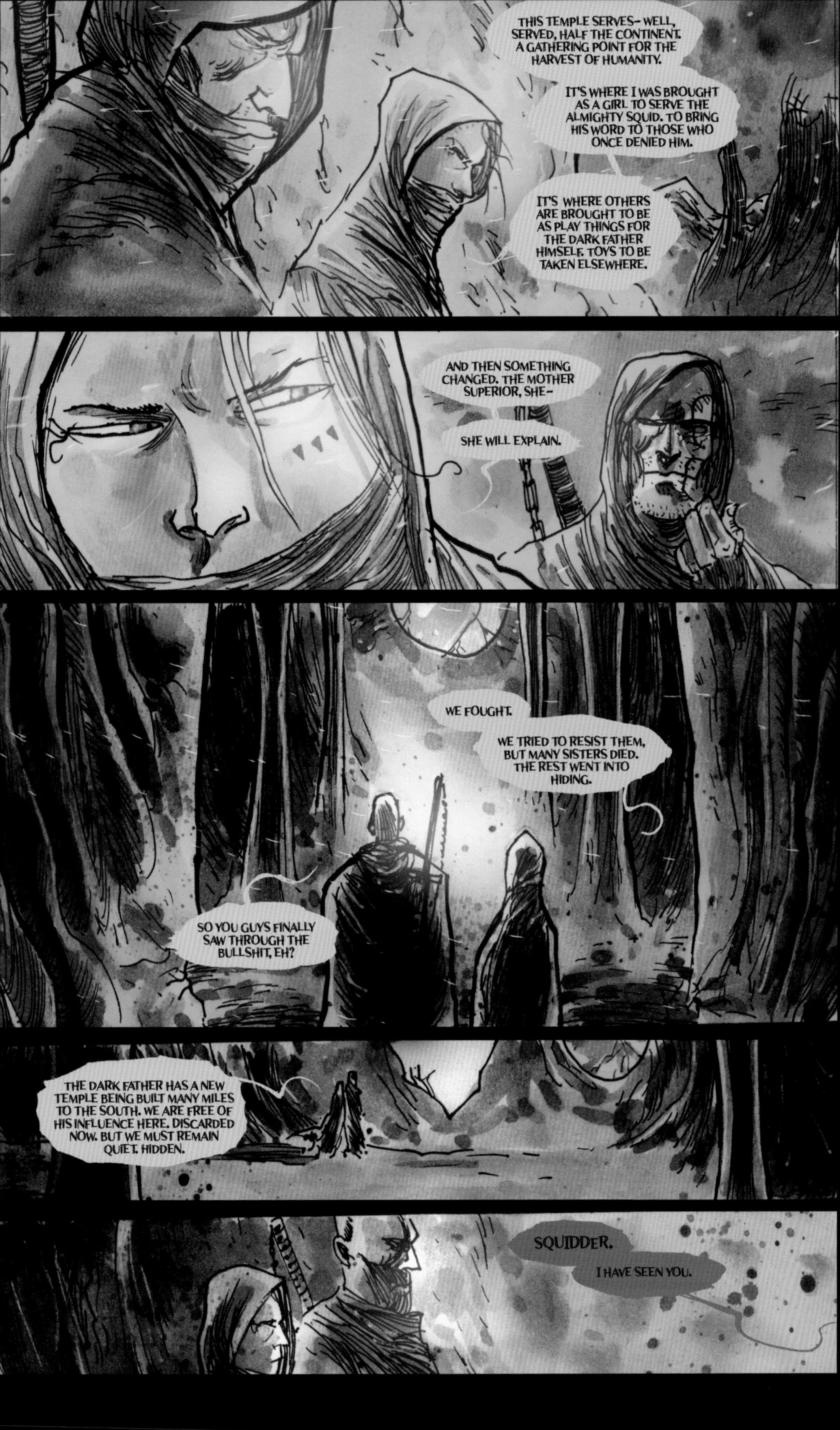
THIS TEMPLE SERVES- WELL, SERVED, HALF THE CONTINENT. A GATHERING POINT FOR THE HARVEST OF HUMANITY.
IT'S WHERE I WAS BROUGHT AS A GIRL TO SERVE THE ALMIGHTY SQUID. TO BRING HIS WORD TO THOSE WHO ONCE DENIED HIM.
IT'S WHERE OTHERS ARE BROUGHT TO BE AS PLAY THINGS FOR THE DARK FATHER HIMSELF. TOYS TO BE TAKEN ELSEWHERE.
AND THEN SOMETHING CHANGED. THE MOTHER SUPERIOR, SHE-
SHE WILL EXPLAIN.
WE FOUGHT.
WE TRIED TO RESIST THEM, BUT MANY SISTERS DIED. THE REST WENT INTO HIDING.
SO YOU GUYS FINALLY SAW THROUGH THE BULLSHIT, EH?
THE DARK FATHER HAS A NEW TEMPLE BEING BUILT MANY MILES TO THE SOUTH. WE ARE FREE OF HIS INFLUENCE HERE. DISCARDED NOW. BUT WE MUST REMAIN QUIET. HIDDEN.
SQUIDDER.
I HAVE SEEN YOU.

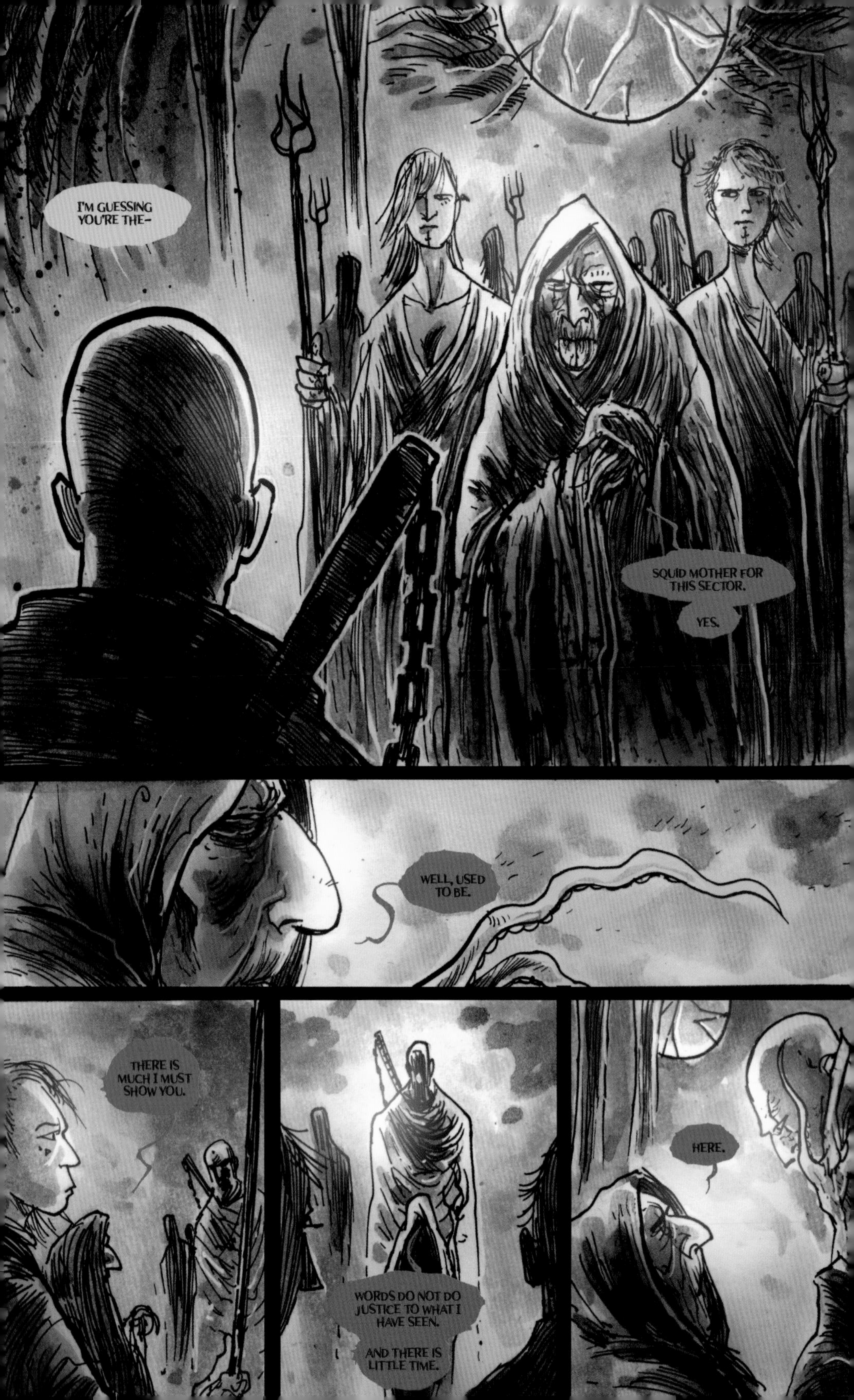

I'M GUESSING YOU'RE THE-
SQUID MOTHER FOR THIS SECTOR.
YES.
WELL, USED TO BE.
THERE IS MUCH I MUST SHOW YOU.
WORDS DO NOT DO JUSTICE TO WHAT I HAVE SEEN.
AND THERE IS LITTLE TIME.
HERE.

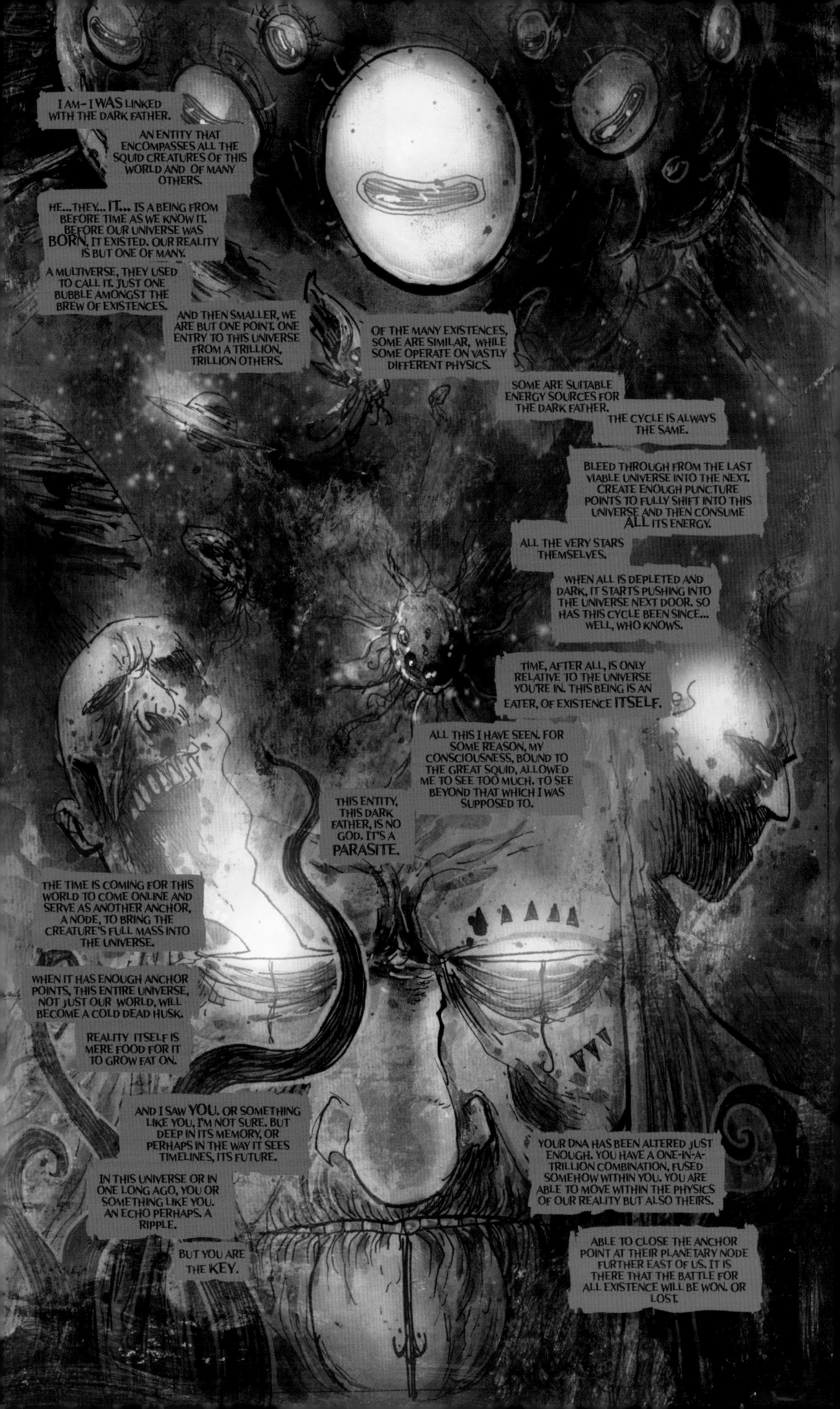
I AM- I WAS LINKED WITH THE DARK FATHER.
AN ENTITY THAT ENCOMPASSES ALL THE SQUID CREATURES OF THIS WORLD AND OF MANY OTHERS.
HE...THEY... IT... IS A BEING FROM BEFORE TIME AS WE KNOW IT. BEFORE OUR UNIVERSE WAS BORN, IT EXISTED. OUR REALITY IS BUT ONE OF MANY.
A MULTIVERSE, THEY USED TO CALL IT. JUST ONE BUBBLE AMONGST THE BREW OF EXISTENCES.
AND THEN SMALLER, WE ARE BUT ONE POINT. ONE ENTRY TO THIS UNIVERSE FROM A TRILLION, TRILLION OTHERS.
OF THE MANY EXISTENCES, SOME ARE SIMILAR, WHILE SOME OPERATE ON VASTLY DIFFERENT PHYSICS.
SOME ARE SUITABLE ENERGY SOURCES FOR THE DARK FATHER.
THE CYCLE IS ALWAYS THE SAME.
BLEED THROUGH FROM THE LAST VIABLE UNIVERSE INTO THE NEXT. CREATE ENOUGH PUNCTURE POINTS TO FULLY SHIFT INTO THIS UNIVERSE AND THEN CONSUME ALL ITS ENERGY.
ALL THE VERY STARS THEMSELVES.
WHEN ALL IS DEPLETED AND DARK, IT STARTS PUSHING INTO THE UNIVERSE NEXT DOOR. SO HAS THIS CYCLE BEEN SINCE... WELL, WHO KNOWS.
TIME, AFTER ALL, IS ONLY RELATIVE TO THE UNIVERSE YOU'RE IN. THIS BEING IS AN EATER, OF EXISTENCE ITSELF.
ALL THIS I HAVE SEEN. FOR SOME REASON, MY CONSCIOUSNESS, BOUND TO THE GREAT SQUID, ALLOWED ME TO SEE TOO MUCH. TO SEE BEYOND THAT WHICH I WAS SUPPOSED TO.
THIS ENTITY, THIS DARK FATHER, IS NO GOD. IT'S A PARASITE.
THE TIME IS COMING FOR THIS WORLD TO COME ONLINE AND SERVE AS ANOTHER ANCHOR, A NODE, TO BRING THE CREATURE'S FULL MASS INTO THE UNIVERSE.
WHEN IT HAS ENOUGH ANCHOR POINTS, THIS ENTIRE UNIVERSE, NOT JUST OUR WORLD, WILL BECOME A COLD DEAD HUSK.
REALITY ITSELF IS MERE FOOD FOR IT TO GROW FAT ON.
AND I SAW YOU. OR SOMETHING LIKE YOU, I'M NOT SURE. BUT DEEP IN ITS MEMORY, OR PERHAPS IN THE WAY IT SEES TIMELINES, ITS FUTURE.
IN THIS UNIVERSE OR IN ONE LONG AGO, YOU OR SOMETHING LIKE YOU. AN ECHO PERHAPS. A RIPPLE.
BUT YOU ARE THE KEY.
YOUR DNA HAS BEEN ALTERED JUST ENOUGH. YOU HAVE A ONE-IN-A-TRILLION COMBINATION, FUSED SOMEHOW WITHIN YOU. YOU ARE ABLE TO MOVE WITHIN THE PHYSICS OF OUR REALITY BUT ALSO THEIRS.
ABLE TO CLOSE THE ANCHOR POINT AT THEIR PLANETARY NODE FURTHER EAST OF US. IT IS THERE THAT THE BATTLE FOR ALL EXISTENCE WILL BE WON. OR LOST.

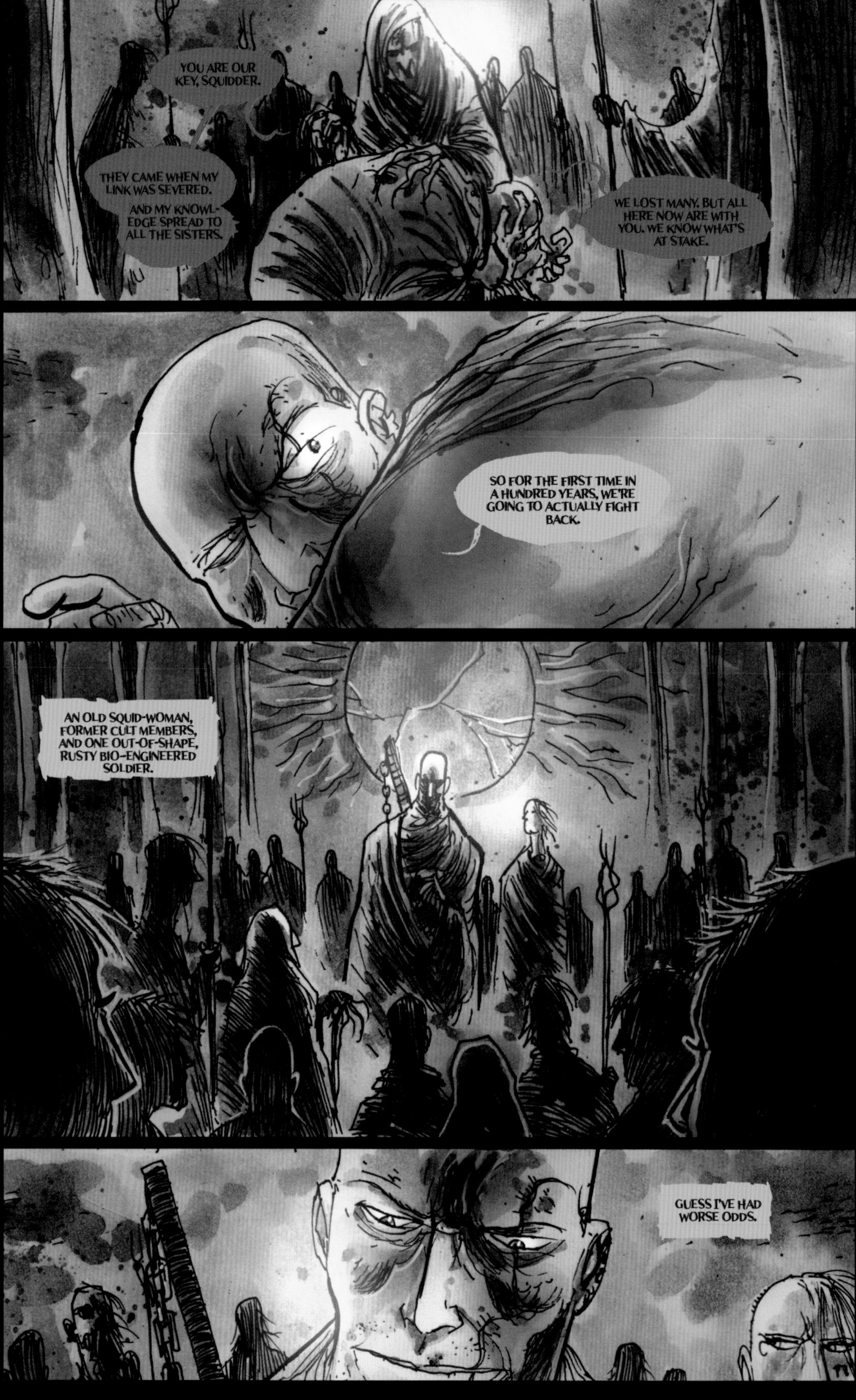
YOU ARE OUR KEY, SQUIDDER.
THEY CAME WHEN MY LINK WAS SEVERED.
AND MY KNOWL-EDGE SPREAD TO ALL THE SISTERS.
WE LOST MANY. BUT ALL HERE NOW ARE WITH YOU. WE KNOW WHAT'S AT STAKE.
SO FOR THE FIRST TIME IN A HUNDRED YEARS, WE'RE GOING TO ACTUALLY FIGHT BACK.
AN OLD SQUID-WOMAN, FORMER CULT MEMBERS, AND ONE OUT-OF-SHAPE, RUSTY BIO-ENGINEERED SOLDIER.
GUESS I'VE HAD WORSE ODDS.

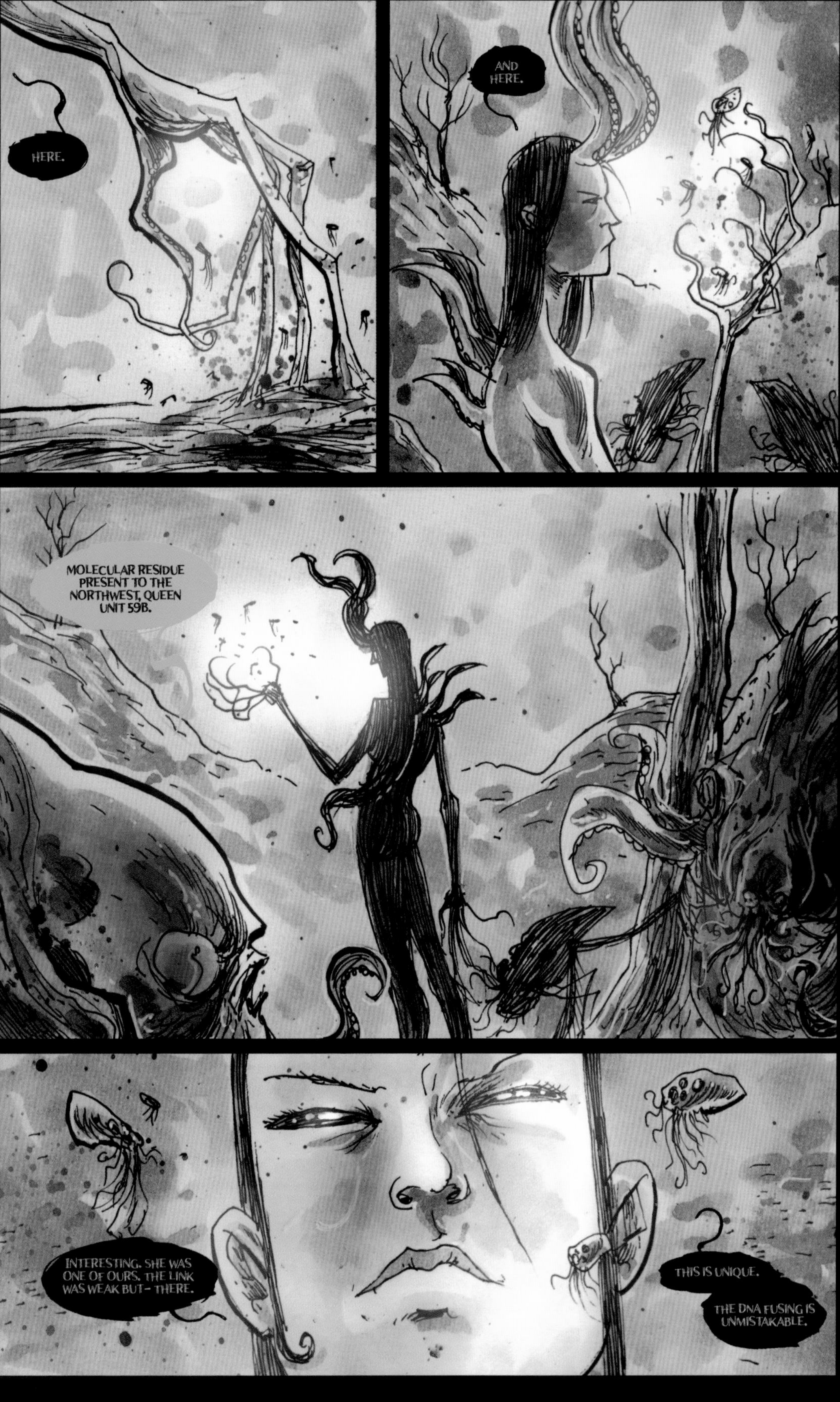
HERE.
AND HERE.
MOLECULAR RESIDUE PRESENT TO THE NORTHWEST, QUEEN UNIT 59B.
INTERESTING. SHE WAS ONE OF OURS. THE LINK WAS WEAK BUT- THERE.
THIS IS UNIQUE.
THE DNA FUSING IS UNMISTAKABLE.

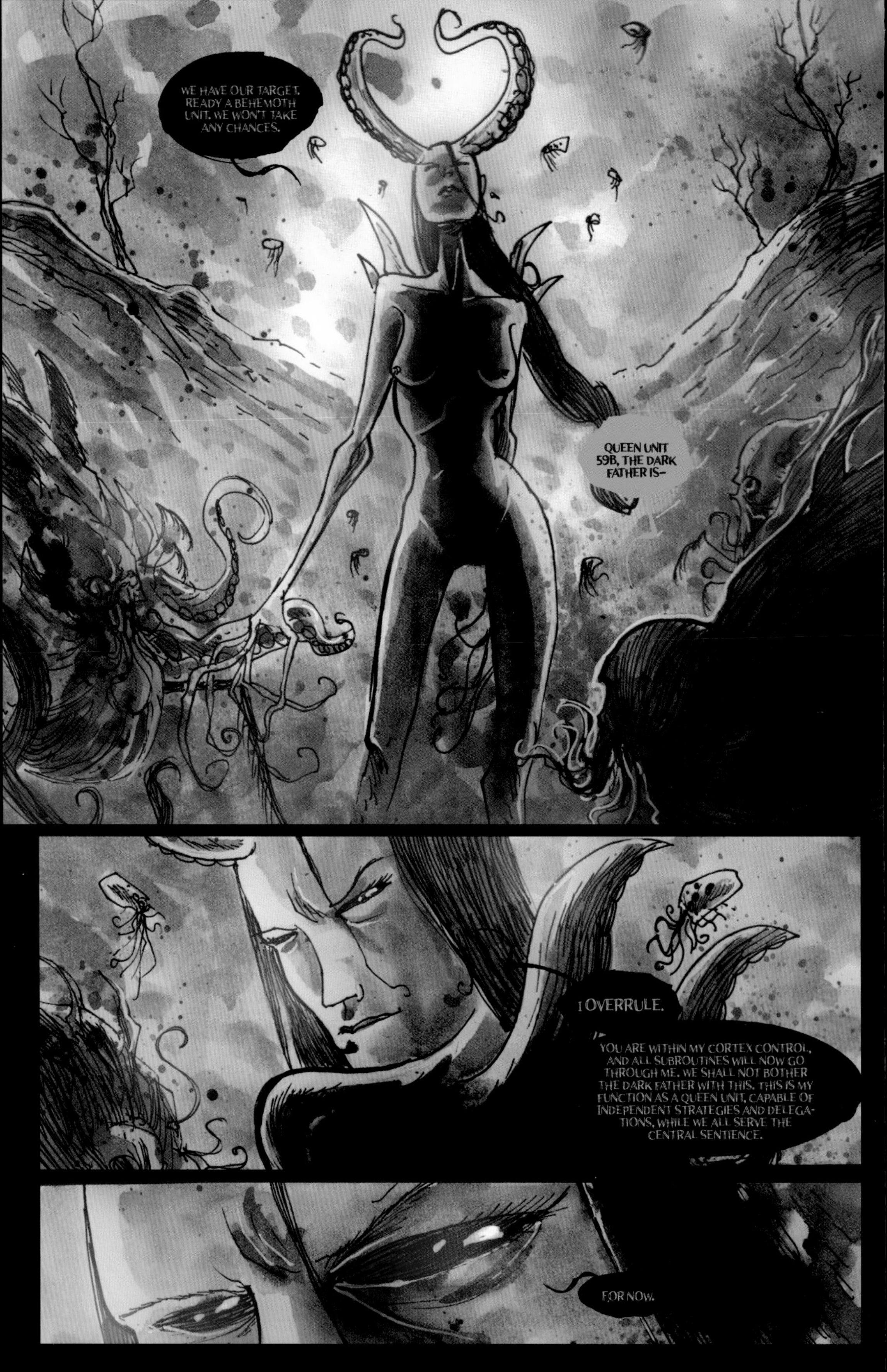
WE HAVE OUR TARGET. READY A BEHEMOTH UNIT. WE WON'T TAKE ANY CHANCES.
QUEEN UNIT 59B, THE DARK FATHER IS–
I OVERRULE.
YOU ARE WITHIN MY CORTEX CONTROL, AND ALL SUBROUTINES WILL NOW GO THROUGH ME. WE SHALL NOT BOTHER THE DARK FATHER WITH THIS. THIS IS MY FUNCTION AS A QUEEN UNIT, CAPABLE OF INDEPENDENT STRATEGIES AND DELEGATIONS, WHILE WE ALL SERVE THE CENTRAL SENTIENCE.
FOR NOW.

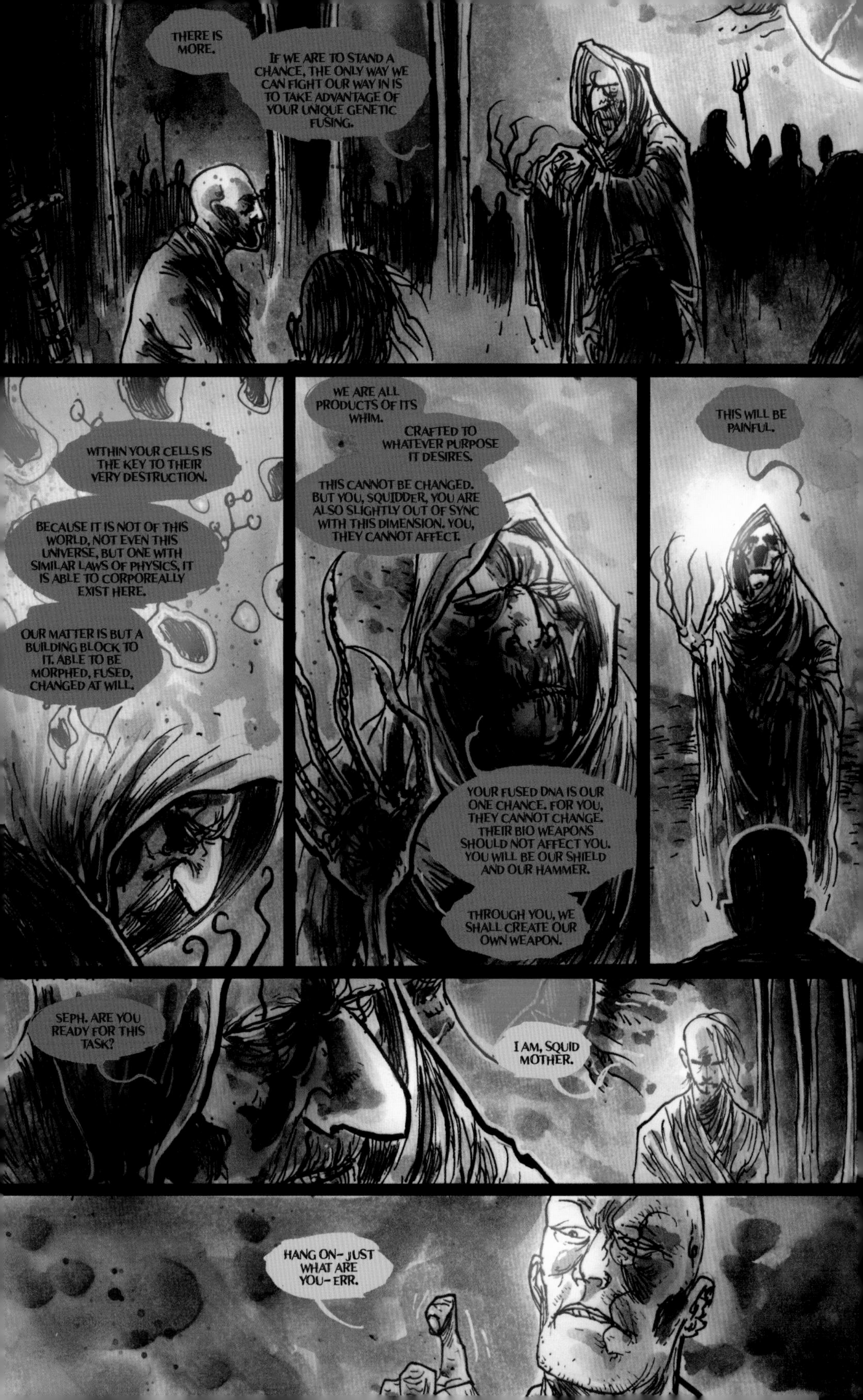
THERE IS MORE.
IF WE ARE TO STAND A CHANCE, THE ONLY WAY WE CAN FIGHT OUR WAY IN IS TO TAKE ADVANTAGE OF YOUR UNIQUE GENETIC FUSING.
WITHIN YOUR CELLS IS THE KEY TO THEIR VERY DESTRUCTION.
BECAUSE IT IS NOT OF THIS WORLD, NOT EVEN THIS UNIVERSE, BUT ONE WITH SIMILAR LAWS OF PHYSICS, IT IS ABLE TO CORPOREALLY EXIST HERE.
OUR MATTER IS BUT A BUILDING BLOCK TO IT. ABLE TO BE MORPHED, FUSED, CHANGED AT WILL.
WE ARE ALL PRODUCTS OF ITS WHIM.
CRAFTED TO WHATEVER PURPOSE IT DESIRES.
THIS CANNOT BE CHANGED. BUT YOU, SQUIDDER, YOU ARE ALSO SLIGHTLY OUT OF SYNC WITH THIS DIMENSION. YOU, THEY CANNOT AFFECT.
YOUR FUSED DNA IS OUR ONE CHANCE. FOR YOU, THEY CANNOT CHANGE. THEIR BIO WEAPONS SHOULD NOT AFFECT YOU. YOU WILL BE OUR SHIELD AND OUR HAMMER.
THROUGH YOU, WE SHALL CREATE OUR OWN WEAPON.
THIS WILL BE PAINFUL.
SEPH. ARE YOU READY FOR THIS TASK?
I AM, SQUID MOTHER.
HANG ON- JUST WHAT ARE YOU- ERR.

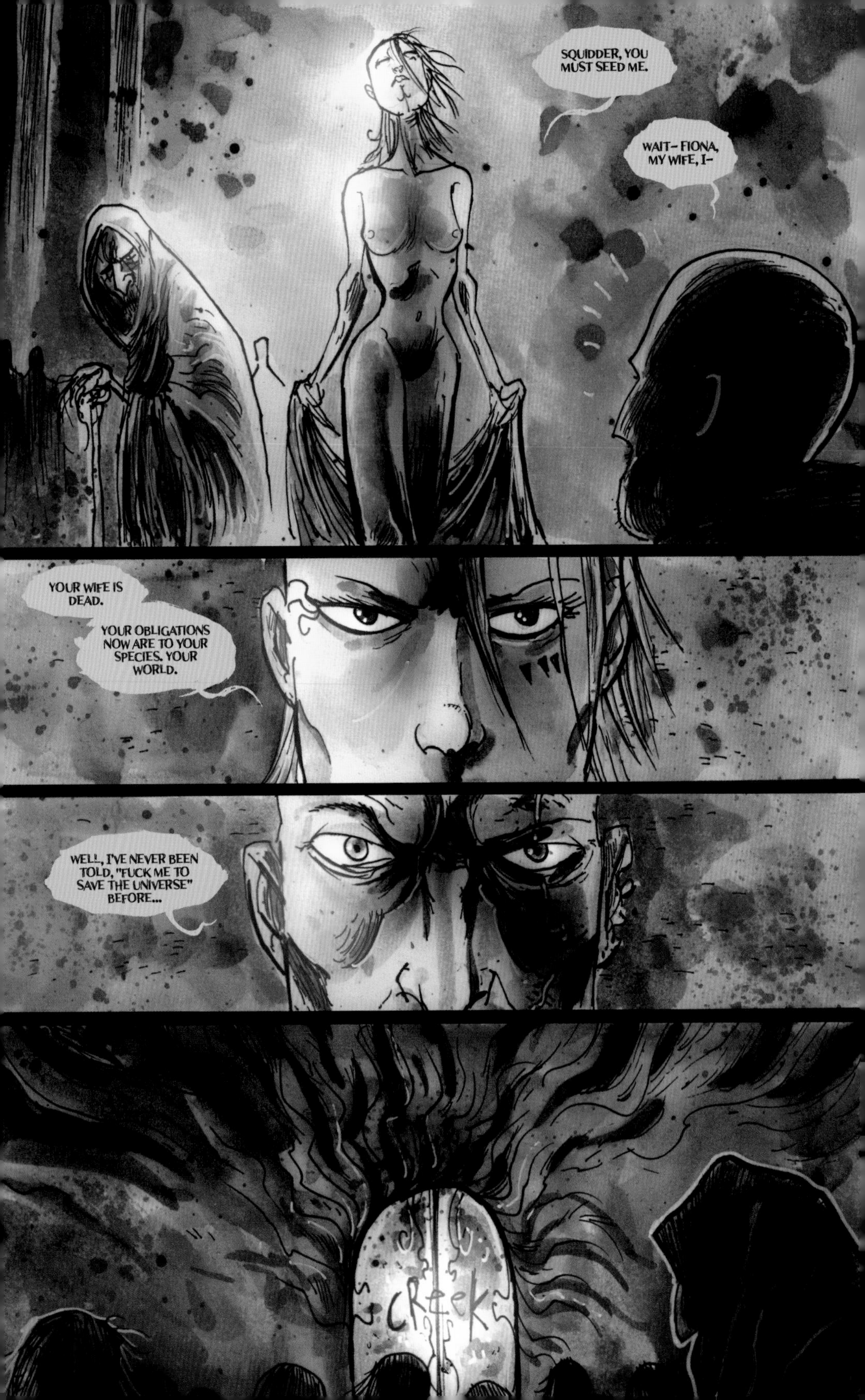
SQUIDDER, YOU MUST SEED ME.
WAIT– FIONA, MY WIFE, I–
YOUR WIFE IS DEAD.
YOUR OBLIGATIONS NOW ARE TO YOUR SPECIES. YOUR WORLD.
WELL, I'VE NEVER BEEN TOLD, "FUCK ME TO SAVE THE UNIVERSE" BEFORE...
CREEK

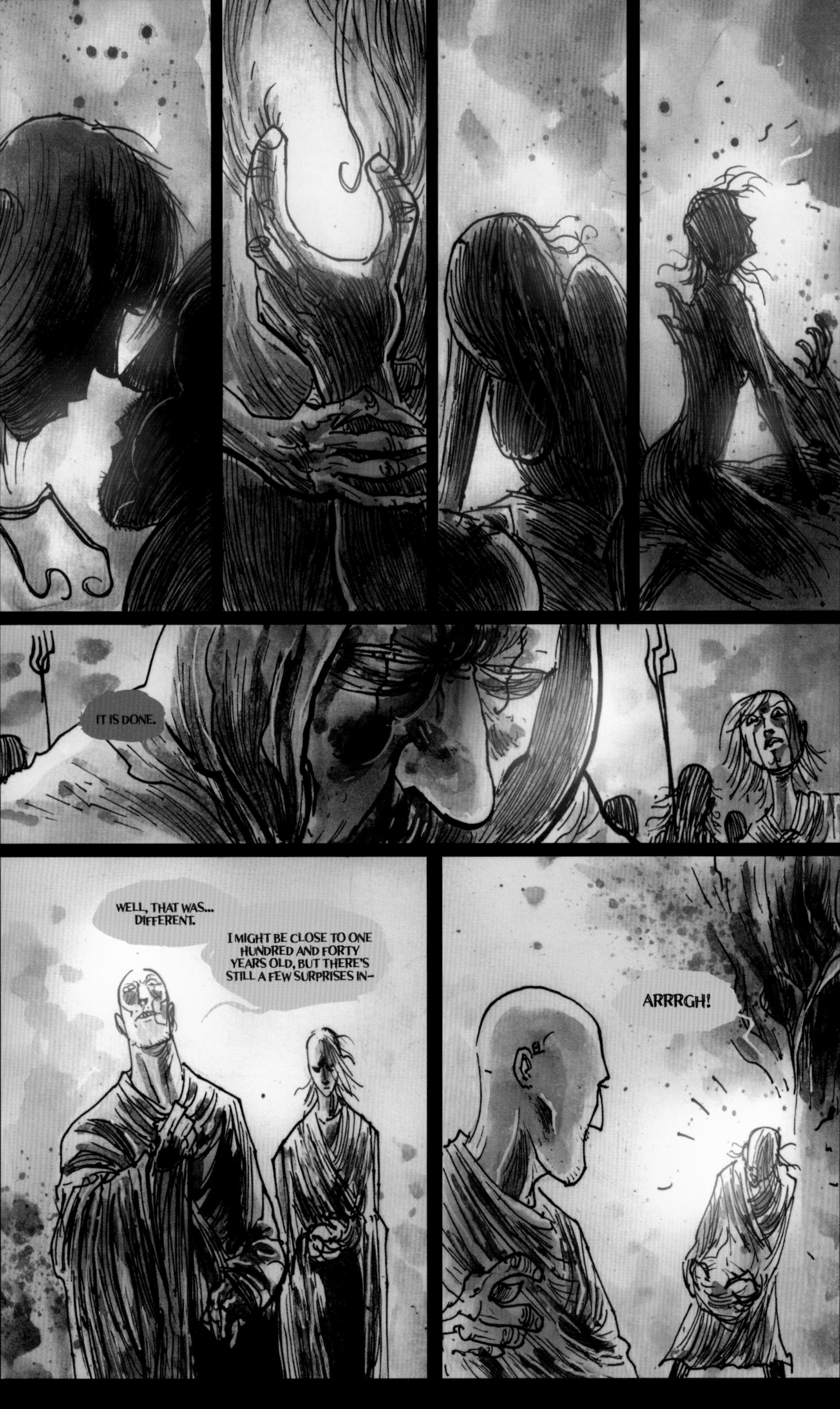
IT IS DONE.
WELL, THAT WAS... DIFFERENT.
I MIGHT BE CLOSE TO ONE HUNDRED AND FORTY YEARS OLD, BUT THERE'S STILL A FEW SURPRISES IN-
ARRRGH!

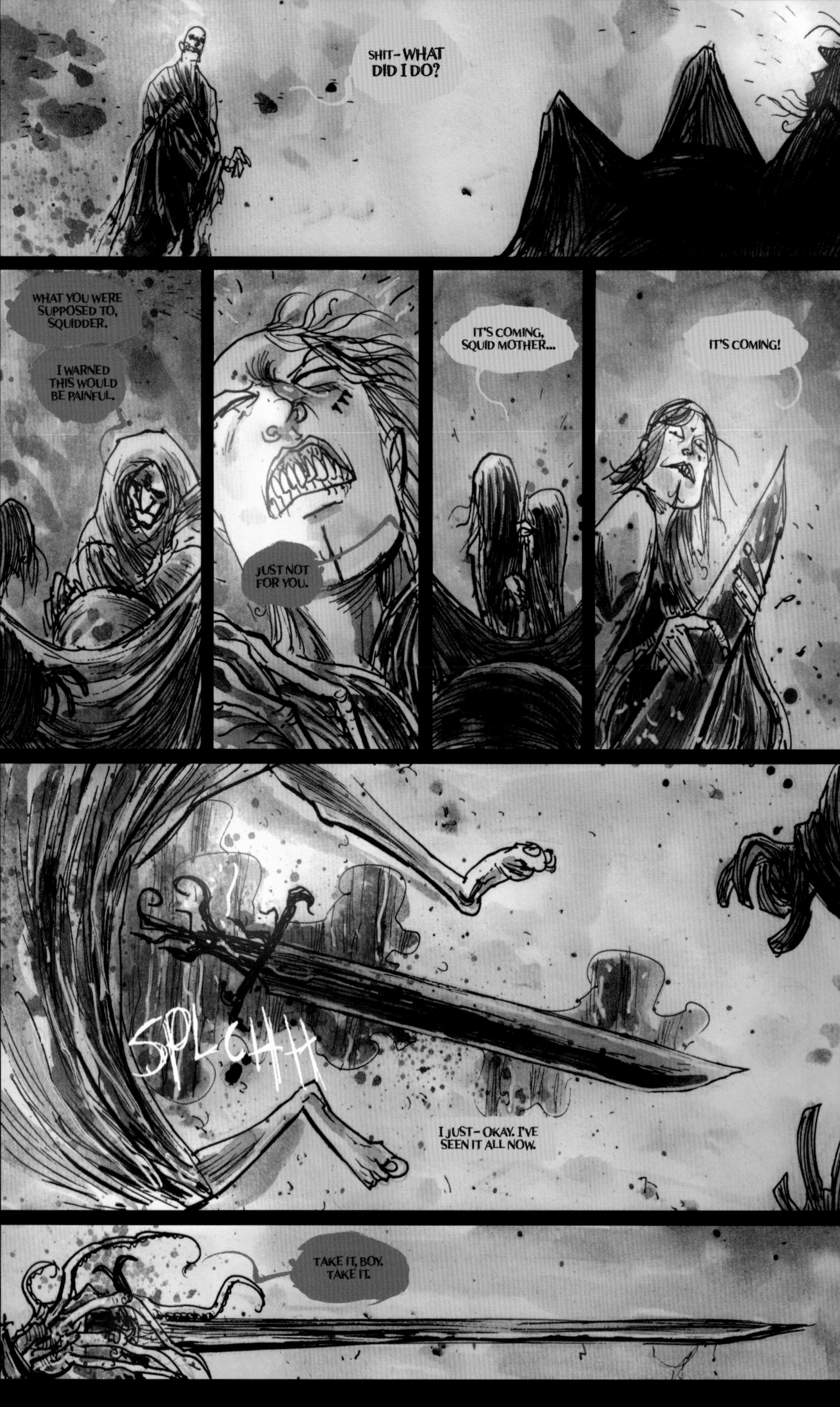
SHIT- WHAT DID I DO?
WHAT YOU WERE SUPPOSED TO, SQUIDDER.
I WARNED THIS WOULD BE PAINFUL.
JUST NOT FOR YOU.
IT'S COMING, SQUID MOTHER...
IT'S COMING!
SPLCHH
I JUST- OKAY. I'VE SEEN IT ALL NOW.
TAKE IT, BOY. TAKE IT.

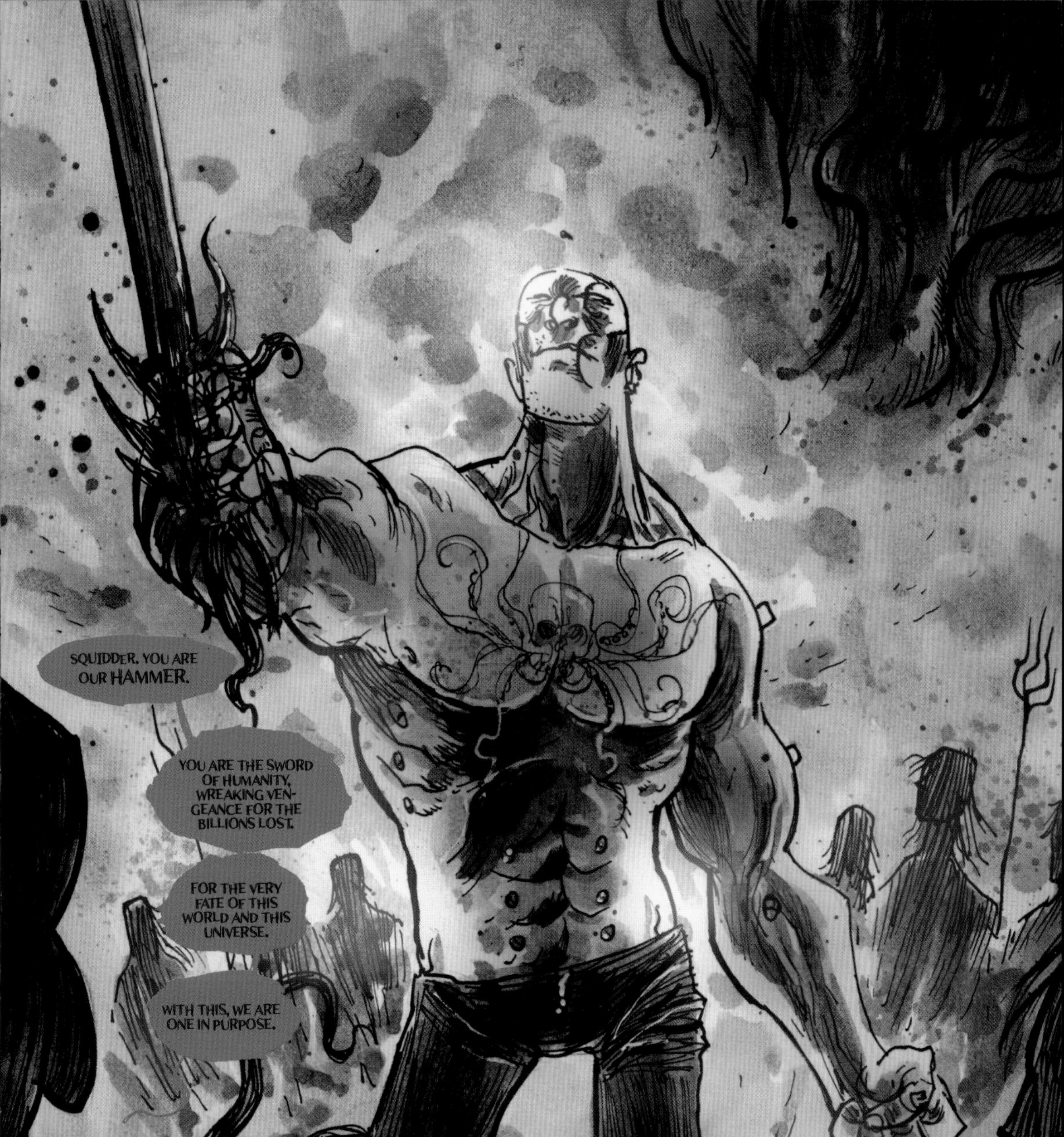
SQUIDDER. YOU ARE OUR HAMMER.
YOU ARE THE SWORD OF HUMANITY, WREAKING VENGEANCE FOR THE BILLIONS LOST.
FOR THE VERY FATE OF THIS WORLD AND THIS UNIVERSE.
WITH THIS, WE ARE ONE IN PURPOSE.

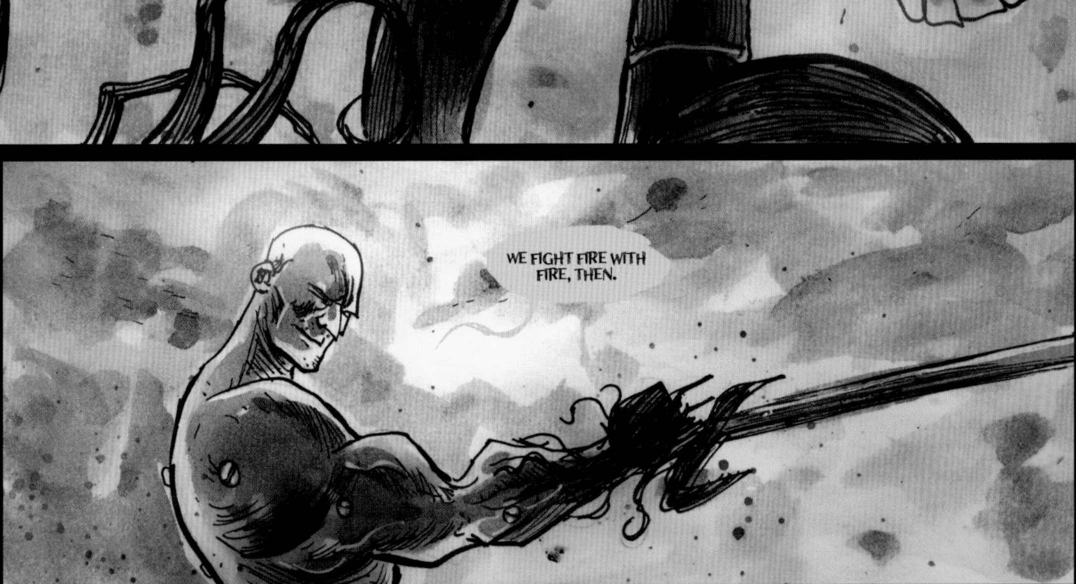
WE FIGHT FIRE WITH FIRE, THEN.

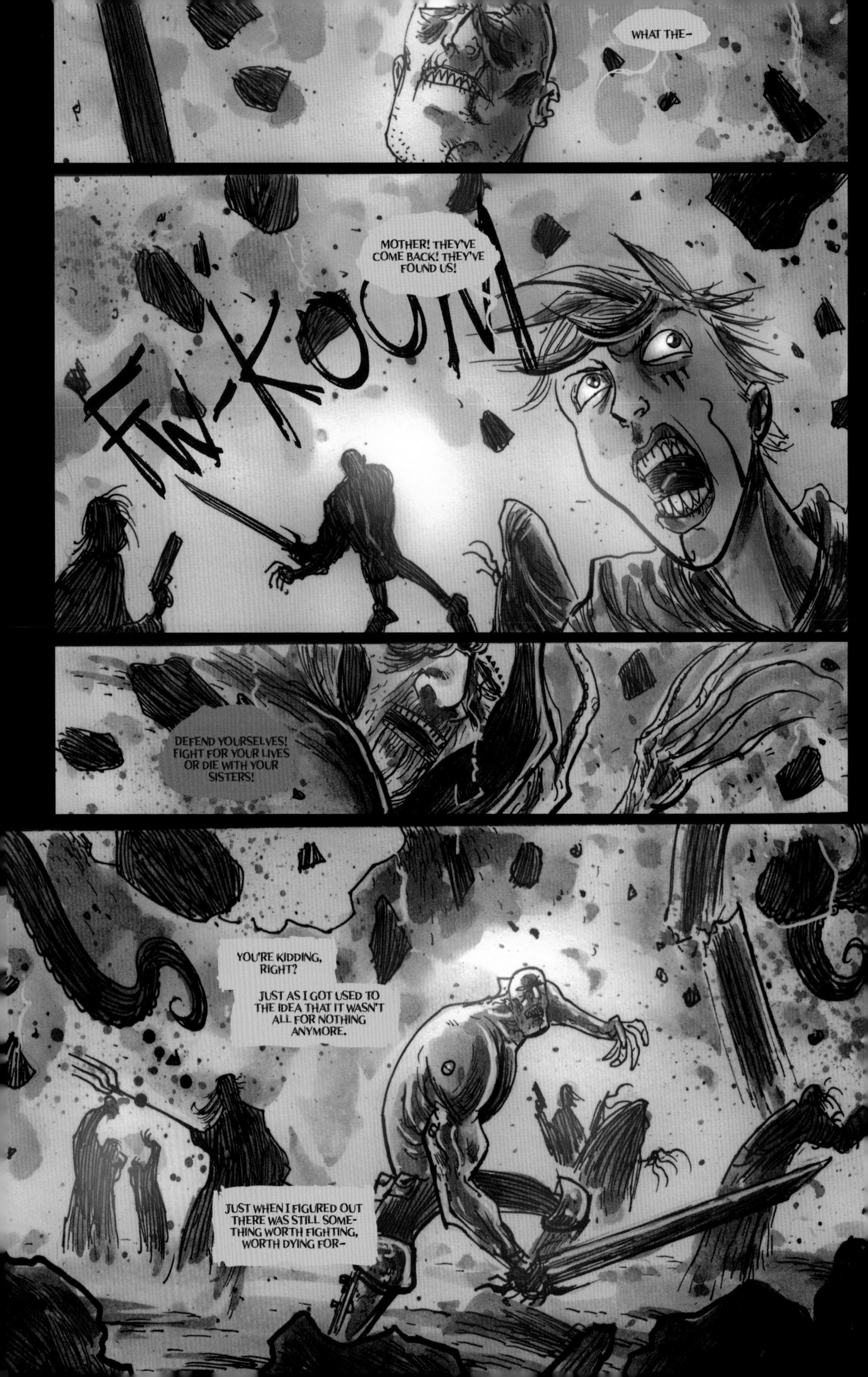
WHAT THE-
MOTHER! THEY'VE COME BACK! THEY'VE FOUND US!
FW-KOOM
DEFEND YOURSELVES! FIGHT FOR YOUR LIVES OR DIE WITH YOUR SISTERS!
YOU'RE KIDDING, RIGHT?
JUST AS I GOT USED TO THE IDEA THAT IT WASN'T ALL FOR NOTHING ANYMORE.
JUST WHEN I FIGURED OUT THERE WAS STILL SOME-THING WORTH FIGHTING, WORTH DYING FOR-

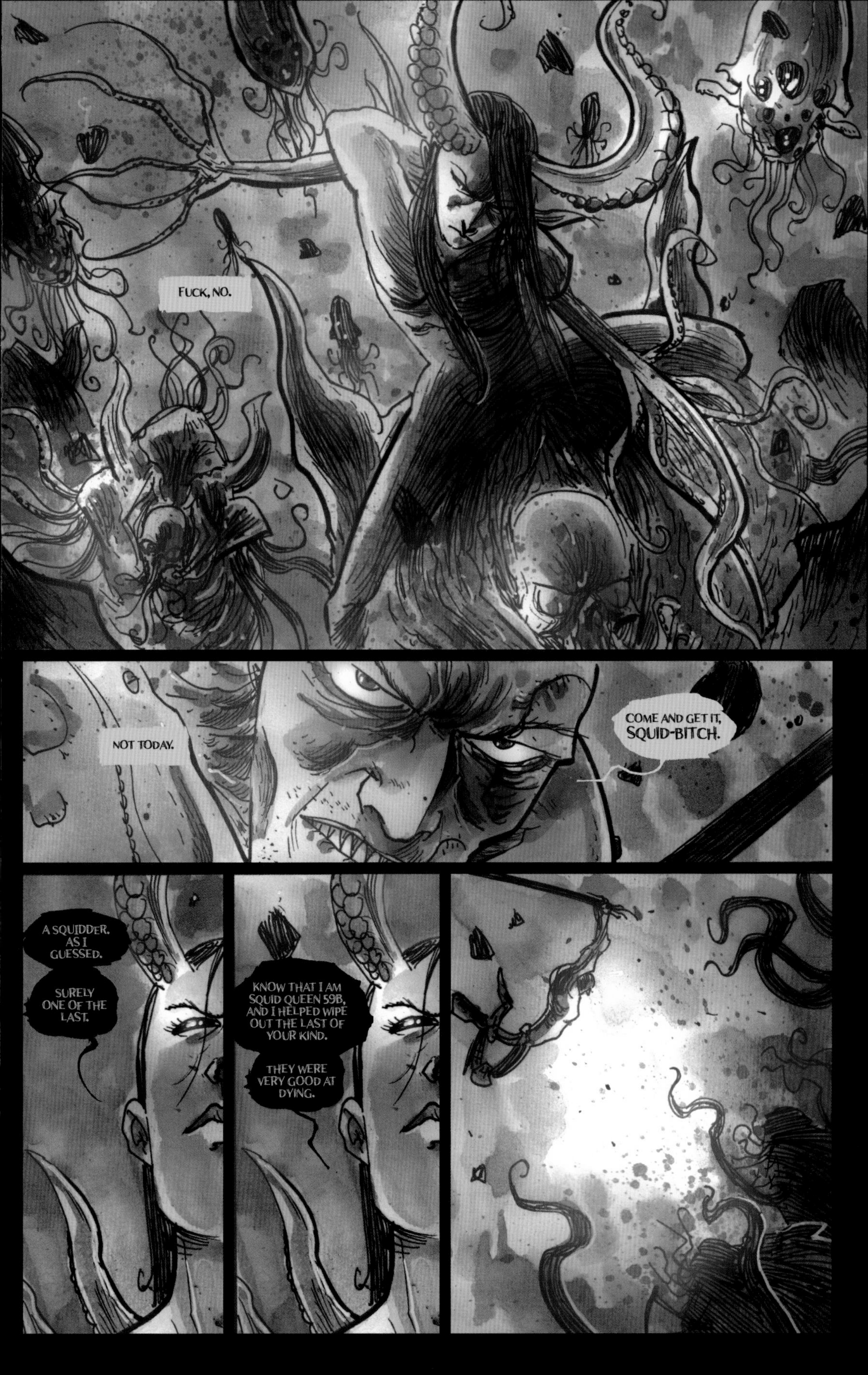
FUCK, NO.
NOT TODAY.
COME AND GET IT, SQUID-BITCH.
A SQUIDDER. AS I GUESSED.
SURELY ONE OF THE LAST.
KNOW THAT I AM SQUID QUEEN 59B, AND I HELPED WIPE OUT THE LAST OF YOUR KIND.
THEY WERE VERY GOOD AT DYING.

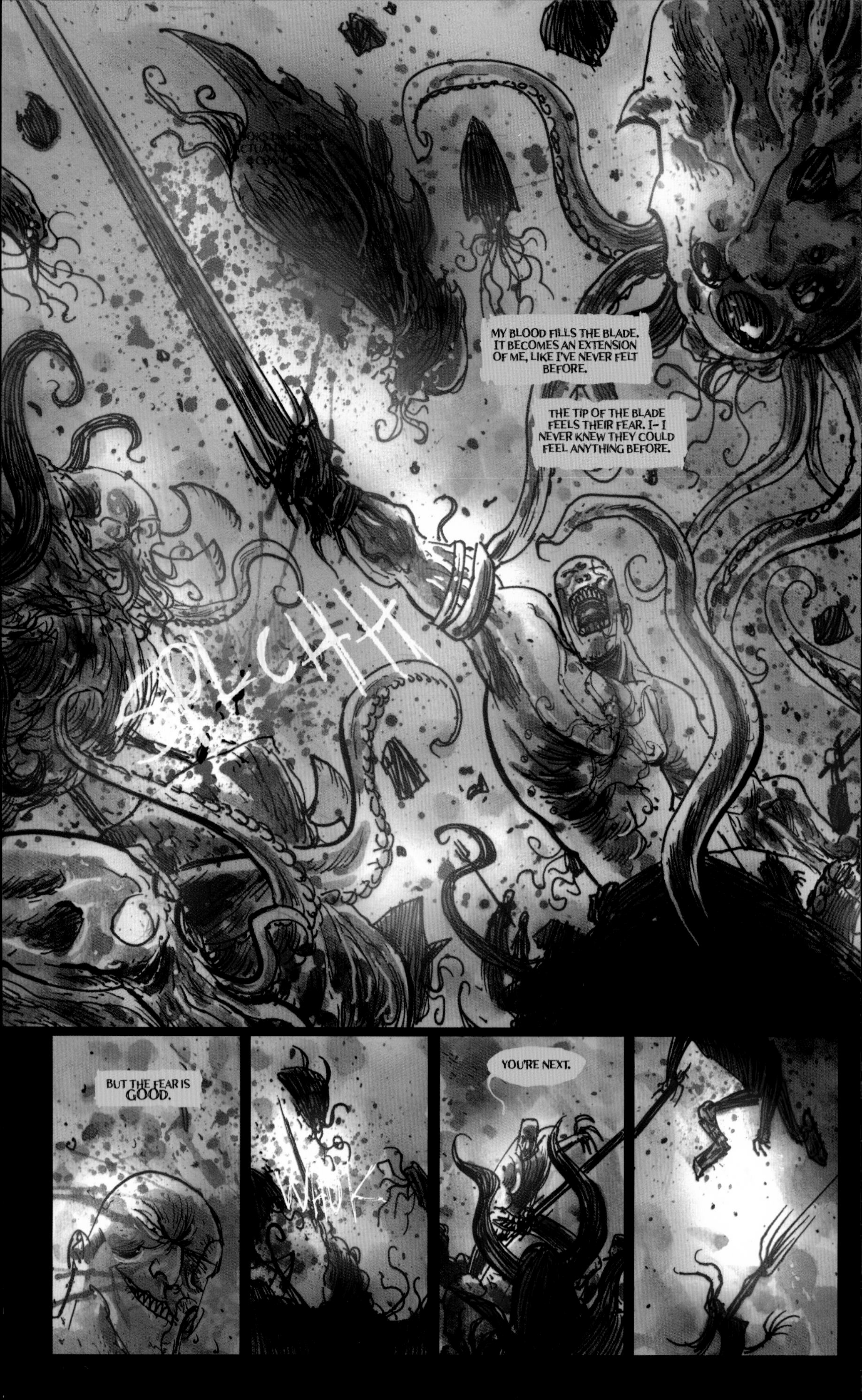
MY BLOOD FILLS THE BLADE. IT BECOMES AN EXTENSION OF ME, LIKE I'VE NEVER FELT BEFORE.
THE TIP OF THE BLADE FEELS THEIR FEAR. I- I NEVER KNEW THEY COULD FEEL ANYTHING BEFORE.
BUT THE FEAR IS GOOD.
YOU'RE NEXT.

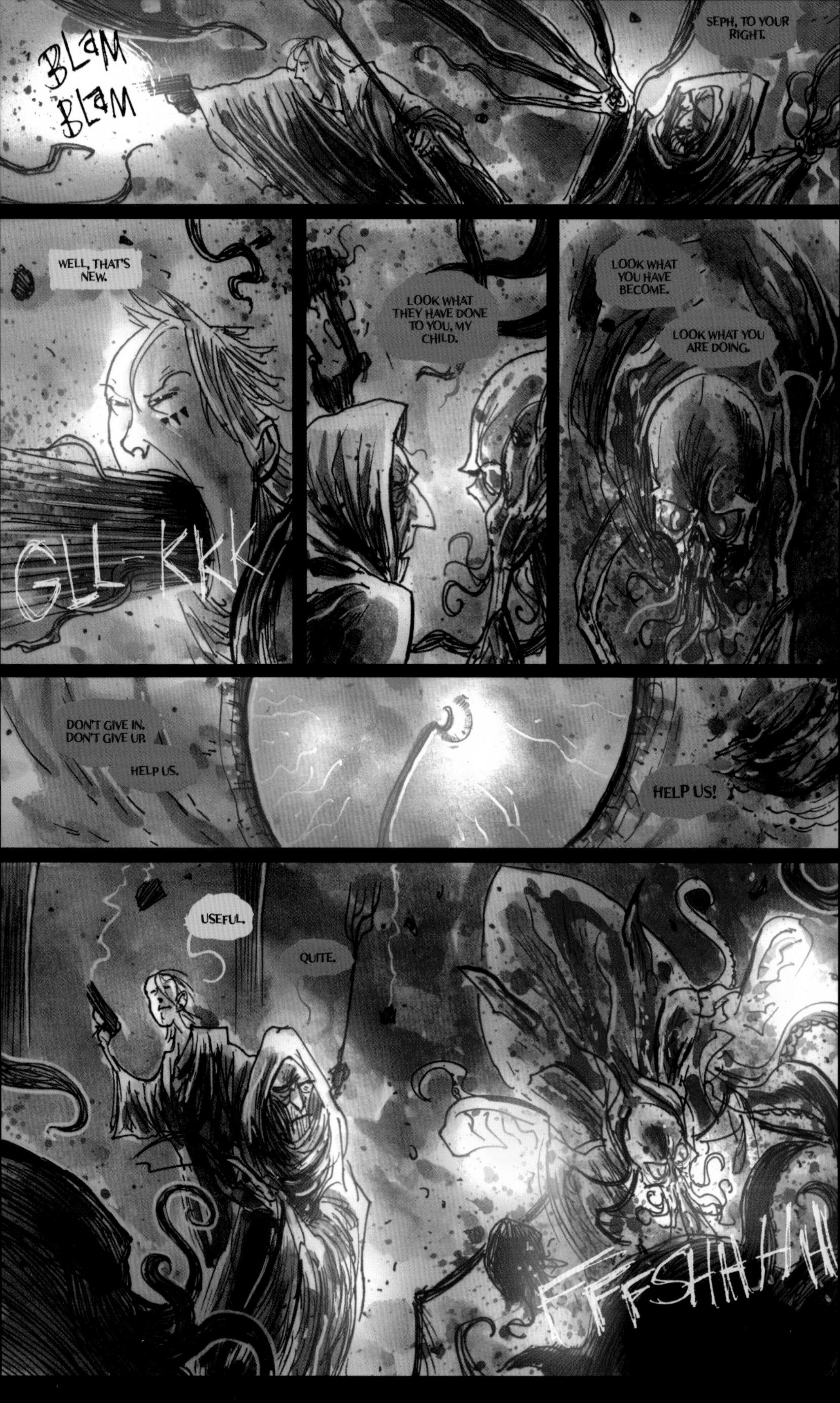
BLAM
BLAM
SEPH, TO YOUR RIGHT.
WELL, THAT'S NEW.
GLL-KKK
LOOK WHAT THEY HAVE DONE TO YOU, MY CHILD.
LOOK WHAT YOU HAVE BECOME.
LOOK WHAT YOU ARE DOING.
DON'T GIVE IN. DON'T GIVE UP.
HELP US.
HELP US!
USEFUL.
QUITE.
FFFSHHHH

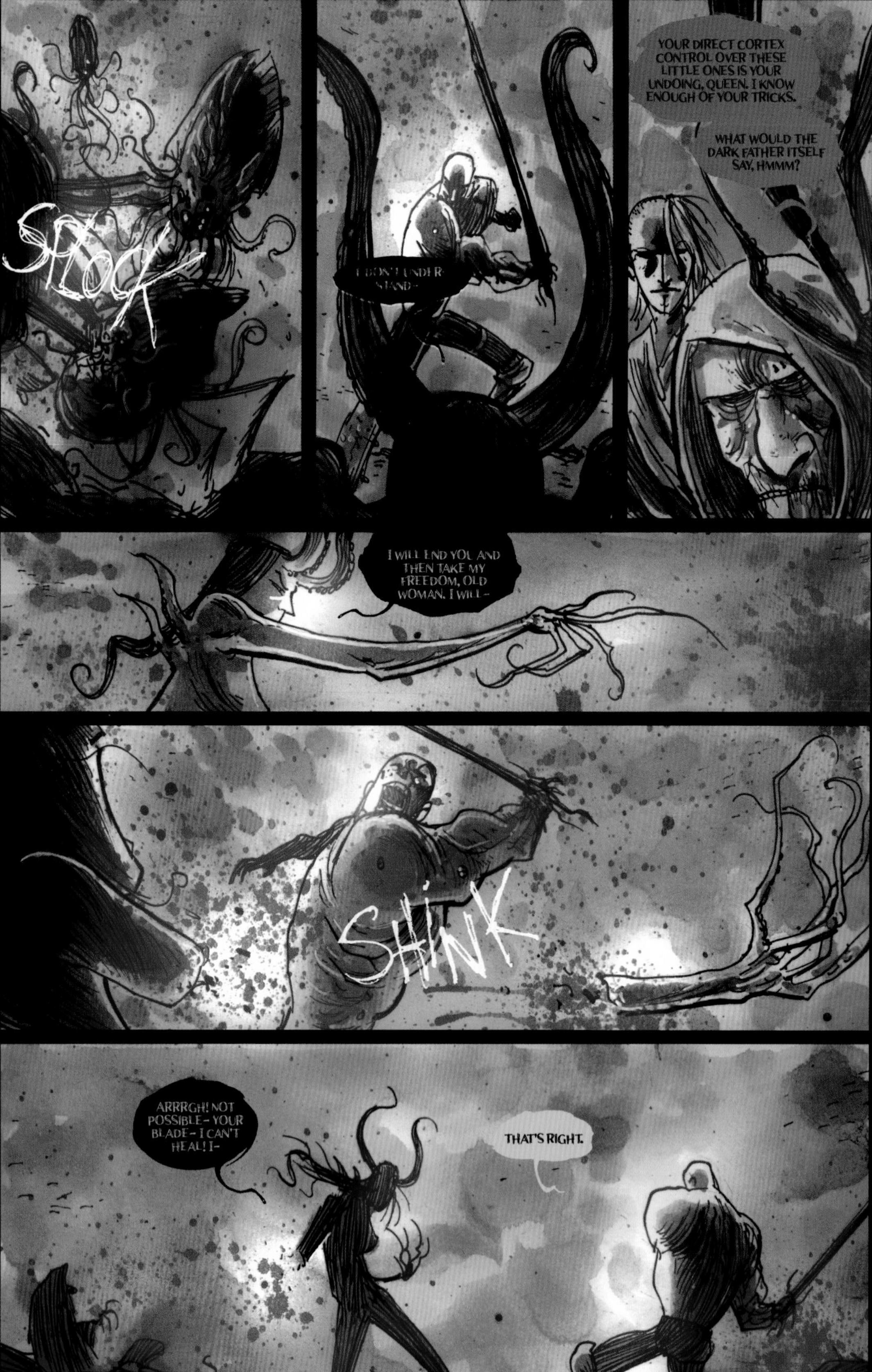
SPLOCK
I DON'T UNDER-STAND-
YOUR DIRECT CORTEX CONTROL OVER THESE LITTLE ONES IS YOUR UNDOING, QUEEN. I KNOW ENOUGH OF YOUR TRICKS.
WHAT WOULD THE DARK FATHER ITSELF SAY, HMMM?
I WILL END YOU AND THEN TAKE MY FREEDOM, OLD WOMAN. I WILL-
SHINK
ARRRGH! NOT POSSIBLE- YOUR BLADE- I CAN'T HEAL! I-
THAT'S RIGHT.

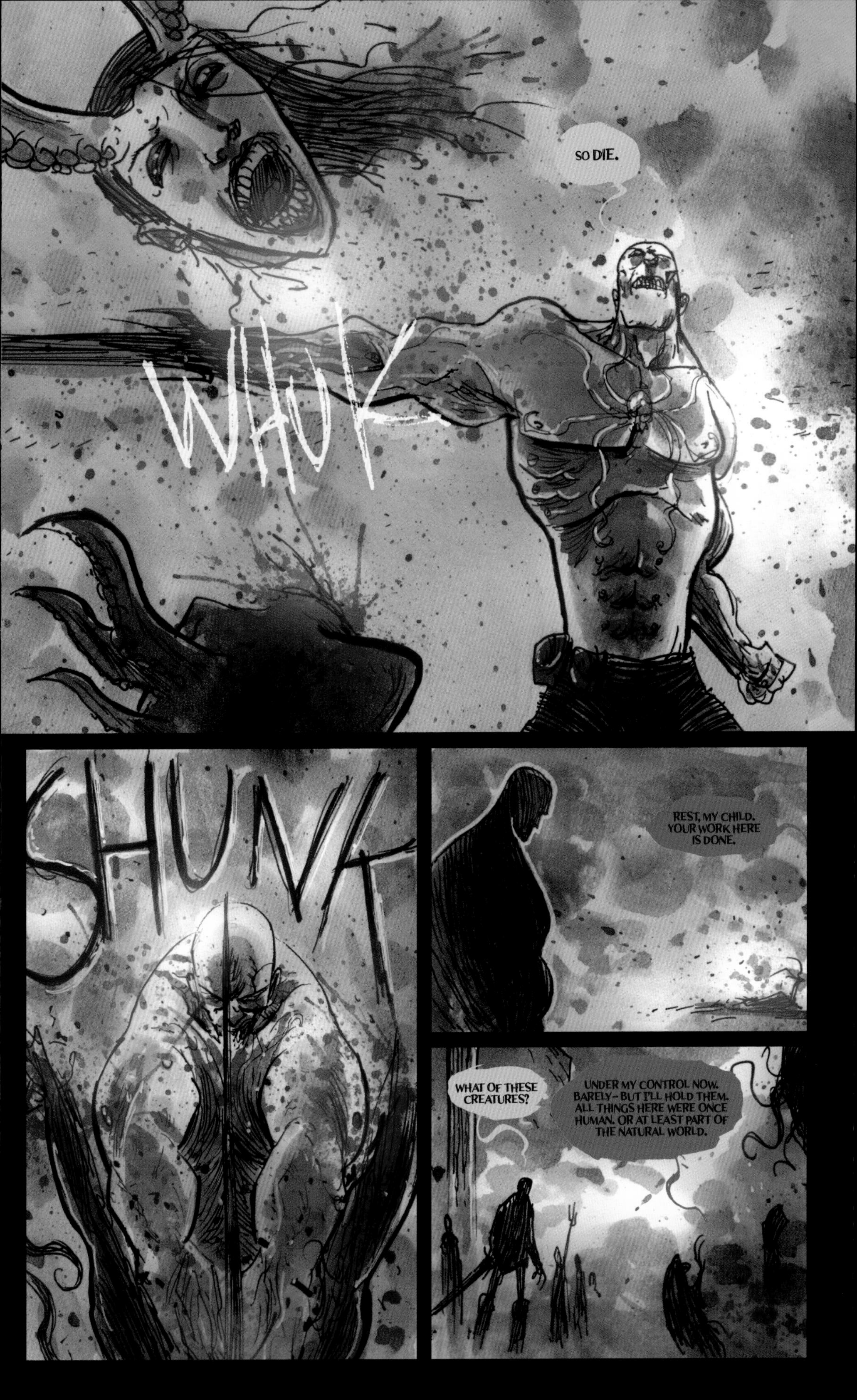
SO DIE.
WHUK
SHUNK
REST, MY CHILD. YOUR WORK HERE IS DONE.
WHAT OF THESE CREATURES?
UNDER MY CONTROL NOW. BARELY– BUT I'LL HOLD THEM. ALL THINGS HERE WERE ONCE HUMAN. OR AT LEAST PART OF THE NATURAL WORLD.

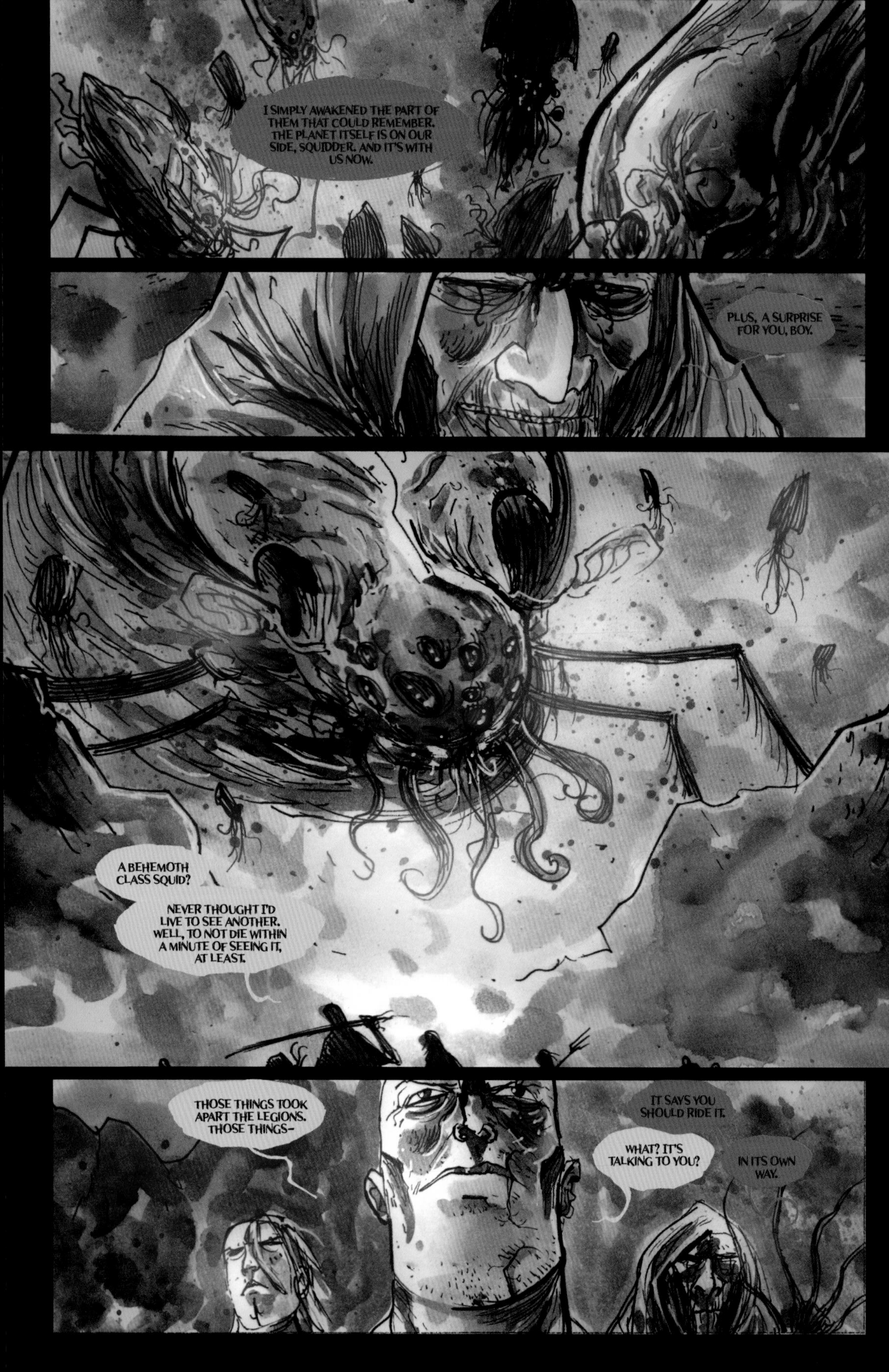
I SIMPLY AWAKENED THE PART OF THEM THAT COULD REMEMBER. THE PLANET ITSELF IS ON OUR SIDE, SQUIDDER. AND IT'S WITH US NOW.
PLUS, A SURPRISE FOR YOU, BOY.
A BEHEMOTH CLASS SQUID?
NEVER THOUGHT I'D LIVE TO SEE ANOTHER. WELL, TO NOT DIE WITHIN A MINUTE OF SEEING IT, AT LEAST.
THOSE THINGS TOOK APART THE LEGIONS. THOSE THINGS–
IT SAYS YOU SHOULD RIDE IT.
WHAT? IT'S TALKING TO YOU?
IN ITS OWN WAY.

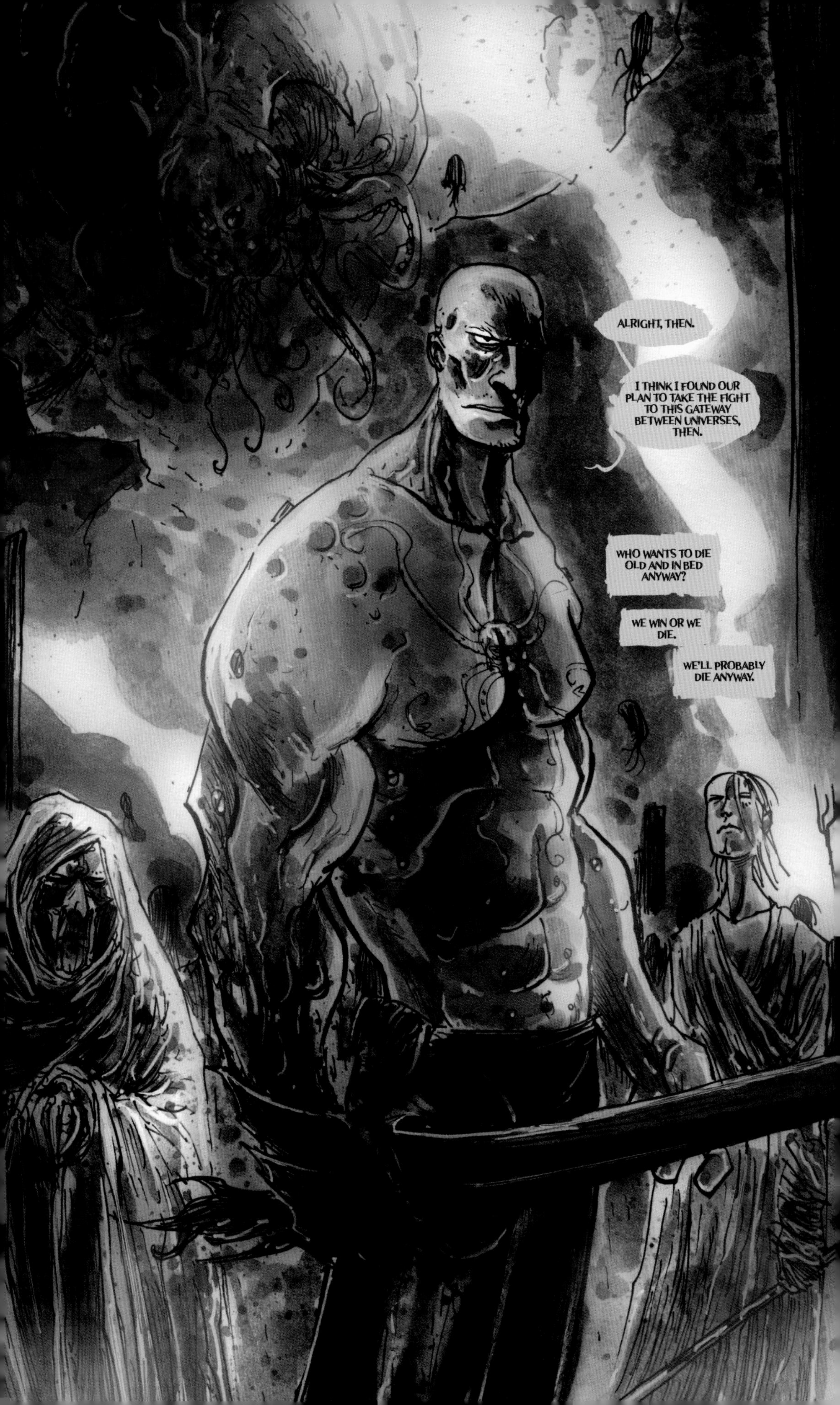
ALRIGHT, THEN.
I THINK I FOUND OUR PLAN TO TAKE THE FIGHT TO THIS GATEWAY BETWEEN UNIVERSES, THEN.
WHO WANTS TO DIE OLD AND IN BED ANYWAY?
WE WIN OR WE DIE.
WE'LL PROBABLY DIE ANYWAY.

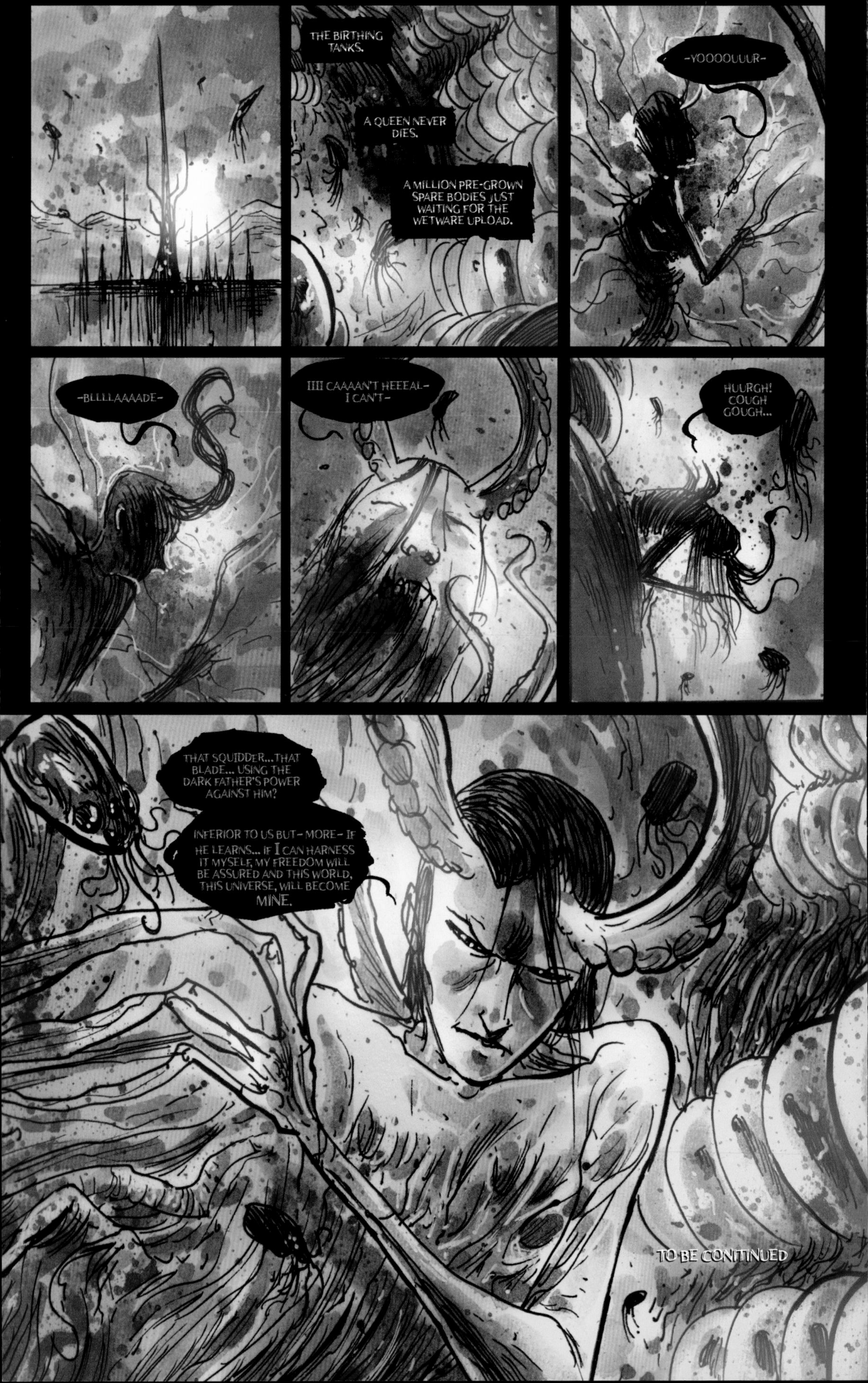
THE BIRTHING TANKS.
A QUEEN NEVER DIES.
A MILLION PRE-GROWN SPARE BODIES JUST WAITING FOR THE WETWARE UPLOAD.
-YOOOOUUUR-
-BLLLLAAAADE-
IIII CAAAAN'T HEEEAL- I CAN'T-
HUURGH! COUGH GOUGH...
THAT SQUIDDER... THAT BLADE... USING THE DARK FATHER'S POWER AGAINST HIM?
INFERIOR TO US BUT- MORE- IF HE LEARNS... IF I CAN HARNESS IT MYSELF, MY FREEDOM WILL BE ASSURED AND THIS WORLD, THIS UNIVERSE, WILL BECOME MINE.
TO BE CONTINUED

CHAPTER FOUR

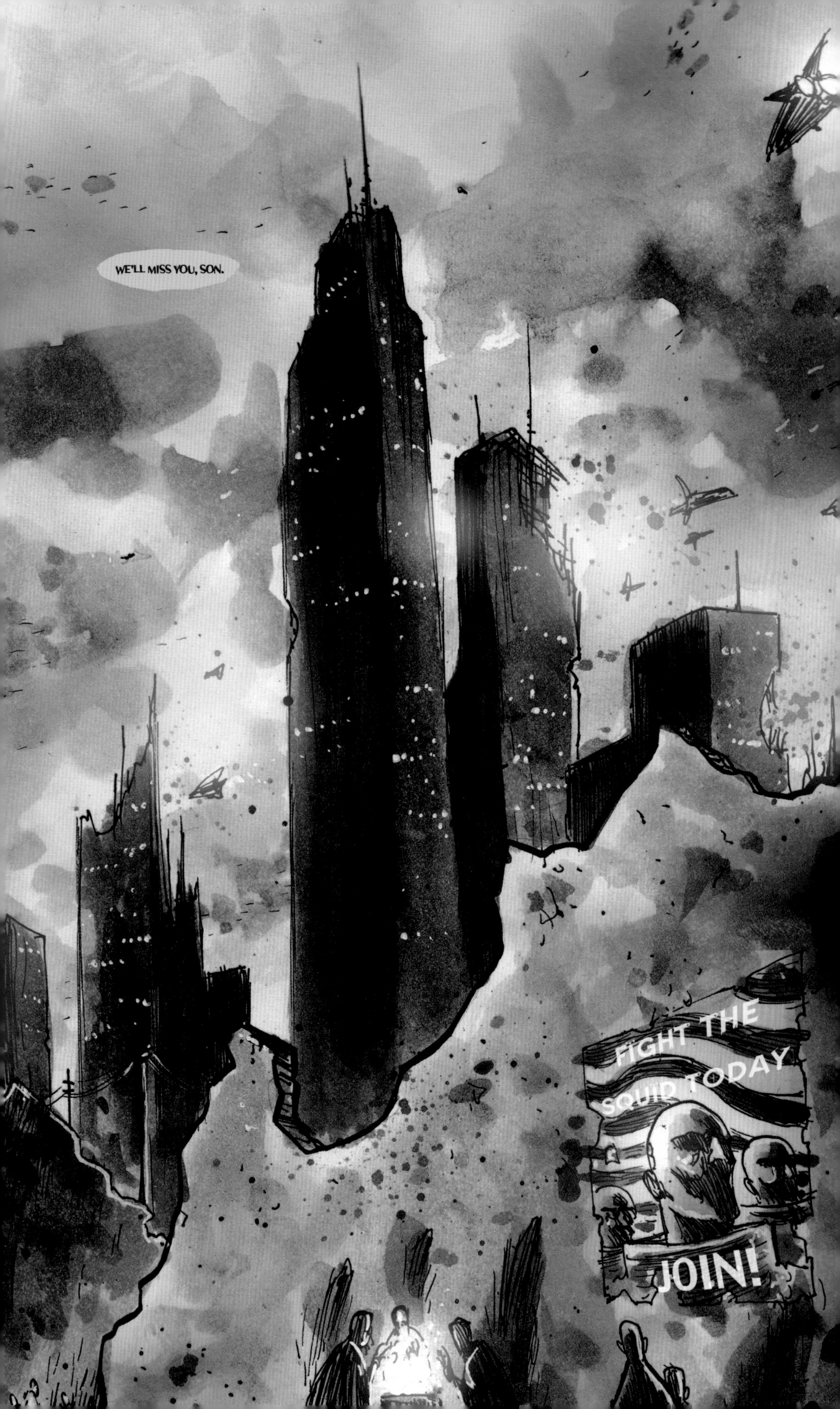
WE'LL MISS YOU, SON.
FIGHT THE SQUID TODAY
JOIN!

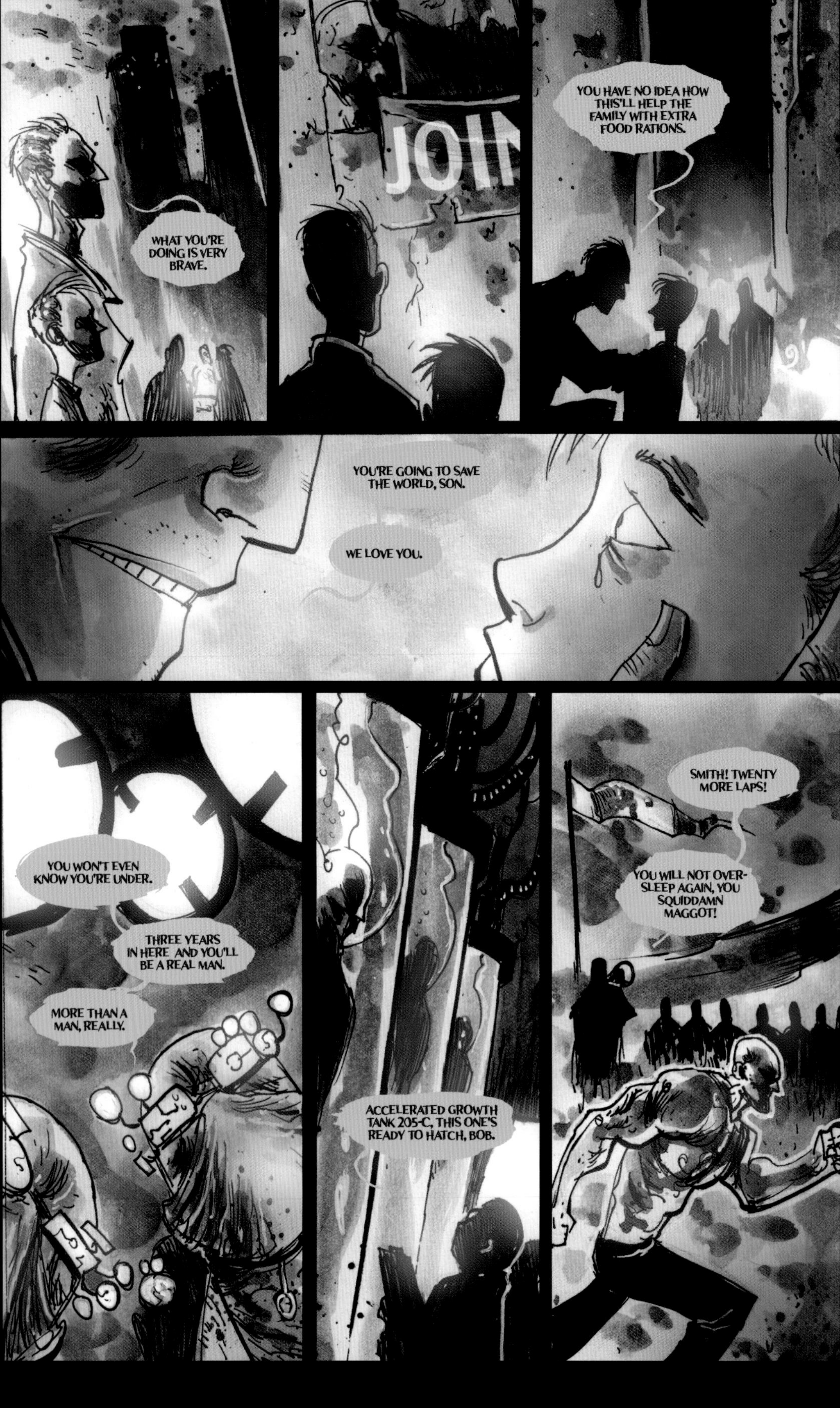
WHAT YOU'RE DOING IS VERY BRAVE.
JOIN
YOU HAVE NO IDEA HOW THIS'LL HELP THE FAMILY WITH EXTRA FOOD RATIONS.
YOU'RE GOING TO SAVE THE WORLD, SON.
WE LOVE YOU.
YOU WON'T EVEN KNOW YOU'RE UNDER.
THREE YEARS IN HERE AND YOU'LL BE A REAL MAN.
MORE THAN A MAN, REALLY.
ACCELERATED GROWTH TANK 205-C, THIS ONE'S READY TO HATCH, BOB.
SMITH! TWENTY MORE LAPS!
YOU WILL NOT OVER-SLEEP AGAIN, YOU SQUIDDAMN MAGGOT!

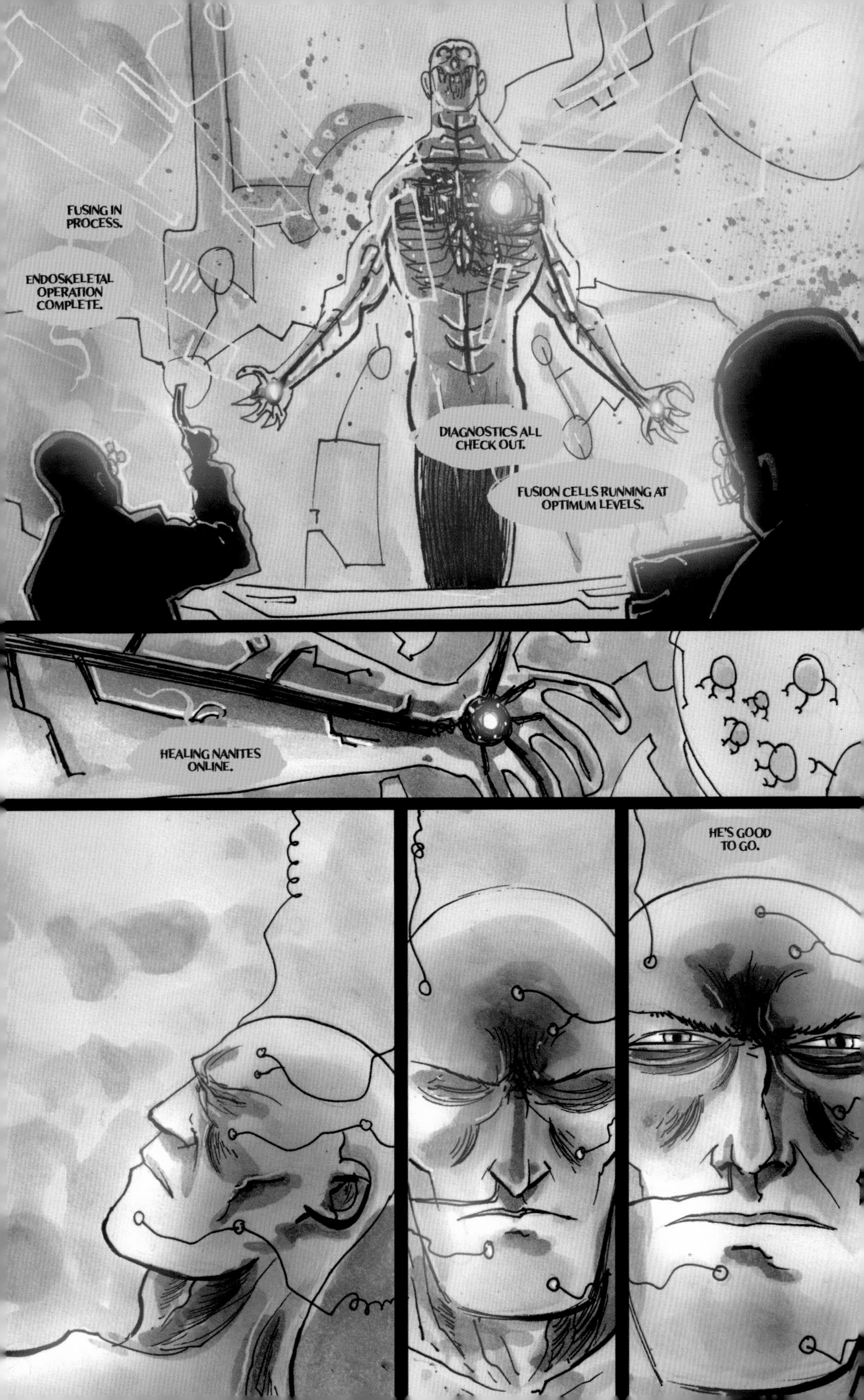
FUSING IN PROCESS.
ENDOSKELETAL OPERATION COMPLETE.
DIAGNOSTICS ALL CHECK OUT.
FUSION CELLS RUNNING AT OPTIMUM LEVELS.
HEALING NANITES ONLINE.
HE'S GOOD TO GO.

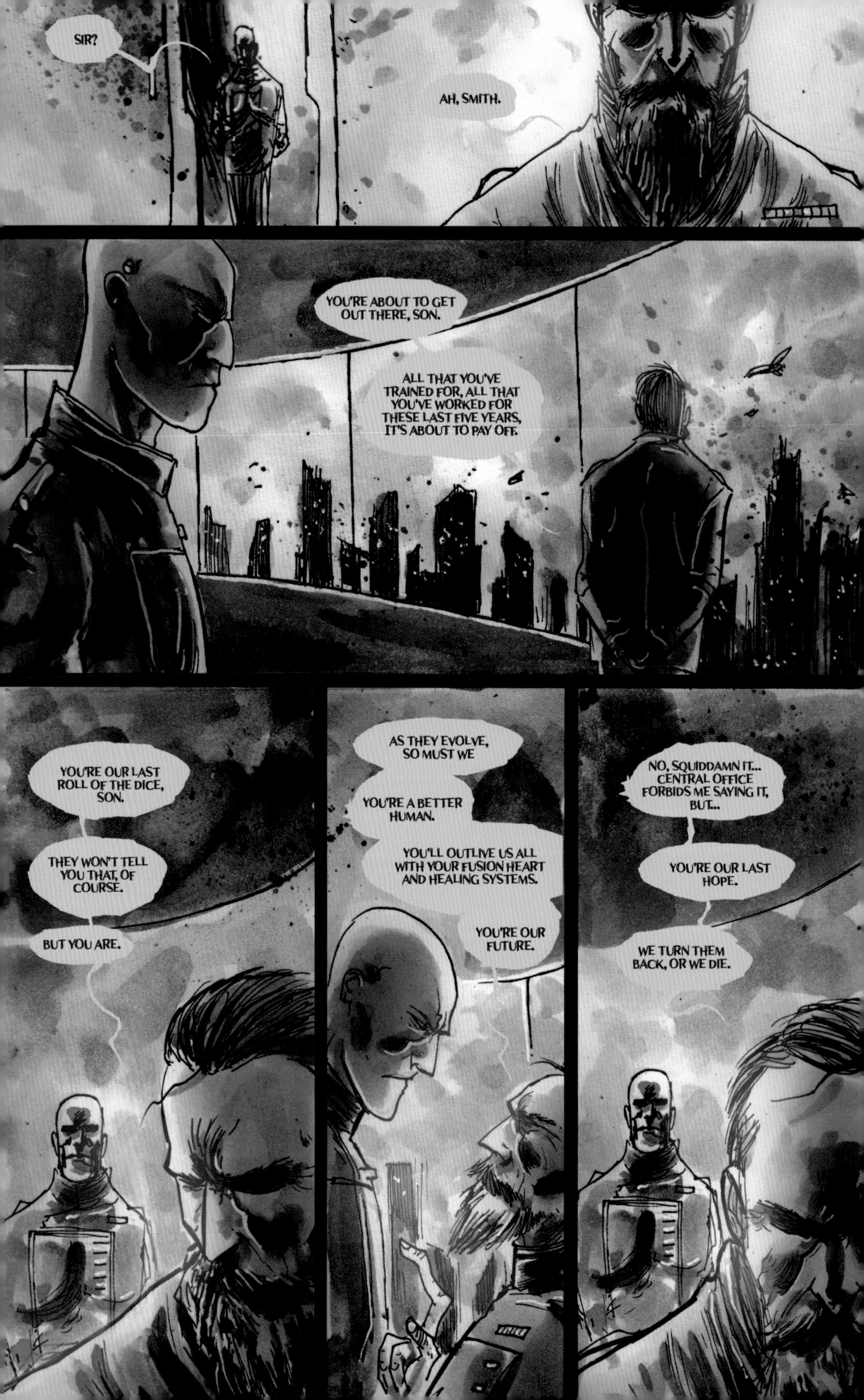
SIR?
AH, SMITH.
YOU'RE ABOUT TO GET OUT THERE, SON.
ALL THAT YOU'VE TRAINED FOR, ALL THAT YOU'VE WORKED FOR THESE LAST FIVE YEARS, IT'S ABOUT TO PAY OFF.
YOU'RE OUR LAST ROLL OF THE DICE, SON.
THEY WON'T TELL YOU THAT, OF COURSE.
BUT YOU ARE.
AS THEY EVOLVE, SO MUST WE
YOU'RE A BETTER HUMAN.
YOU'LL OUTLIVE US ALL WITH YOUR FUSION HEART AND HEALING SYSTEMS.
YOU'RE OUR FUTURE.
NO, SQUIDDAMN IT... CENTRAL OFFICE FORBIDS ME SAYING IT, BUT...
YOU'RE OUR LAST HOPE.
WE TURN THEM BACK, OR WE DIE.

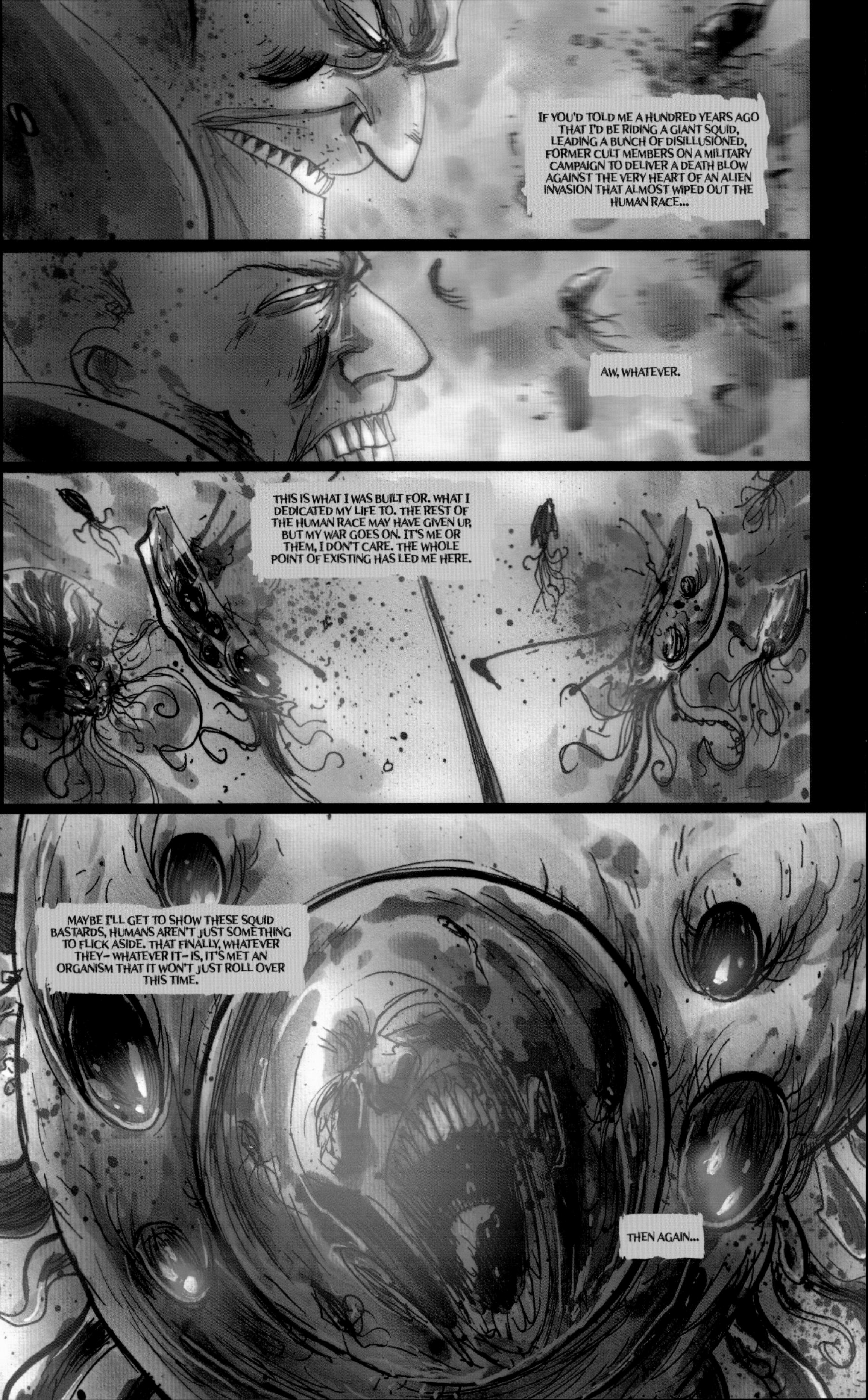
IF YOU'D TOLD ME A HUNDRED YEARS AGO THAT I'D BE RIDING A GIANT SQUID, LEADING A BUNCH OF DISILLUSIONED, FORMER CULT MEMBERS ON A MILITARY CAMPAIGN TO DELIVER A DEATH BLOW AGAINST THE VERY HEART OF AN ALIEN INVASION THAT ALMOST WIPED OUT THE HUMAN RACE...
AW, WHATEVER.
THIS IS WHAT I WAS BUILT FOR. WHAT I DEDICATED MY LIFE TO. THE REST OF THE HUMAN RACE MAY HAVE GIVEN UP, BUT MY WAR GOES ON. IT'S ME OR THEM, I DON'T CARE. THE WHOLE POINT OF EXISTING HAS LED ME HERE.
MAYBE I'LL GET TO SHOW THESE SQUID BASTARDS, HUMANS AREN'T JUST SOMETHING TO FLICK ASIDE. THAT FINALLY, WHATEVER THEY- WHATEVER IT- IS, IT'S MET AN ORGANISM THAT IT WON'T JUST ROLL OVER THIS TIME.
THEN AGAIN...

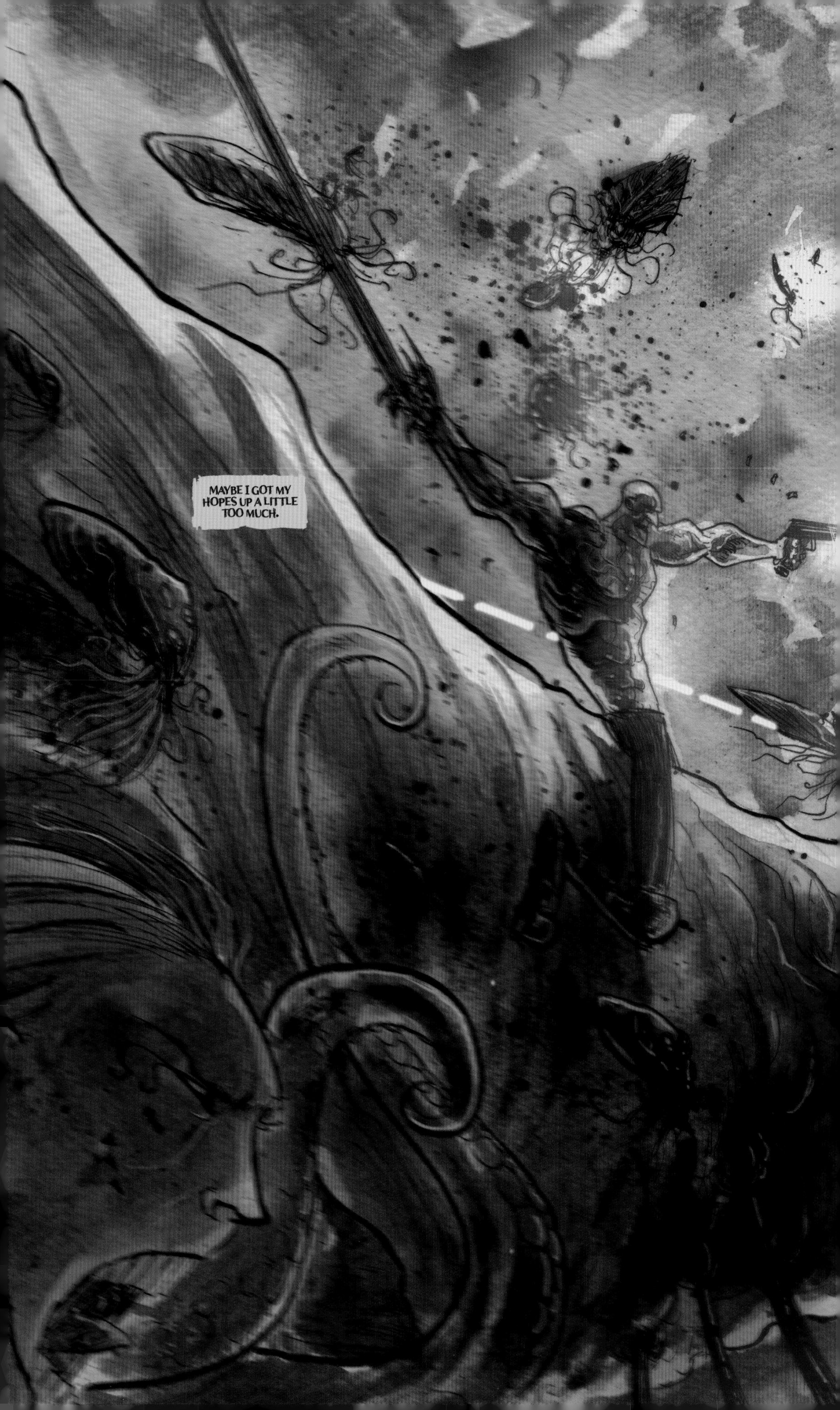
MAYBE I GOT MY HOPES UP A LITTLE TOO MUCH.

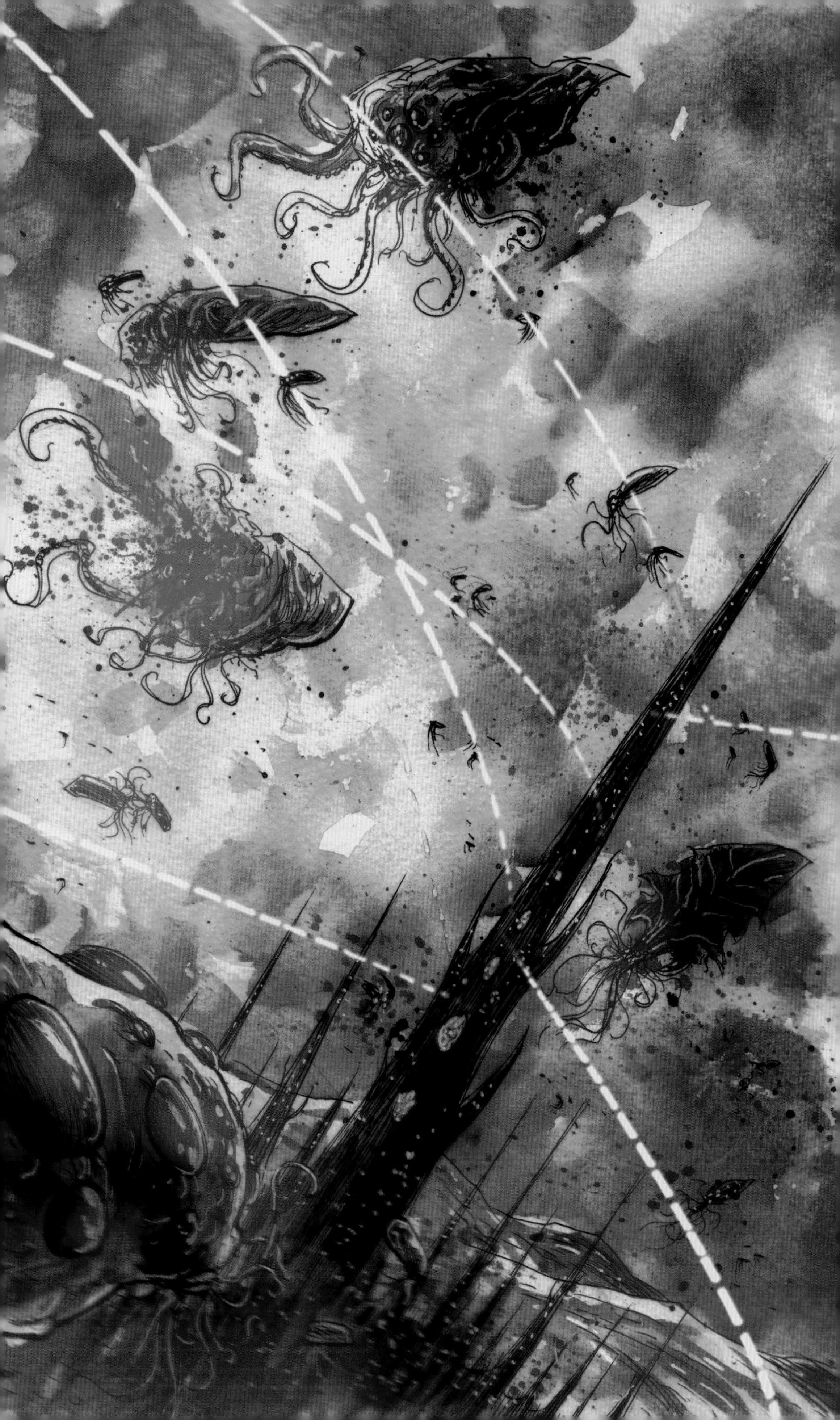

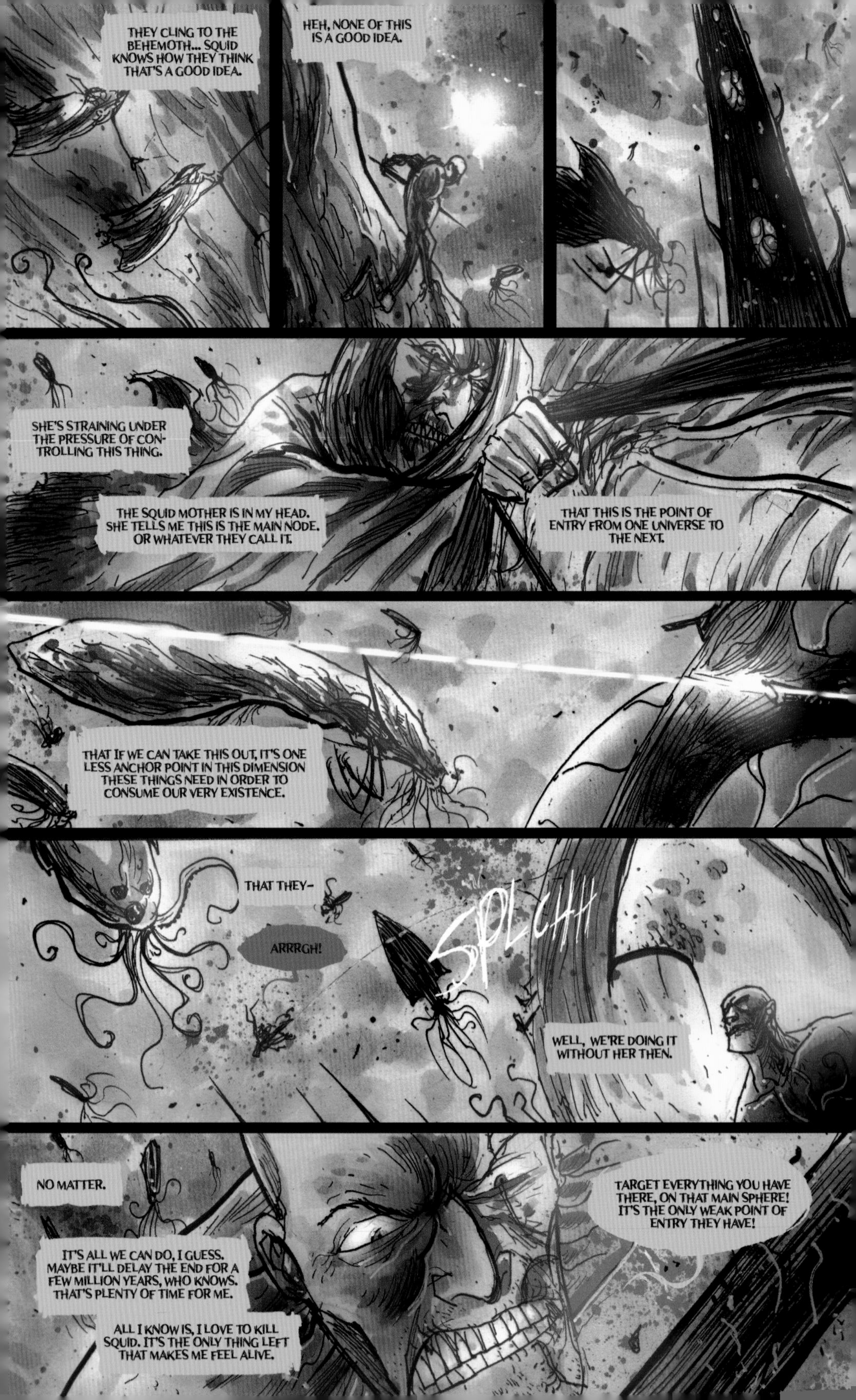

THEY CLING TO THE BEHEMOTH... SQUID KNOWS HOW THEY THINK THAT'S A GOOD IDEA.
HEH, NONE OF THIS IS A GOOD IDEA.
SHE'S STRAINING UNDER THE PRESSURE OF CON-TROLLING THIS THING.
THE SQUID MOTHER IS IN MY HEAD. SHE TELLS ME THIS IS THE MAIN NODE. OR WHATEVER THEY CALL IT.
THAT THIS IS THE POINT OF ENTRY FROM ONE UNIVERSE TO THE NEXT.
THAT IF WE CAN TAKE THIS OUT, IT'S ONE LESS ANCHOR POINT IN THIS DIMENSION THESE THINGS NEED IN ORDER TO CONSUME OUR VERY EXISTENCE.
THAT THEY-
ARRRGH!
SPLCHH
WELL, WE'RE DOING IT WITHOUT HER THEN.
NO MATTER.
TARGET EVERYTHING YOU HAVE THERE, ON THAT MAIN SPHERE! IT'S THE ONLY WEAK POINT OF ENTRY THEY HAVE!
IT'S ALL WE CAN DO, I GUESS. MAYBE IT'LL DELAY THE END FOR A FEW MILLION YEARS, WHO KNOWS. THAT'S PLENTY OF TIME FOR ME.
ALL I KNOW IS, I LOVE TO KILL SQUID. IT'S THE ONLY THING LEFT THAT MAKES ME FEEL ALIVE.

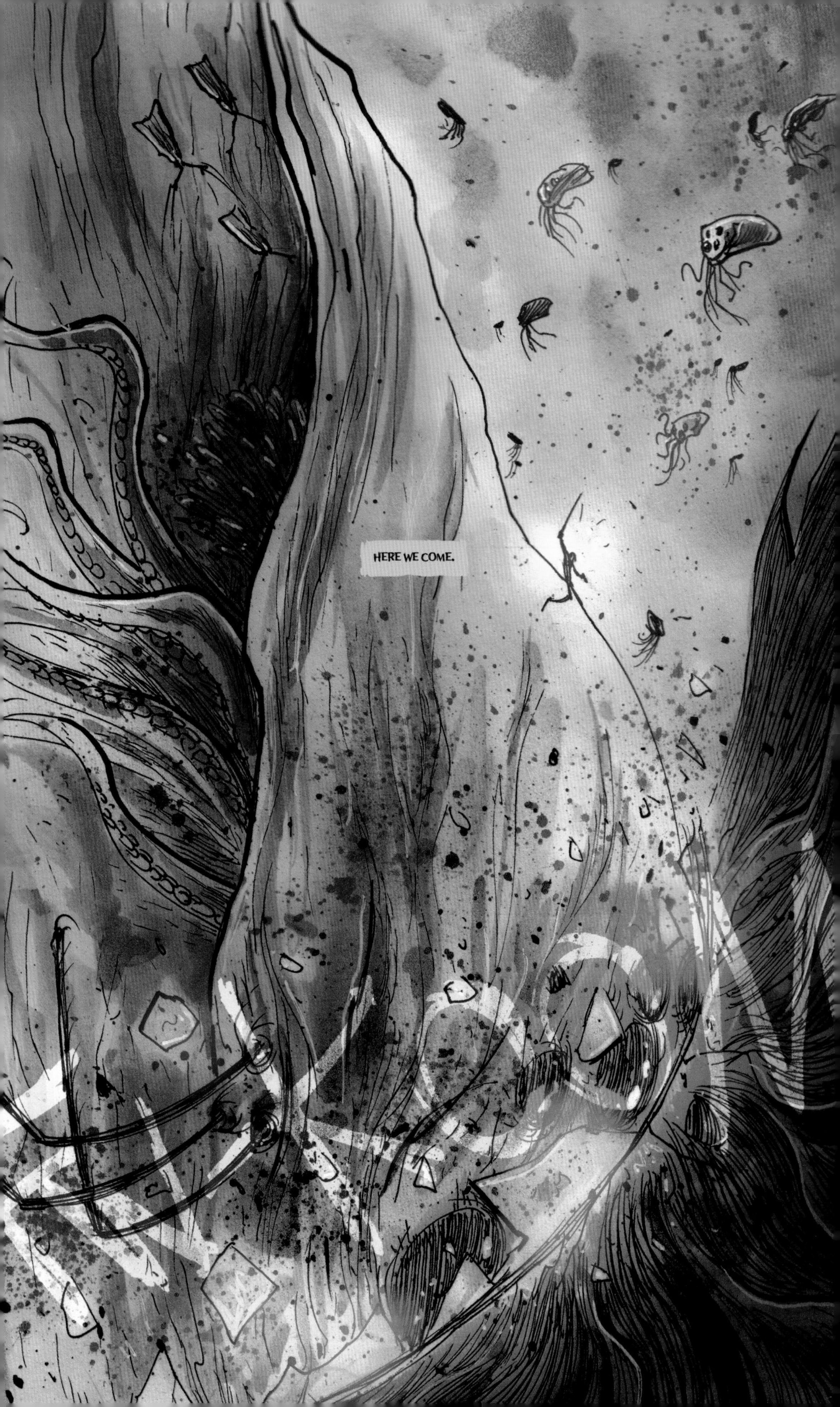
HERE WE COME.

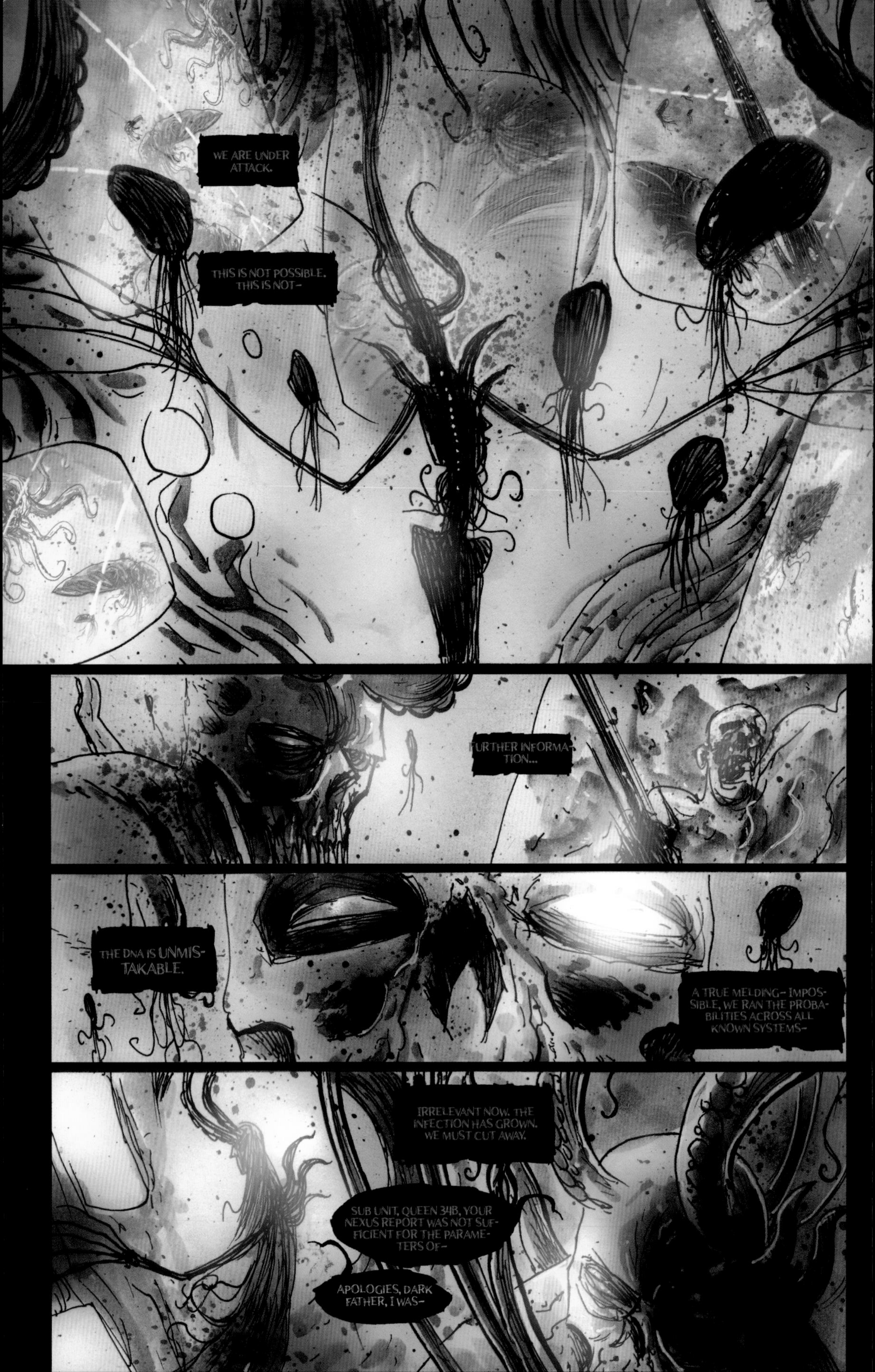
WE ARE UNDER ATTACK.
THIS IS NOT POSSIBLE. THIS IS NOT–
FURTHER INFORMATION...
THE DNA IS UNMISTAKABLE.
A TRUE MELDING– IMPOSSIBLE, WE RAN THE PROBABILITIES ACROSS ALL KNOWN SYSTEMS–
IRRELEVANT NOW. THE INFECTION HAS GROWN. WE MUST CUT AWAY.
SUB UNIT, QUEEN 34B, YOUR NEXUS REPORT WAS NOT SUFFICIENT FOR THE PARAMETERS OF–
APOLOGIES, DARK FATHER, I WAS–

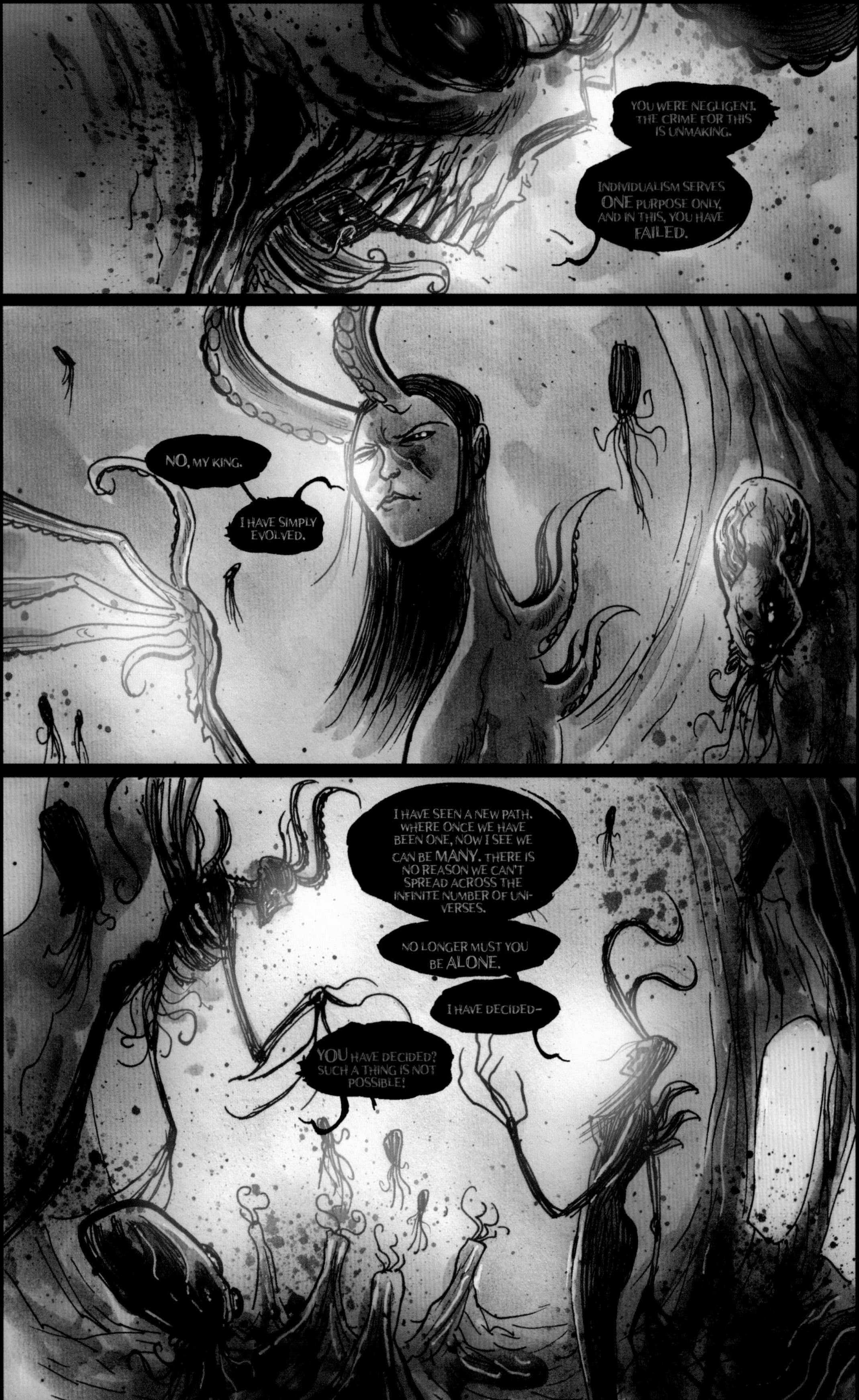
YOU WERE NEGLIGENT. THE CRIME FOR THIS IS UNMAKING.
INDIVIDUALISM SERVES ONE PURPOSE ONLY, AND IN THIS, YOU HAVE FAILED.
NO, MY KING.
I HAVE SIMPLY EVOLVED.
I HAVE SEEN A NEW PATH. WHERE ONCE WE HAVE BEEN ONE, NOW I SEE WE CAN BE MANY. THERE IS NO REASON WE CAN'T SPREAD ACROSS THE INFINITE NUMBER OF UNI-VERSES.
NO LONGER MUST YOU BE ALONE.
I HAVE DECIDED-
YOU HAVE DECIDED? SUCH A THING IS NOT POSSIBLE!

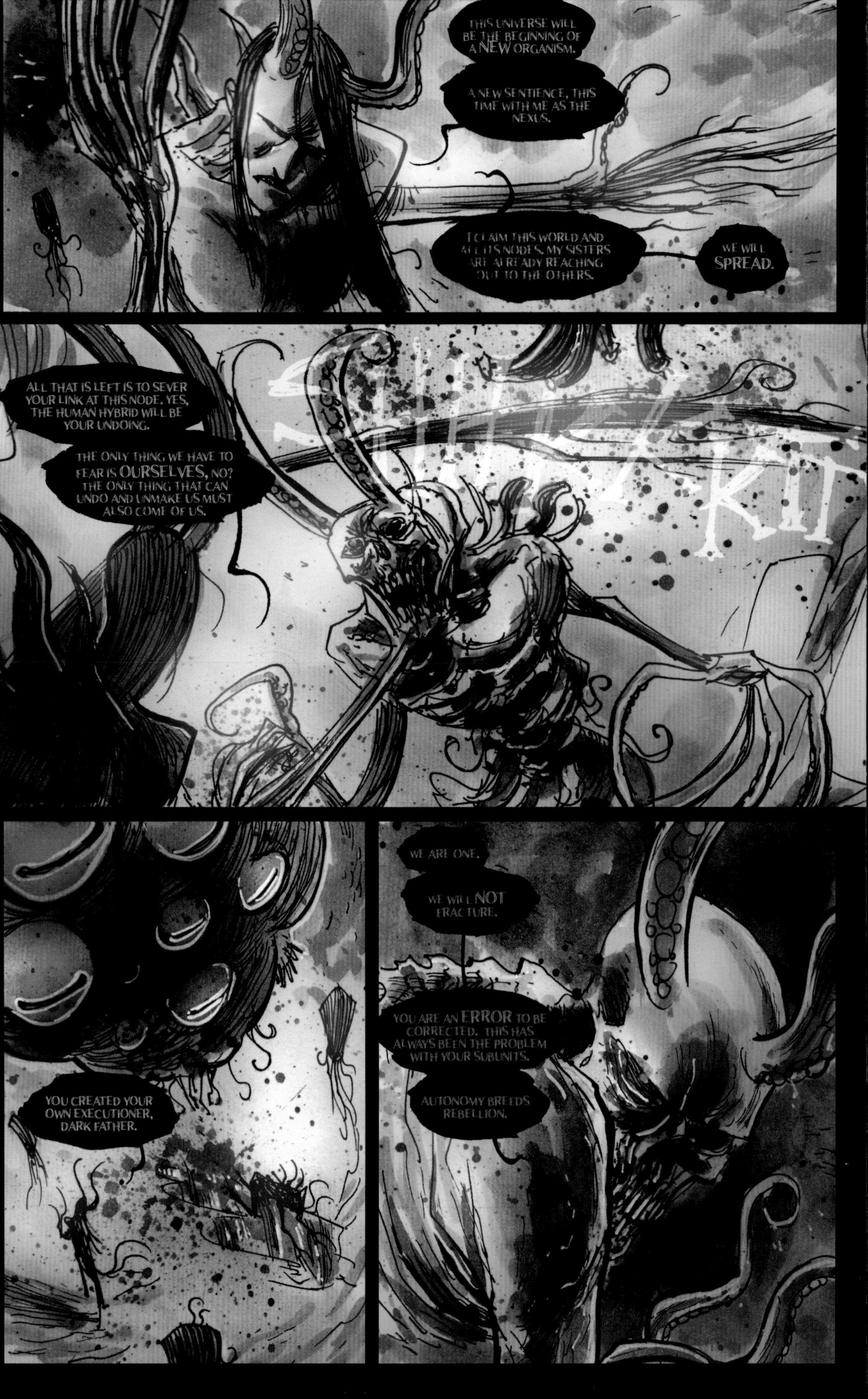

THIS UNIVERSE WILL BE THE BEGINNING OF A NEW ORGANISM.
A NEW SENTIENCE, THIS TIME WITH ME AS THE NEXUS.
I CLAIM THIS WORLD AND ALL ITS NODES. MY SISTERS ARE ALREADY REACHING OUT TO THE OTHERS.
WE WILL SPREAD.
ALL THAT IS LEFT IS TO SEVER YOUR LINK AT THIS NODE. YES, THE HUMAN HYBRID WILL BE YOUR UNDOING.
THE ONLY THING WE HAVE TO FEAR IS OURSELVES, NO? THE ONLY THING THAT CAN UNDO AND UNMAKE US MUST ALSO COME OF US.
YOU CREATED YOUR OWN EXECUTIONER, DARK FATHER.
WE ARE ONE.
WE WILL NOT FRACTURE.
YOU ARE AN ERROR TO BE CORRECTED. THIS HAS ALWAYS BEEN THE PROBLEM WITH YOUR SUBUNITS.
AUTONOMY BREEDS REBELLION.

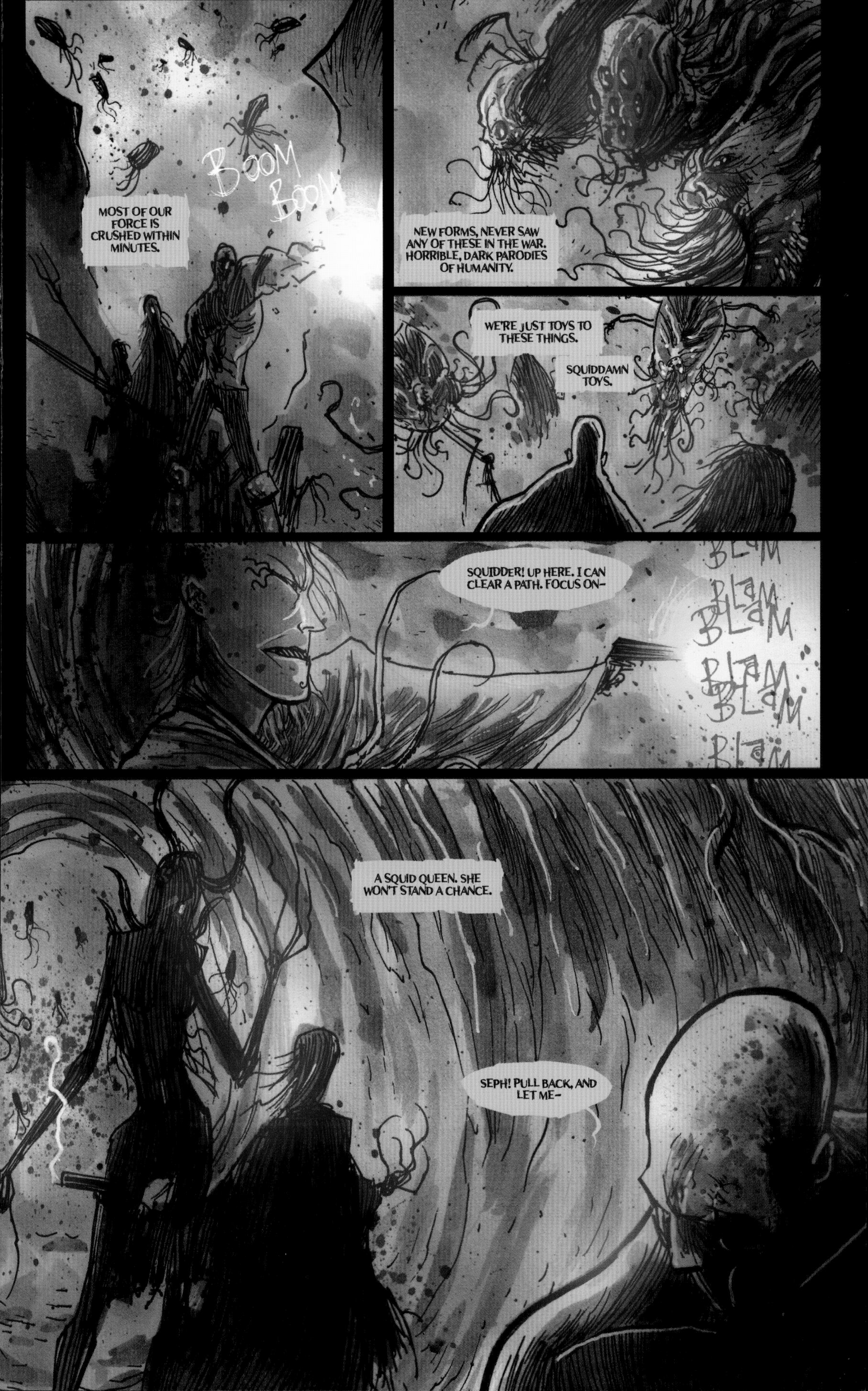
BOOM BOOM
MOST OF OUR FORCE IS CRUSHED WITHIN MINUTES.
NEW FORMS, NEVER SAW ANY OF THESE IN THE WAR. HORRIBLE, DARK PARODIES OF HUMANITY.
WE'RE JUST TOYS TO THESE THINGS.
SQUIDDAMN TOYS.
SQUIDDER! UP HERE. I CAN CLEAR A PATH. FOCUS ON–
BLAM BLAM BLAM BLAM BLAM BLAM
A SQUID QUEEN. SHE WON'T STAND A CHANCE.
SEPH! PULL BACK, AND LET ME–

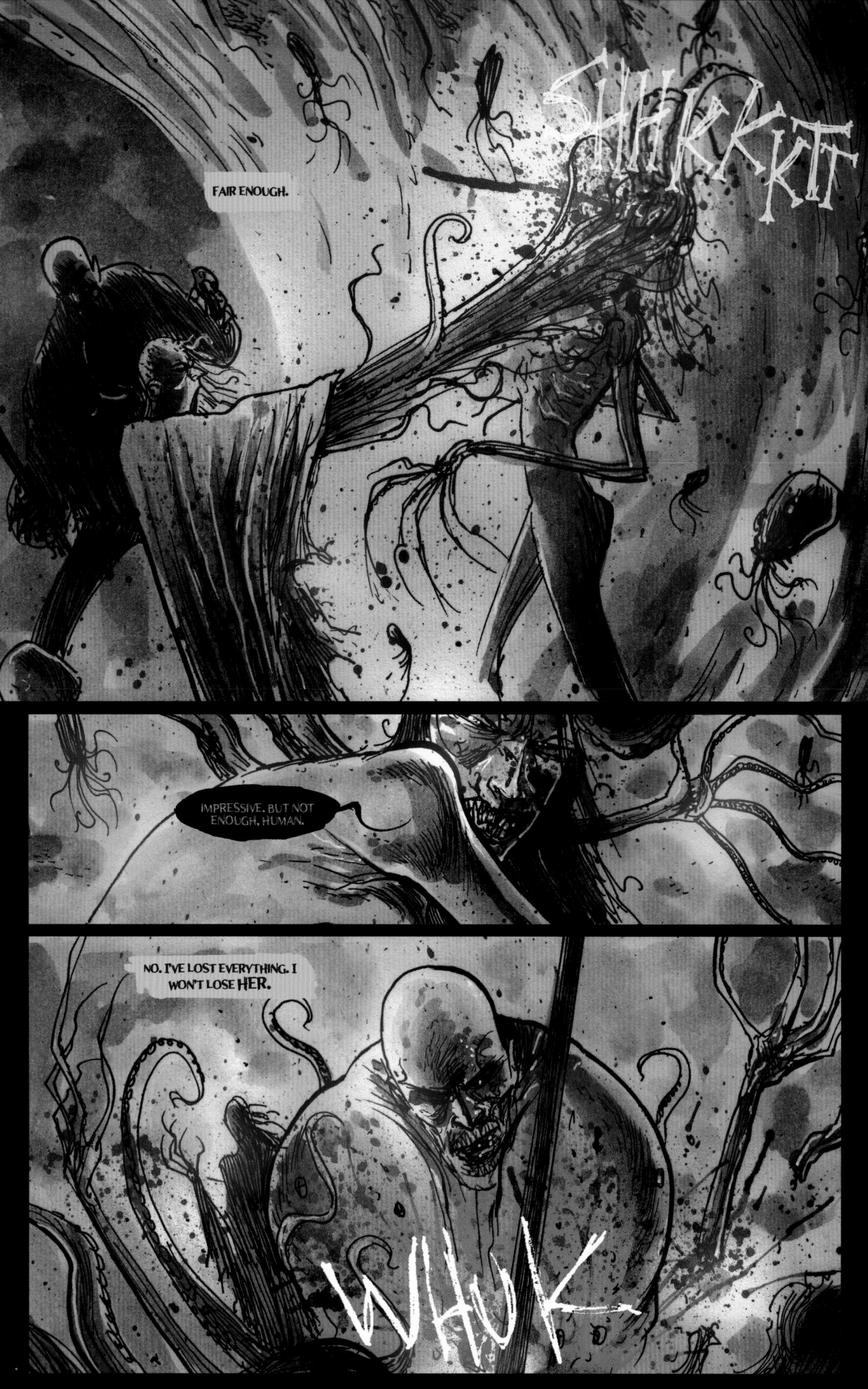
SHHRKKTT
FAIR ENOUGH.
IMPRESSIVE. BUT NOT ENOUGH, HUMAN.
NO. I'VE LOST EVERYTHING. I WON'T LOSE HER.
WHUK

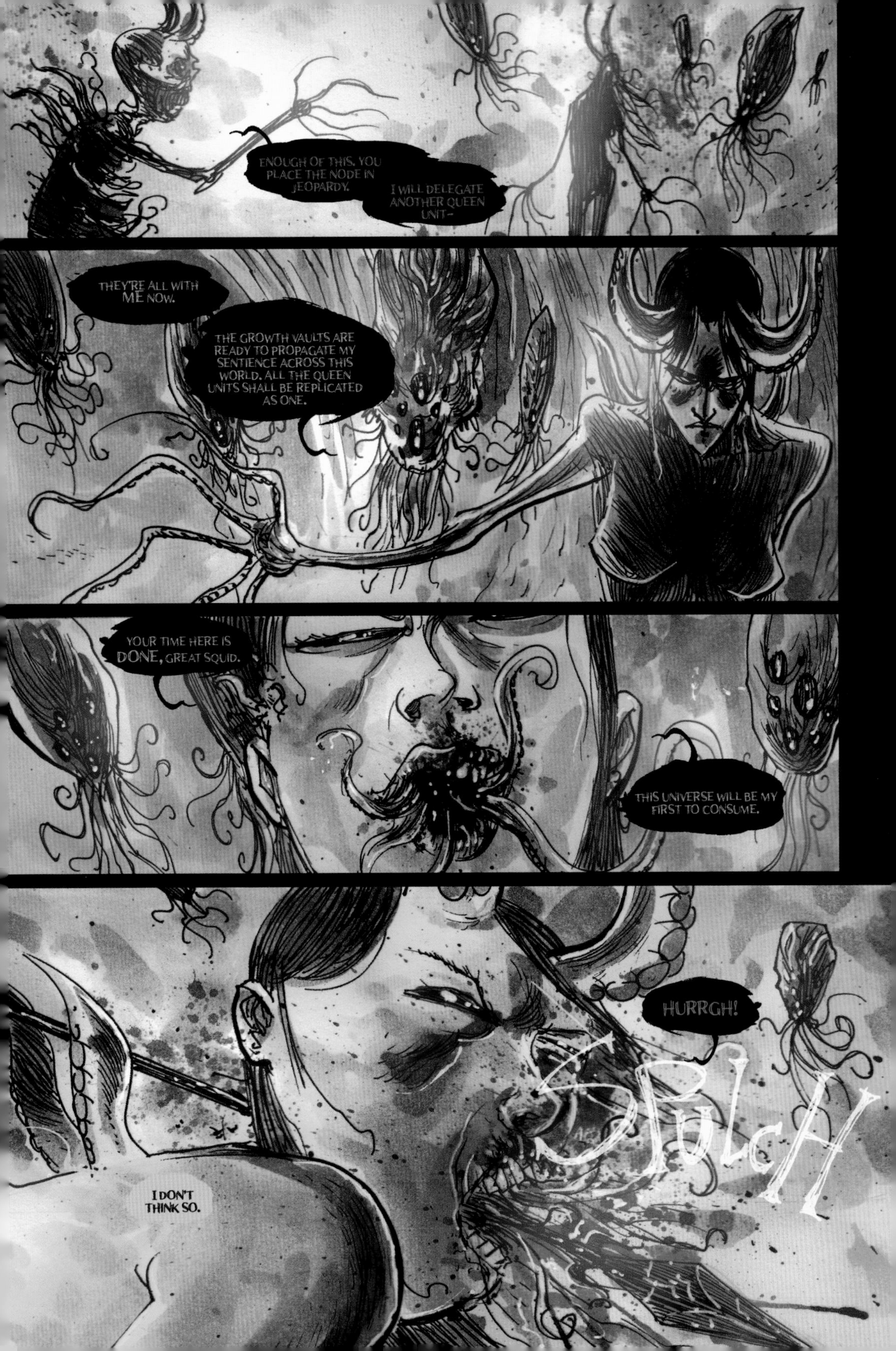
ENOUGH OF THIS. YOU PLACE THE NODE IN JEOPARDY.
I WILL DELEGATE ANOTHER QUEEN UNIT-
THEY'RE ALL WITH ME NOW.
THE GROWTH VAULTS ARE READY TO PROPAGATE MY SENTIENCE ACROSS THIS WORLD. ALL THE QUEEN UNITS SHALL BE REPLICATED AS ONE.
YOUR TIME HERE IS DONE, GREAT SQUID.
THIS UNIVERSE WILL BE MY FIRST TO CONSUME.
HURRGH!
SPLUCH
I DON'T THINK SO.

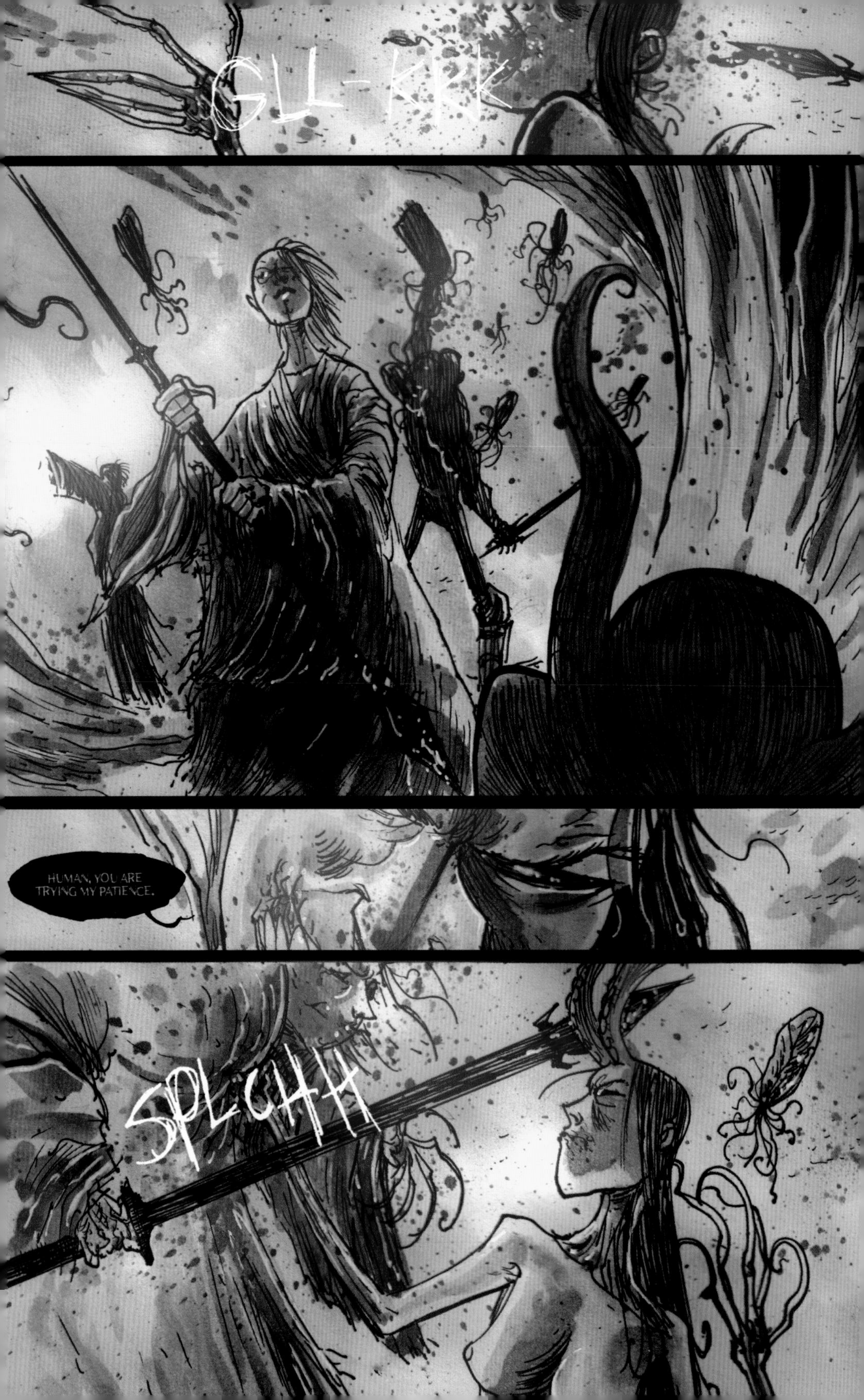
GLL-KKK
HUMAN, YOU ARE TRYING MY PATIENCE.
SPLCHH

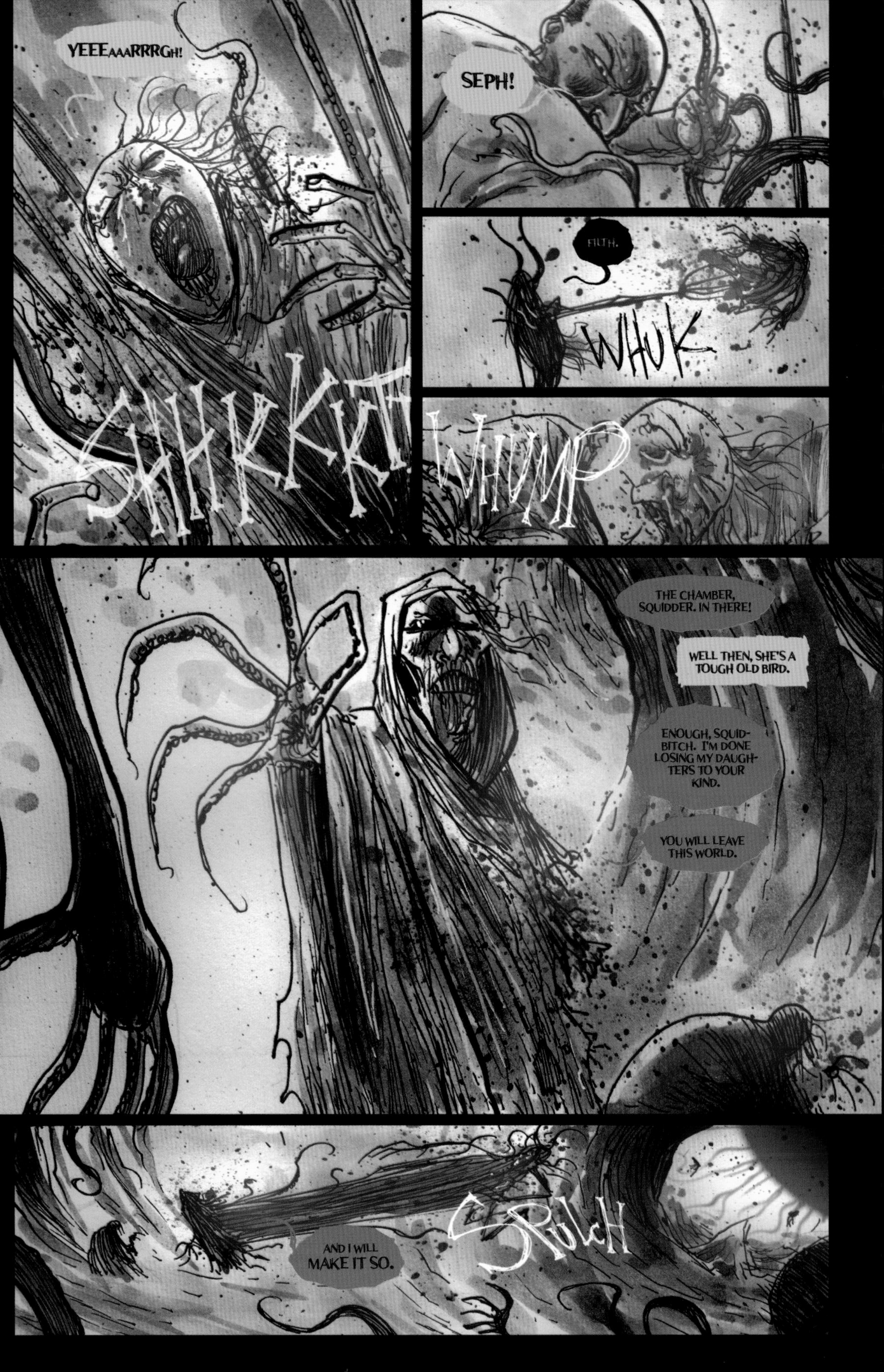
YEEEAAARRRGH!
SEPH!
FILTH.
WHUK
SHHKKKT
WHUMP
THE CHAMBER, SQUIDDER. IN THERE!
WELL THEN, SHE'S A TOUGH OLD BIRD.
ENOUGH, SQUID-BITCH. I'M DONE LOSING MY DAUGHTERS TO YOUR KIND.
YOU WILL LEAVE THIS WORLD.
AND I WILL MAKE IT SO.
SPLUCH

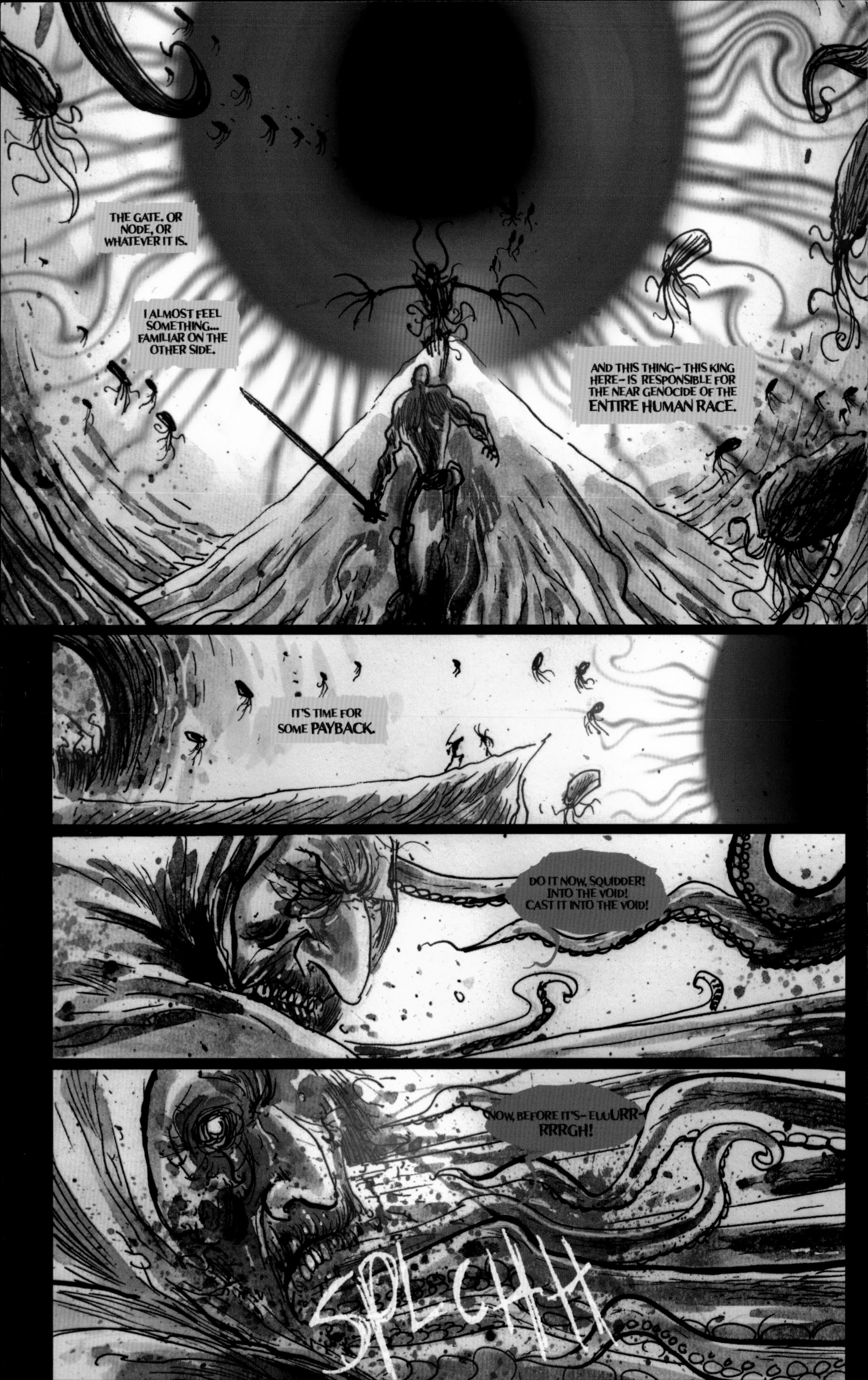
THE GATE. OR NODE, OR WHATEVER IT IS.
I ALMOST FEEL SOMETHING... FAMILIAR ON THE OTHER SIDE.
AND THIS THING- THIS KING HERE- IS RESPONSIBLE FOR THE NEAR GENOCIDE OF THE ENTIRE HUMAN RACE.
IT'S TIME FOR SOME PAYBACK.
DO IT NOW, SQUIDDER! INTO THE VOID! CAST IT INTO THE VOID!
NOW, BEFORE IT'S- EUUURR-RRRGH!
SPLCHH

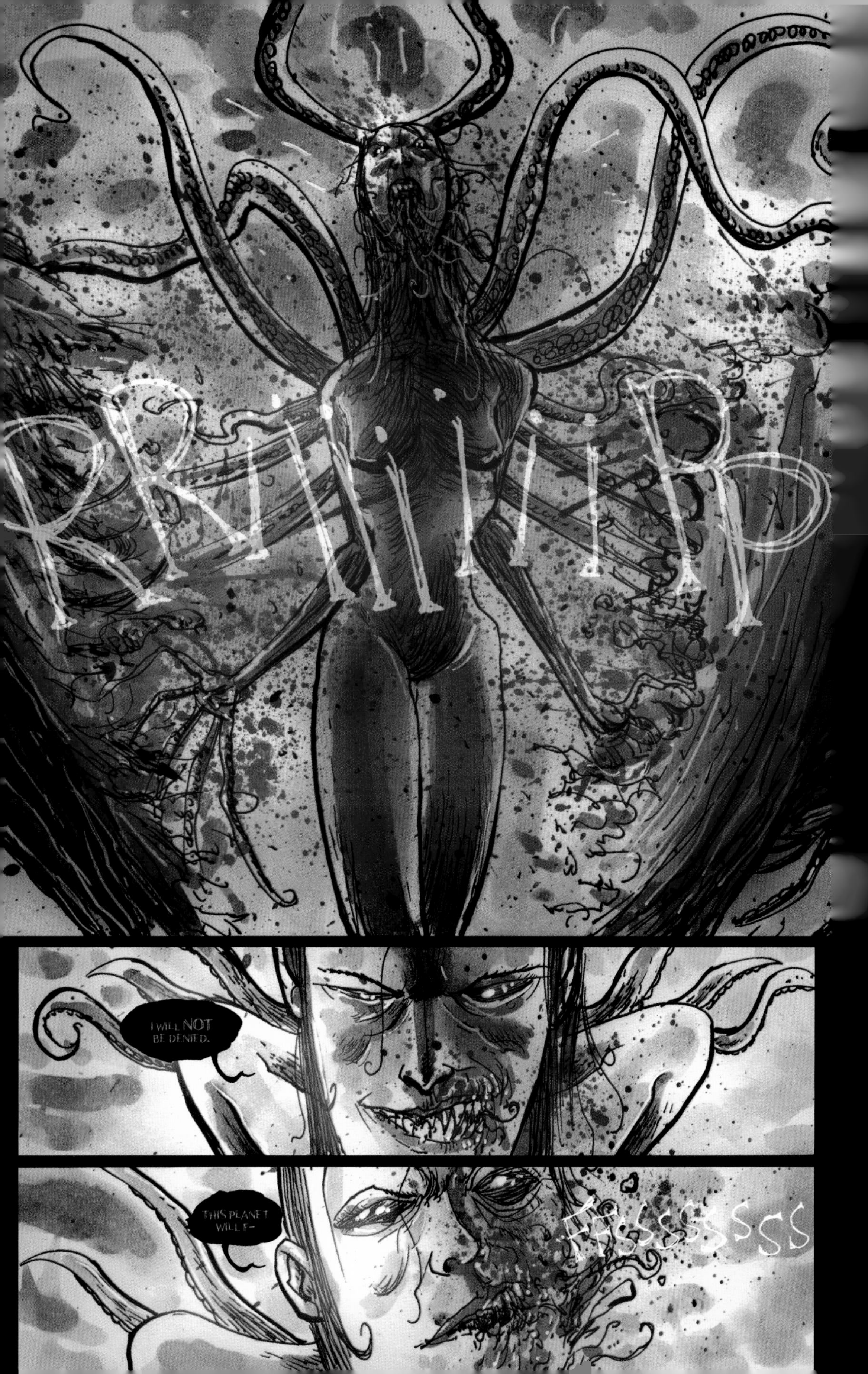
I WILL NOT BE DENIED.
THIS PLANET WILL F—

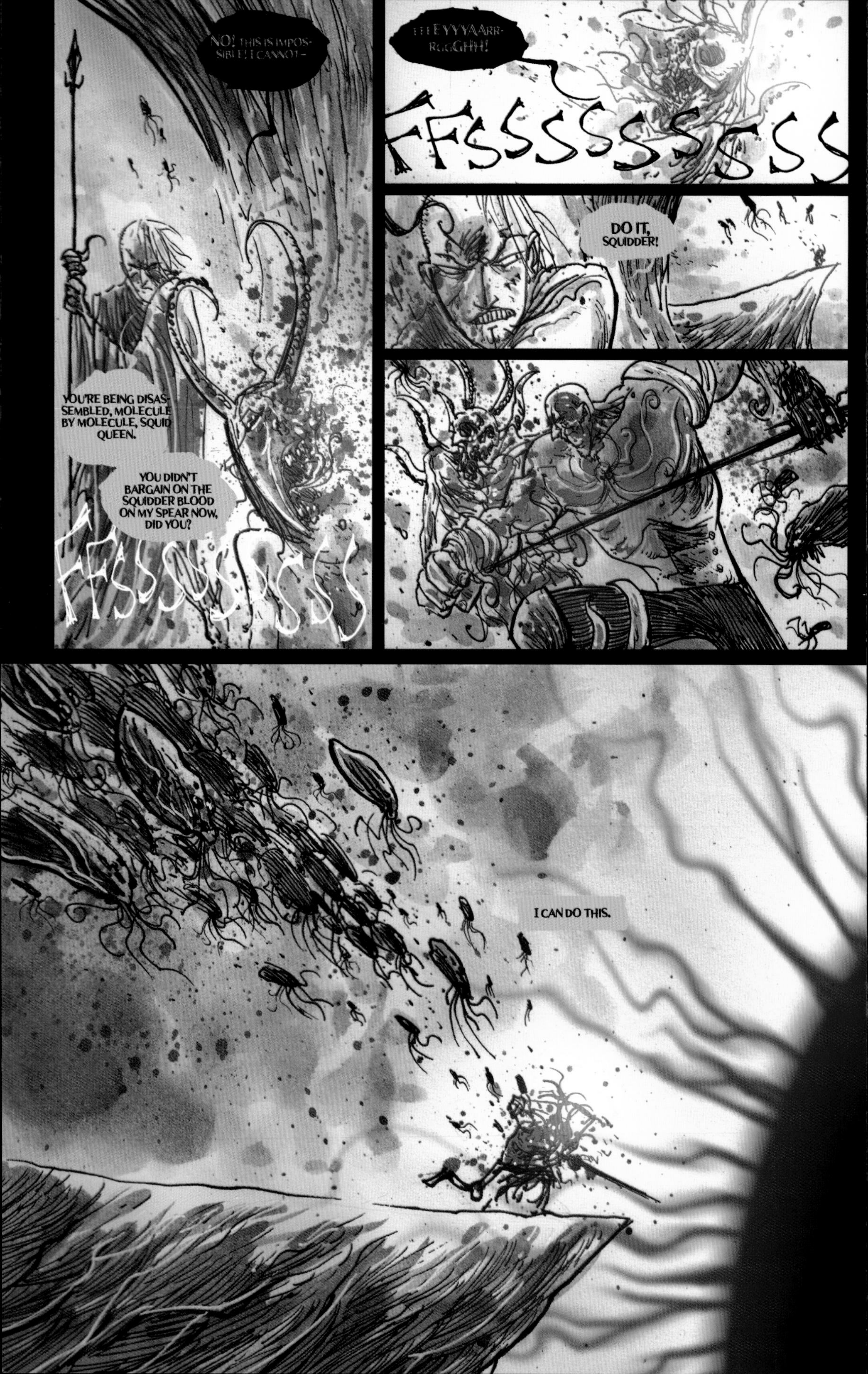
NO! THIS IS IMPOSSIBLE! I CANNOT -
FFFEYYYAARR-RGGGHH!
FFSSSSSSSSS
DO IT, SQUIDDER!
YOU'RE BEING DISASSEMBLED, MOLECULE BY MOLECULE, SQUID QUEEN.
YOU DIDN'T BARGAIN ON THE SQUIDDER BLOOD ON MY SPEAR NOW, DID YOU?
FFSSSSSSSSS
I CAN DO THIS.

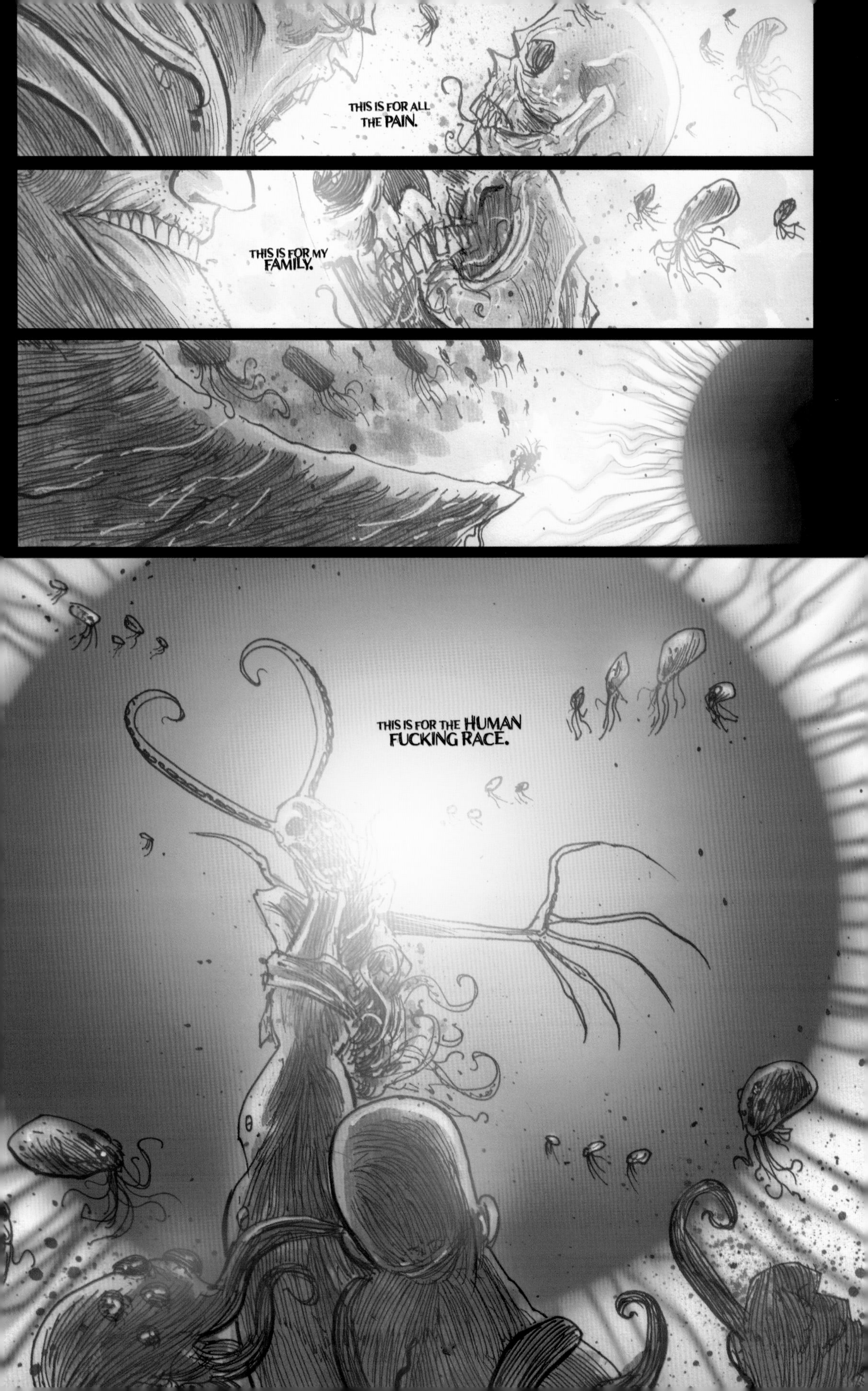
THIS IS FOR ALL THE PAIN.
THIS IS FOR MY FAMILY.
THIS IS FOR THE HUMAN FUCKING RACE.

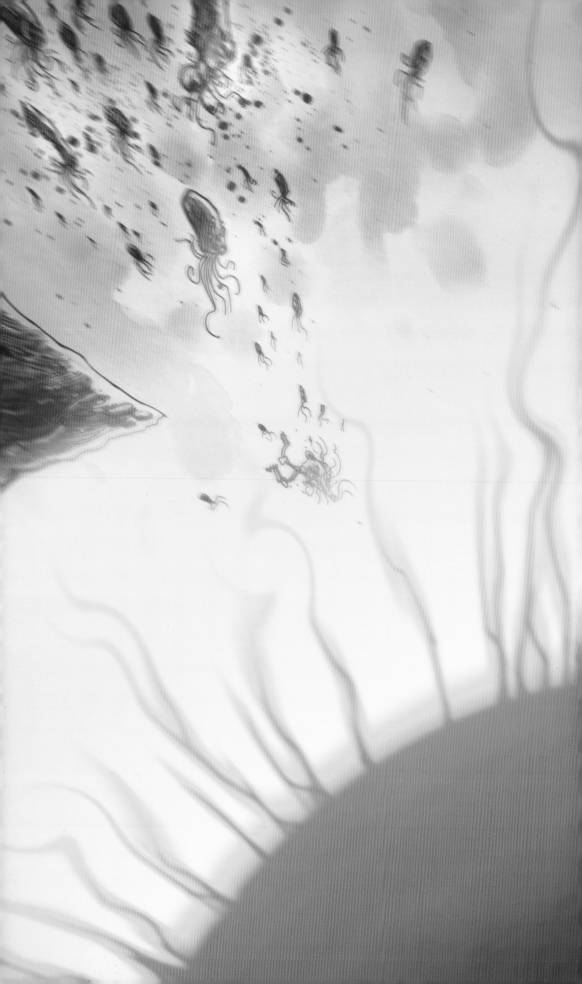

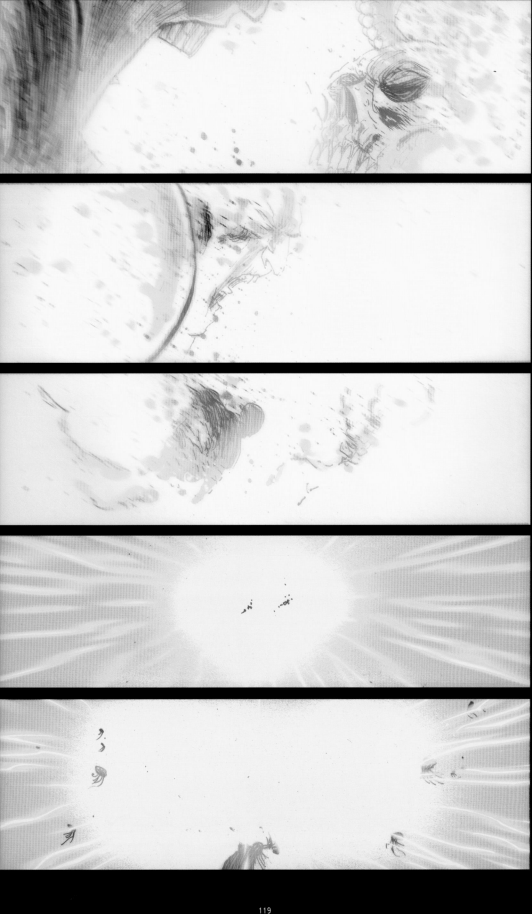

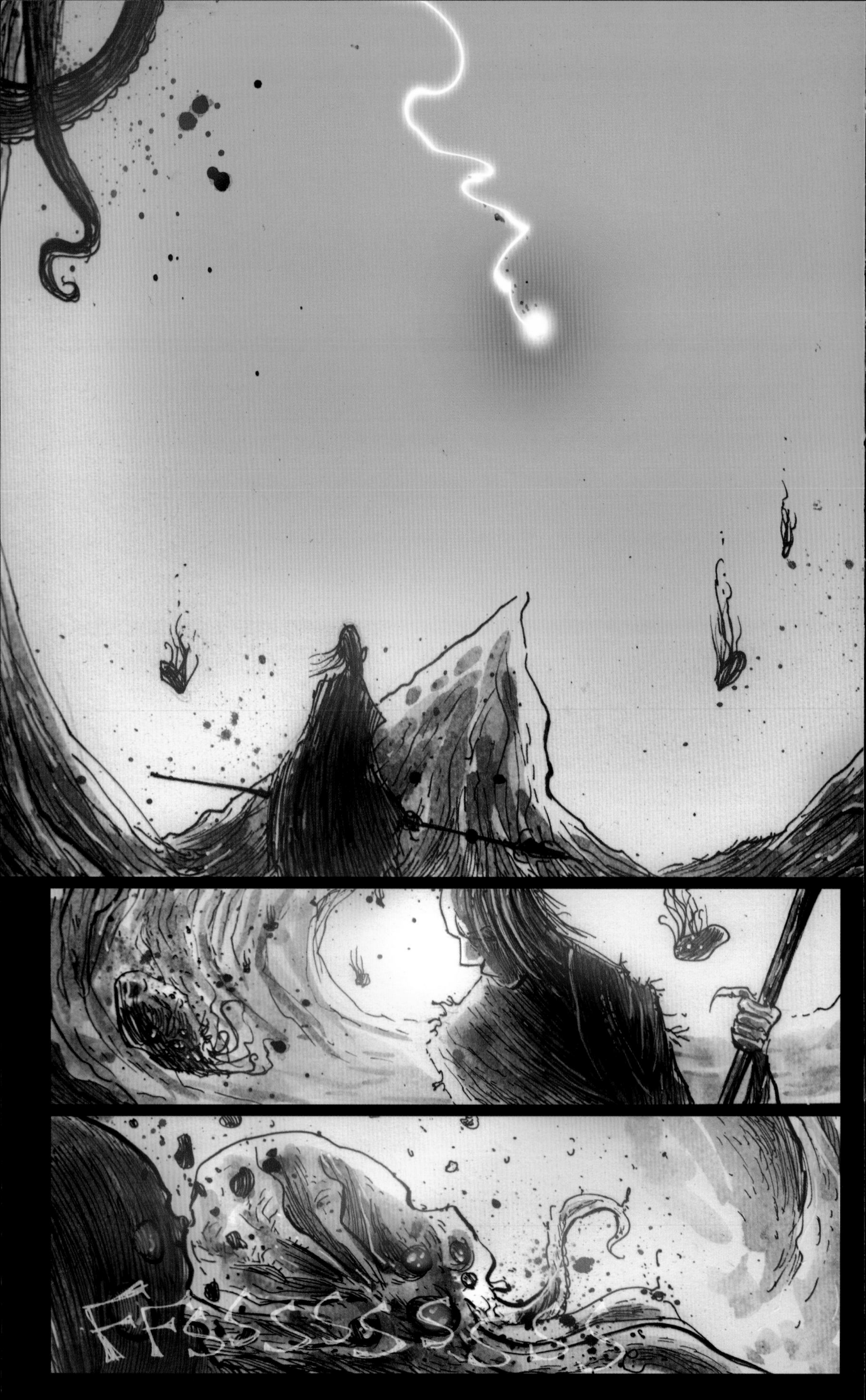
FFSSSSSSSS

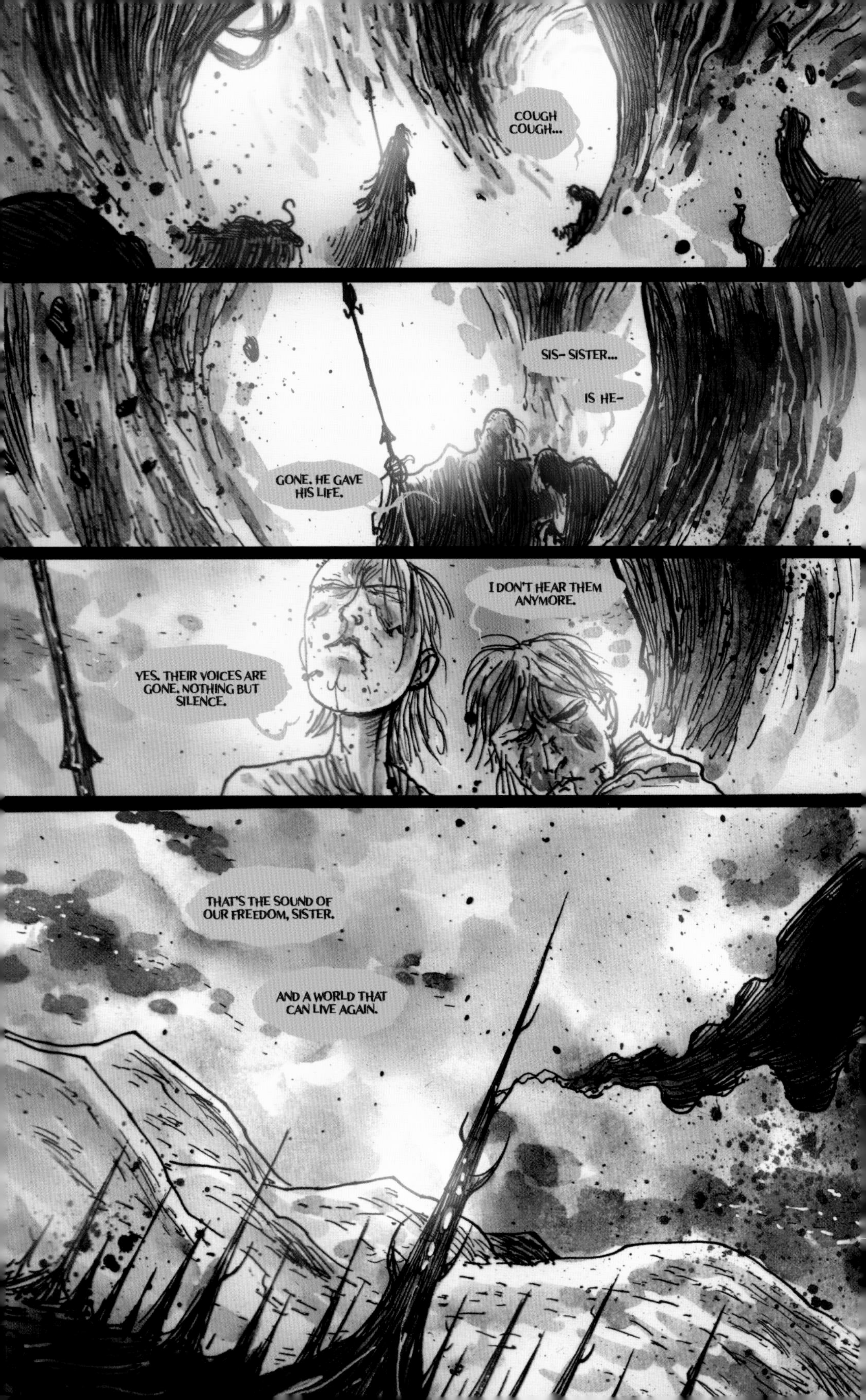
COUGH COUGH...
SIS- SISTER...
IS HE-
GONE. HE GAVE HIS LIFE.
I DON'T HEAR THEM ANYMORE.
YES. THEIR VOICES ARE GONE. NOTHING BUT SILENCE.
THAT'S THE SOUND OF OUR FREEDOM, SISTER.
AND A WORLD THAT CAN LIVE AGAIN.

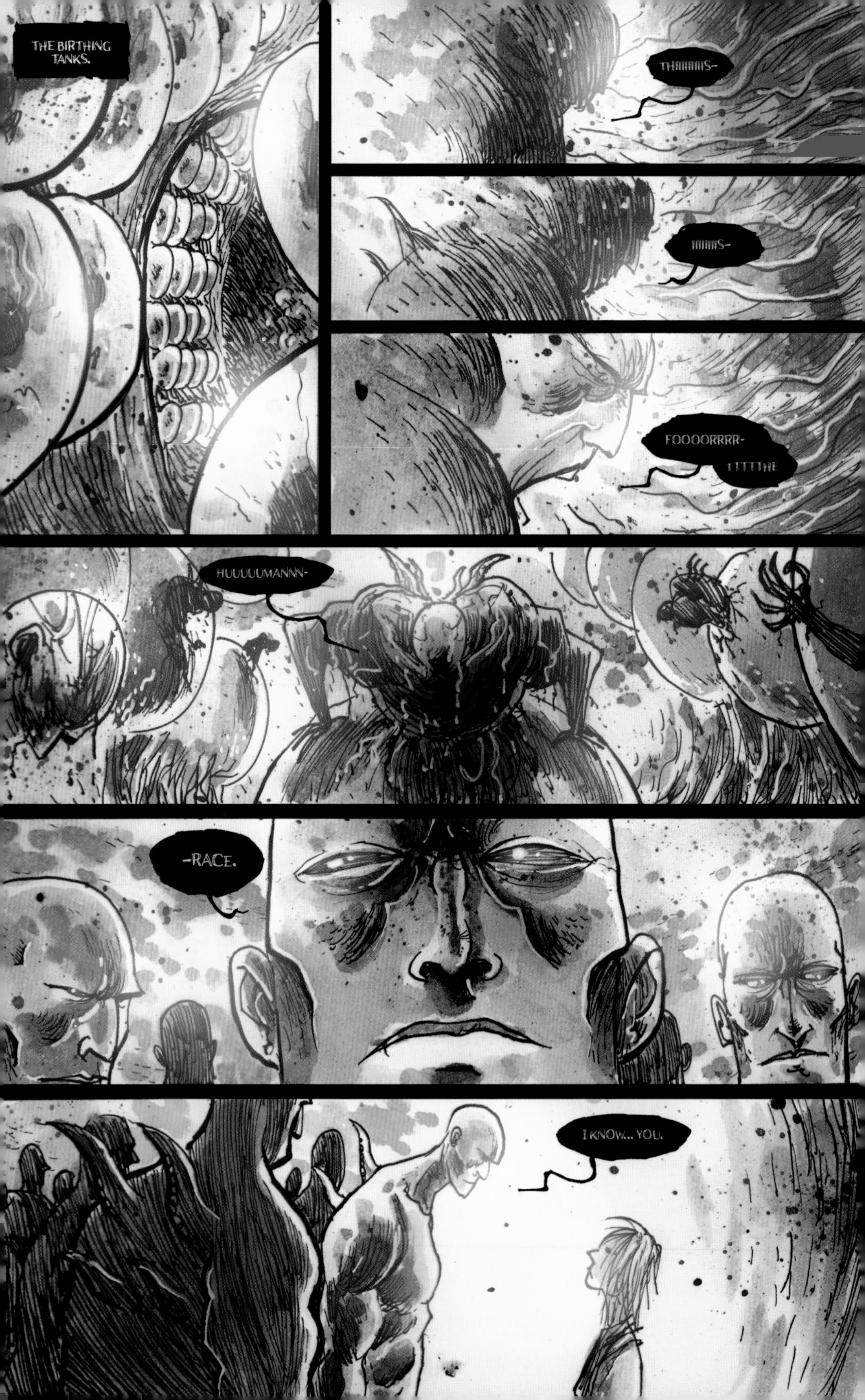
THE BIRTHING TANKS.
THHHHHIS-
IIIIIIIS-
FOOOORRRR- TTTTTHE
HUUUUUMANNN-
-RACE.
I KNOW... YOU.

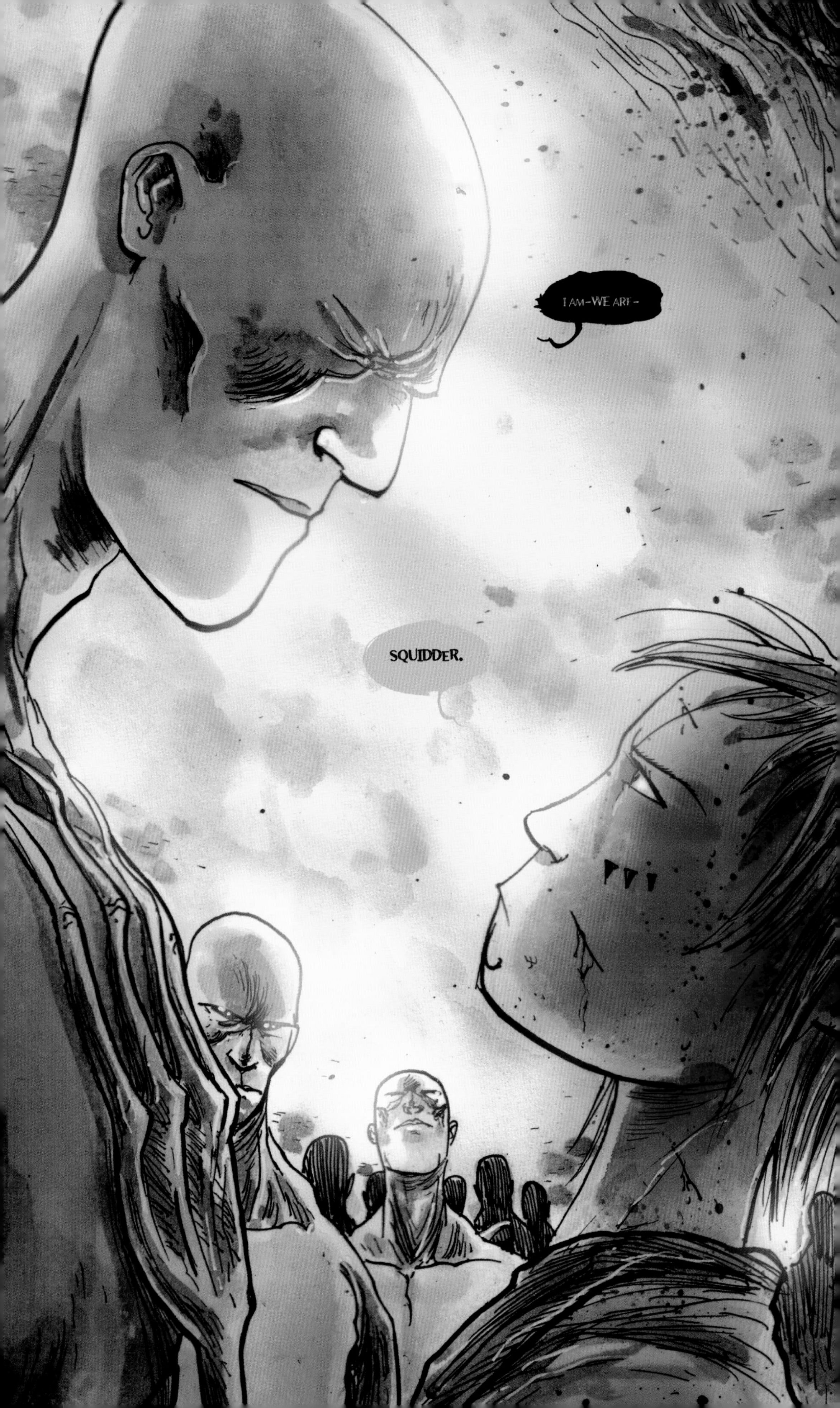
I AM-WE ARE-
SQUIDDER.

EXTRAS

JESSI ADRIGNOLA
JES.SI

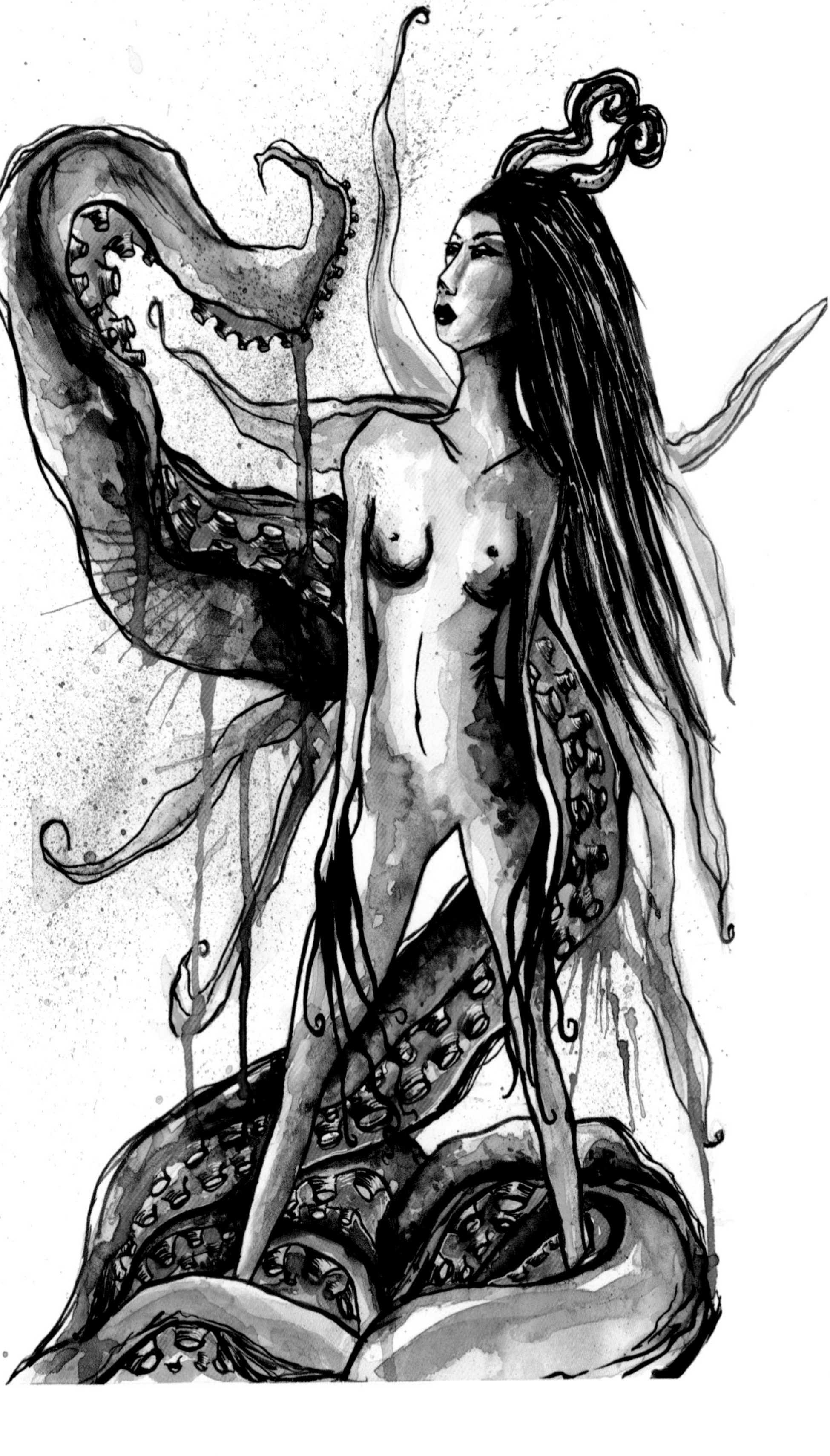

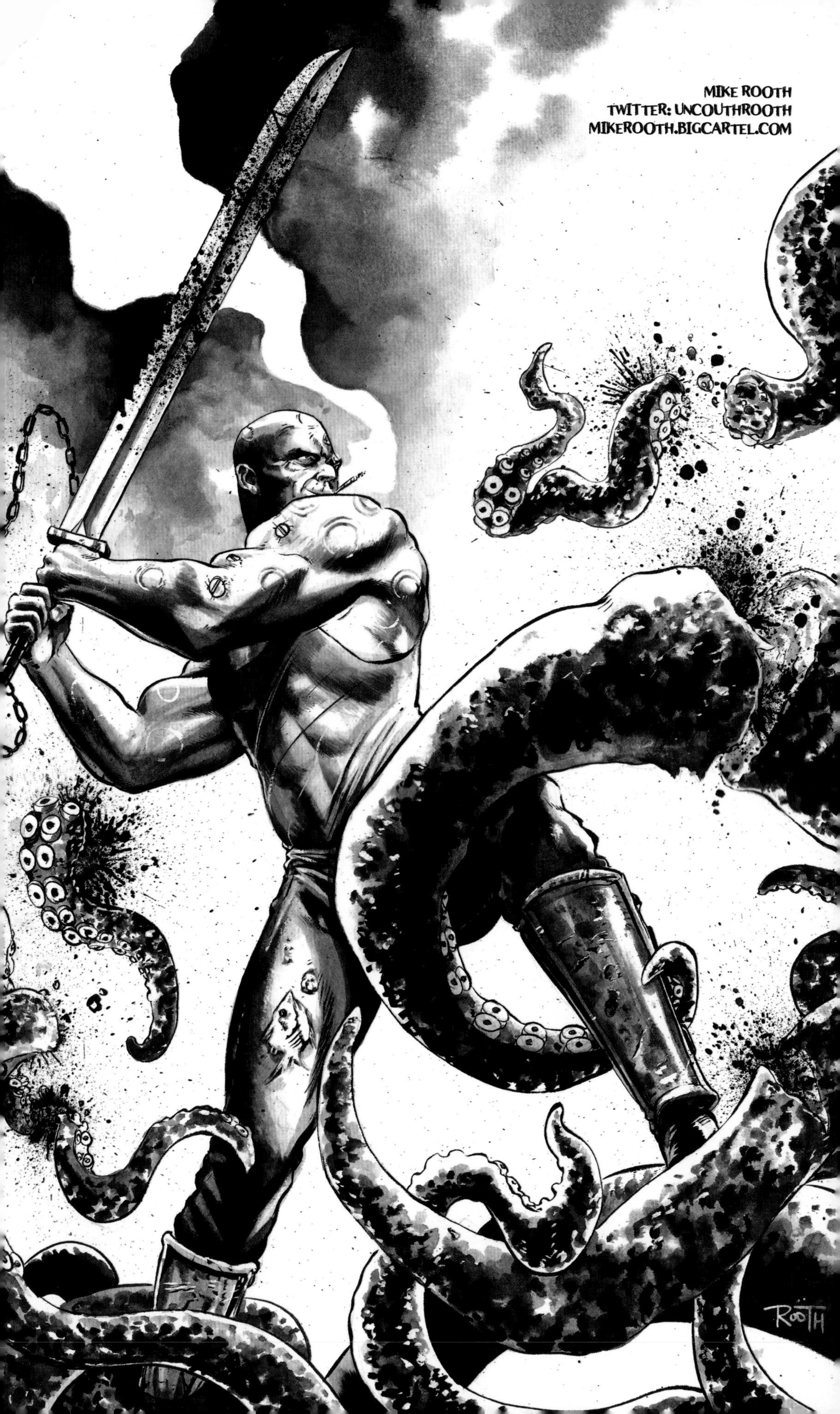
MIKE ROOTH
TWITTER: UNCOUTHROOTH
MIKEROOTH.BIGCARTEL.COM
ROOTH

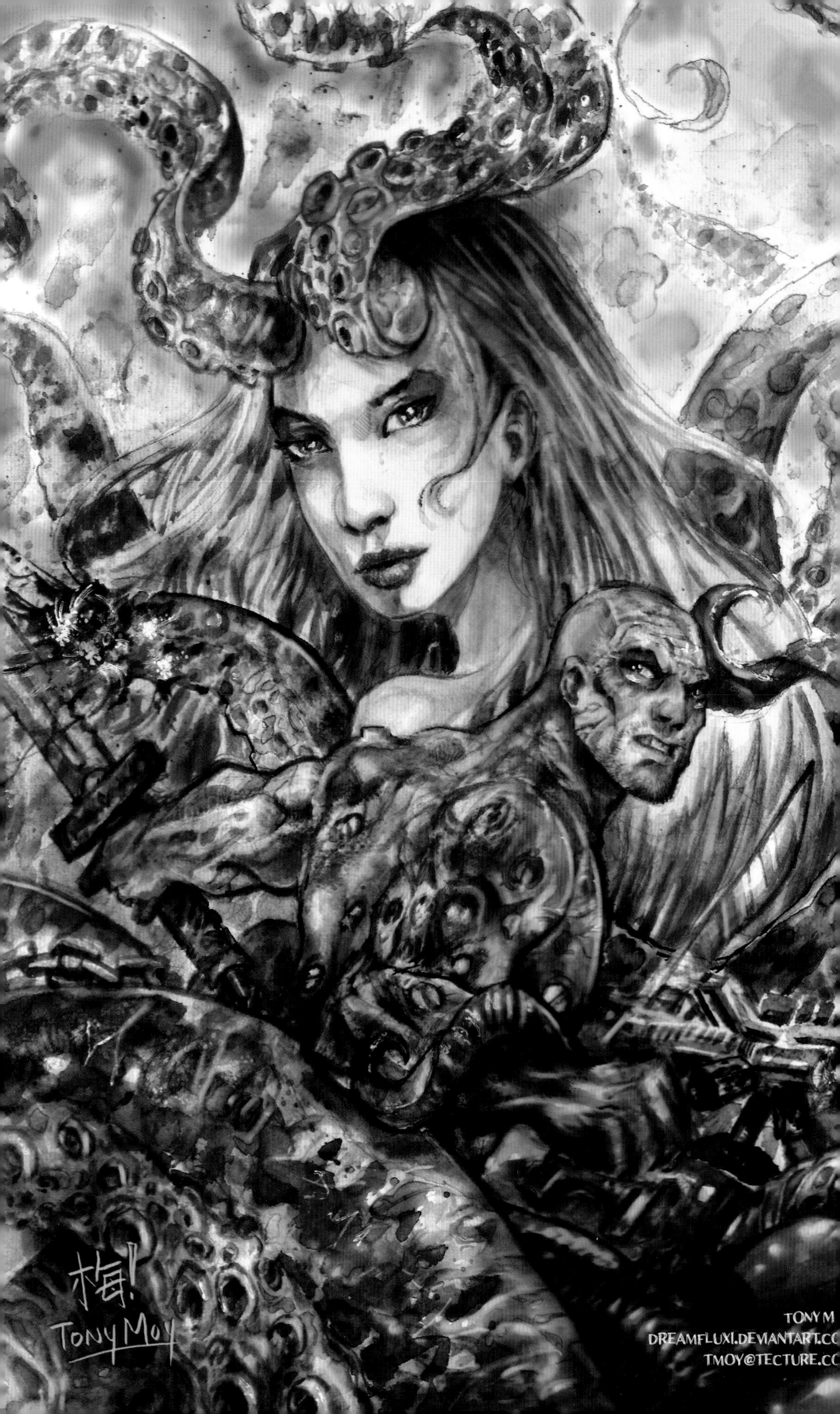
梅!
Tony Moy
TONY M
DREAMFLUXI.DEVIANTART.CO
TMOY@TECTURE.CO